Woman of the River

Georgie White Clark
White-Water Pioneer

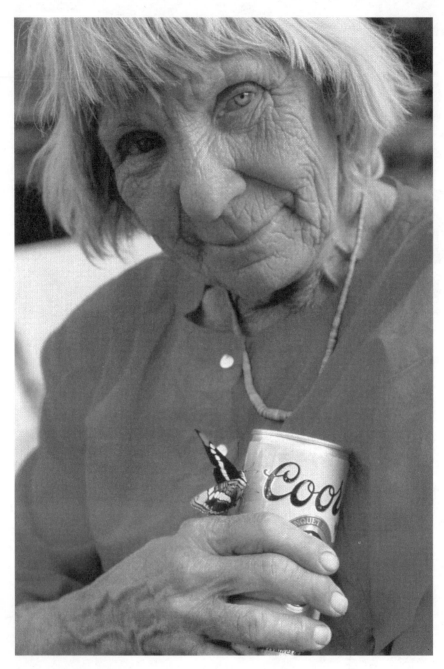

Even butterflies were attracted to Georgie. *Courtesy of Teresa Yates.*

Woman of the River

Georgie White Clark
White-Water Pioneer

Richard E. Westwood

Foreword by
Roy Webb

Utah State University Press
Logan, Utah
1997

Utah State University Press
Logan, Utah 84322–7800

Typography by WolfPack

Library of Congress Cataloging-in-Publication Data

Westwood, Dick, 1921-
    Woman of the river : Georgie White Clark, white water pioneer /
Richard E. Westwood ; foreword by Roy Webb.
        p.   cm.
    Includes bibliographical references and index.
    ISBN 0-87421-234-0
    1. Clark, Georgie White. 2. West (U.S.)—Biography. 3. Adventure
and adventurers—West (U.S.)—Biography. 4. Rafting (Sports)—West
(U.S.) I. Title.
CT275.C6265W47   1997
917.804'33—dc21   97-21169
                                                                    CIP

Contents

Illustrations

Foreword
Roy Webb

$\mathcal{T}$he first time I met Georgie was in 1986 on my first Grand Canyon trip. I had heard of her, of course, having been a student of river history for a couple of years by then, but I didn't know her to see her. Not knowing what to do, and not wanting to get in the way as the crew rigged our boat, I walked down the ramp to where a huge pontoon raft was moored. I walked around it, marveling at the intricate lacework of ropes. Then I noticed, standing in the water on the other side, a little, wiry, gnome-like figure in a shapeless hat and leopard tights. She looked at me sharply and asked me my business. Just looking around, I told her; by now, even a first-trip canyon swamper could guess who she was. I said I was a historian interested in the river, and she warmed instantly. I spent the rest of the morning listening to yarn after yarn and finally had to tear myself away when my boat was ready to leave.

After that first meeting I saw her almost every trip, either rigging her boat at Lee's Ferry (a three-day event that other boatmen would gather to watch) or holding court on the end of her boat while her passengers hiked the popular trail at Deer Creek Falls. I was even lucky enough to catch her a couple of times with an empty spot in the motor well of her boat—usually crowded with other boatmen who wanted to meet her—where she would offer me one of her trademark Coors and give me cause to reflect that of such moments was a river historian's life made. The apotheosis of my experiences with Georgie, though, had to be at her eightieth birthday party at Hatchland—the Hatch River Expeditions warehouse near Lee's Ferry—in 1990. It was a night to be remembered; more fun, I reflected later, than anyone should have while a Republican is in the White House. The river community came together (a rare enough event in what is perforce a trade practiced by individuals and iconoclasts) and finally honored her as one of their own. There were those who worshiped her, those who abhorred her—all joined to celebrate her success, or at least to admit that she had endured in what they knew was a difficult but rewarding life.

Georgie obviously made an impression on me; how much more so, then, did she impress those who came to know her well, for good or ill. For it would be disingenuous to say that being well known meant that she was equally well liked. Georgie was one of those Colorado River characters who, like her predecessor John Wesley Powell and her contemporary Otis "Dock" Marston, aroused great passions in the hearts of those who knew her. Thousands, from one-time passengers to long-term boatmen, loved her and are warmed by their memories of her. Many others, some guests, but more river professionals, felt equally strongly that her contribution was not positive—that she was indifferent to environmental concerns and passengers' safety. Suffice it to say all who met her can hardly fail to remember her, and mostly for doing what she was best at, being utterly and indubitably Georgie, the "Woman of the River."

And if the impression she made on her fellow river rats was indelible, so too is her place in the history of the Colorado River, for Georgie not only made history, she changed it. Before her, women went down the river solely as passengers and even, in those less enlightened times, were made to walk around rapids since they were "the weaker sex." Georgie would have none of that; she wanted to run her own boat, and the opinions of the men on the river be damned. At the time she made her famous swim down the Grand Canyon with Harry Aleson, wooden boats patterned after Norm Nevills's cataract boats were the standard river craft in the Grand Canyon. They were stable and manueverable and all-around good boats but could only carry three passengers at most. Georgie, like many others just after World War II, took advantage of cheap surplus boats and created— after a number of experiments, some more successful than others— her big boat, a mammoth contraption that could carry up to forty passengers at a time and plow through virtually any rapid. During the winters, Georgie began touring the country promoting her share-the-expense river trips, which were the forerunner to modern mass tourism in the Grand Canyon. By 1950 less than one hundred people had run the Colorado River through the Grand Canyon; by the end of that decade, in no small part due to Georgie's efforts, that number had jumped into the thousands, and it continued to climb until the Park Service put a ceiling on the number of people who could run the canyon every year. Those who were able to share in her excitement at running the wild rapids flocked to her trips in droves; those who abhorred the idea of thousands of tourists in "their" canyon called her "that woman" or other, less printable names.

Happily, it's the real Georgie, wrinkles and bright blue eyes and all, who comes through in Dick Westwood's thorough and balanced account of her interesting life. I know his research is thorough, having been on the other end of the phone when he was looking for something. His description of Georgie's early life (always a clouded subject), the development of her boats, and the complicated genealogies of Colorado River outfitters are first-rate and completely original. Westwood is not only thorough, but insightful; he goes below the surface of people in boats on the water to reach the dynamics that underlie the whole Grand Canyon/Colorado River community. Even more importantly for a book like this, his account is balanced—writing about rivers is in Dick Westwood's blood. He comes from a river family; his maternal grandfather, H. E. Blake, Sr., was a pioneer motorboater on the Green and Colorado rivers. Dick's uncle H. E. Blake, Jr., was a boatman for the U.S. Geological Survey and others throughout the 1920s, and he was the subject of Dick's earlier book, *Rough-Water Man: Elwyn Blake's Colorado River Expeditions*. So Dick grew up with tales of the Green and the Colorado told at the kitchen table, and he didn't confine his knowledge of the river to listening to oft-told yarns. He has been around the Colorado most of his life, from boyhood explorations of the river marshes near Moab to high adventure on a raft in the middle of Hance Rapid in the Grand Canyon. Dick Westwood knows the rhythms of the river life, knows there are good moments and those not so good, and knows that any trip through life, like any river trip, contains some of both. Who better than someone of such broad background and sure knowledge of the river to write about such an important figure in Colorado and other western river history?

Vividly I remember one damp morning on the calm but achingly beautiful Conquistador Isle, midway down the Grand Canyon. Georgie was camped just upstream in her big boat, and as we got ready to go she passed by. Riverside rumor had it that there was a Park Service patrol trip on the river that she didn't care if she didn't see, and all the boatmen were laughing about how she avoided seeing them. We pulled out shortly afterward and followed her boat for several miles, watching her vanish and reappear in the morning mist. At the time it seemed that she *was* the mist, already fading from history at that moment. But it has struck me since that she had more in common with Conquistador Isle and the canyon itself than the ephemeral vapors. For better or for worse, Georgie's image and memory are forever wed to the Grand Canyon and the rivers of the West. As long as people in boats are running those marvelous rivers, Georgie will be right there too. And that's just the way she would want it.

Acknowledgments

I have had the generous help and cooperation of many people in getting this book together. Karen Underhill and the staff at Cline Library, Northern Arizona University, got me started and helped along the way by guiding me through the Georgie Clark collection and putting me in touch with Rosalyn J. (Roz) Jirge. This book would have been incomplete without the input and help from Roz. She not only told me of her own experiences, but collected others' diaries, did interviews, transcribed tapes of my interviews, and supplied me with names and addresses of passengers and boatmen that were invaluable in my research. She also read and commented on more than one version of the manuscript. William P. Frank, associate curator of Western Manuscripts at the Huntington Library, was extremely helpful in guiding me through the Marston collection. Deborah Whiteford generously shared her interviews with Georgie, as well as her research file.

My daughter Beth Davies went through the Harry Aleson collection at the Utah State Historical Society and sent me copies of Georgie's letters to Aleson and other references to Georgie. I owe thanks to the Grand Canyon River Guides Association for inviting me to their meetings and outings, where I mingled with and interviewed many people who knew Georgie, and where I learned more about the Grand Canyon and the river community. My thanks also to the Colorado Plateau River Guides. Orville Miller, long-time boatman and friend of Georgie, invited me to reunions at his home in Sacramento for friends of Georgie. Not only was I able to do interviews while there, but I felt the love and devotion that many people had for Georgie.

My niece, Shannon Cruthers of Denver, searched the records there, which revealed that most of Georgie's early life was spent in that area. Roy Webb and others filled me in on Georgie's eightieth birthday party at the Hatch warehouse at Marble Canyon. I am especially grateful to Dr. William Phillips, retired professor of history at Arizona State University, for reading different versions of the manuscript and guiding me in the proper form of a work of this nature. He also allowed me to go with him and his family group on a float trip through Grand Canyon.

Without the sixty or more people who agreed to interviews and supplied copies of their logs and diaries, this book would not have been possible. I wish to thank all of them. I am grateful to Beky Quintero for reading and copyediting the final version of the manuscript.

I owe a special debt of thanks to two readers for Utah State University Press for their valuable comments and recommendations to have the book published. Thomas Zajkowski of the University of Utah made maps, and the University of Nevada Press allowed use of other maps.

Last but not least, I want to thank editor John Alley for the yeoman work he did in comparing the long and short manuscripts to get the final version together. I apologize to those I have failed to mention. Any mistakes in this work are mine alone.

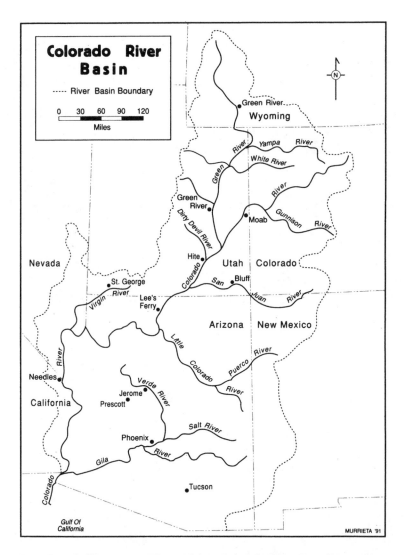

From Rough-Water Man: Elwyn Blake's Colorado River Expeditions, *by Richard E. Westwood. Copyright © 1992 by University of Nevada Press. Used with permission.*

Georgie White and Harry Aleson ready for their 1945 swim of the Colorado River. *Harry Aleson Collection, C-187. Used by permission, Utah State Historical Society, all rights reserved.*

Georgie White and Harry Aleson demonstrate wrist lock that held them together during their Colorado River swim of 1945. *Harry Aleson Collection, C-187. Used by permission, Utah State Historical Society, all rights reserved.*

1 Swimming Rapids in Grand Canyon, 1944–1945

Georgie White and Harry Aleson stared at the raging, silt-laden Colorado River. The awesome beauty of Grand Canyon would be lost on the pair for the next four days as they fought the swirling brown water. It was June of 1945, just a month after V.E. Day, and the two had decided to swim the lower reaches of the Grand Canyon from Diamond Creek[1] to Lake Mead.

From Boulder City, Nevada, they had taken a bus to Peach Springs, Arizona, on U.S. 66, where they stripped down to swimsuits, tennis shoes, and shirts. Each wore a life preserver and a backpack which held a malt can containing a light jacket, sugar candy, powdered coffee, dehydrated soup, and their cameras and film. They had asked the sheriff in Peach Springs to ship the rest of their clothes back to Boulder City. After a hot twenty-mile hike down to the Colorado River, they were faced with a rampaging, debris-filled stream at the height of spring runoff. The swift current carried along trees and other driftwood the rains had washed down from side canyons. Lashing waves crashed against the shore rocks with an ominous roar.[2] And, as happens with all floods of this kind, the air was filled with the pungent odor of rotting vegetation.

The pair had planned to swim awhile and climb out whenever they were tired, but with the current so strong this would be risky. Their swim began at about Mile 221.[3] Harry waded in first; the current grabbed him, knocked off his hat, and soon swept him out of sight around a bend. There was nothing for Georgie to do but follow. She jumped in and immediately felt quite helpless as she was carried along by the powerful current. Until then she did not know

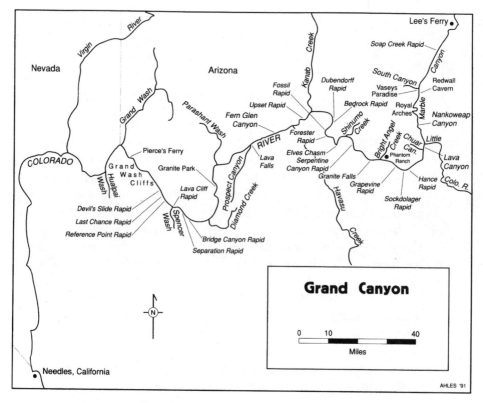

From Rough-Water Man: Elwyn Blake's Colorado River Expeditions, *by Richard E. Westwood.*
Copyright © 1992 by University of Nevada Press. Used with permission.

the great power of the water. She soon realized that she was at the mercy of the river.

Eventually Georgie was swept into an eddy near the edge of the river where she was able to swim to shore and climb out. Along the way she thought she had seen Harry in an eddy she had passed. As she sat gasping for breath she stared at the river, hoping to catch sight of him. Soon after, she heard a shout from downstream. Apparently Harry had passed by while she was climbing out of the river. Harry had spotted her and gotten to shore as soon as he could.

They knew that from then on they should stay together if at all possible. As the pair sat resting, they devised a hand and wrist lock that proved to work very well. One would grip the other's right wrist with his or her left hand while the other hung onto the left wrist with the right hand. They then reentered the river, and it sped them downstream at a terrific pace. Georgie recalled, "For the next six hours we careened through the rapids, fought giant waves and bounced around like two bobbing corks. It was like riding a roller coaster made of water."[4]

The wrist grip worked well and the two swimmers stayed locked together. They tried repeatedly to get to shore to rest, but the powerful current kept them moving. Near dark they were swept into a giant whirlpool that swirled them viciously around. Georgie later said, "In that water, passing at 125,000 cubic feet a second, those giant whirlpools had a life of their own."[5] The wrist lock which had worked so well all afternoon now worked against them. The eye of the whirlpool sucked them down like a flushed toilet, one feet first and the other head first. When they were able to come up for a breath of air, the order was reversed. As Georgie remembers it, "The first time I plunged into the hole, time stood still, and my lungs began to burn. When I thought I couldn't hold my breath any longer, I burst out, gulped for air, and went under again."[6]

Georgie and Harry were on top just long enough to gasp some air before being sucked down again. The third time down, Georgie thought it was the end. She held her nose with her free hand, trying to stave off the inevitable, and then suddenly they were on top again and close enough to shore to grab onto a rock ledge. They hung on desperately until they could gain enough strength to climb out.

They wanted to build a fire, but there wasn't a single piece of driftwood on the narrow ledge where they were stranded. So they both had to settle for instant coffee made from cold, muddy river water. The rest of their supper was made up of a few pieces of candy. Huddled together on the narrow rock ledge, they tried to get some rest. They kept on their cold, wet life preservers lest they should fall into the river during the night. There would be little sleep for either of them.

At dawn they drank more cold coffee and ate a few more pieces of candy. When they got a good look at the river they were amazed and delighted to see that the whirlpool had disappeared during the night. Adjusting their packs, they resumed their wrist lock and jumped in. The pair encountered little trouble the rest of the way but were half-starved by the end of the second day, having eaten only a little candy, soup, and coffee.

A few years earlier Harry had established a tent camp in Quartermaster Canyon, which he christened "My Home, Arizona."[7] Harry had come up by boat a short time earlier and cached food there, so he and Georgie planned to stop and have a solid meal. By then they would be in the calmer waters of Lake Mead and anticipated no problems getting ashore. As they approached Quartermaster Canyon they worked their way toward shore, but as hard as they swam, the current still carried them almost a mile downstream before they were able to land. Exhausted, they then had to scramble back over the rocks to reach Harry's camp. Georgie said, "It was worth the effort, however, and to this day I'll never forget how good that meal tasted."

After eating and resting they continued to swim the waters of Lake Mead. On the third day they encountered a huge log jam created by the large amount of driftwood coming down the river. The logs would not hold them up and there was no way to swim between them, so they had to walk around. Headwinds also slowed their progress, but the two were able to swim most of the time. Their swim ended on the lake at Pierce Ferry,[8] about five miles from the Grand Wash Cliffs. From there they hiked out to the highway where they could flag down a Greyhound bus.

In those days bus drivers would stop for anyone who waved them down. Harry and Georgie were wearing only bathing suits, shirts, and tennis shoes. Harry had not shaved for several days, and Georgie had not even brought a comb for her hair. Passengers on the bus must have done some tall wondering about the two of them. But soon the pair was back in Boulder City where they could recover the rest of their clothes.

Harry Aleson

Fate had brought these two adventurers together a year earlier. Harry was a man of medium build and thinning hair. Born Harry Leroy

Asleson on March 9, 1899, in Waterloo, Iowa, he later changed his name to Aleson. While serving in World War I he had been gassed. This left him with chronic stomach problems, for which he received a small pension. During the Great Depression he worked at a number of jobs, including some with various geophysical firms searching for oil in the Southwest. This brought him into contact with the Colorado River and Grand Canyon, and "he soon gave up any desires for a life apart from the river."[9] It also cost him his marriage. He and his wife, Thursa Arnold, whom he married in 1928, were separated in 1940.

From his tent camp in Quartermaster Canyon, Aleson made explorations of the Grand Canyon and the lower Colorado River system. This made him a popular river guide and somewhat of an authority on that section of the river.

In 1945 Aleson changed his winter headquarters to the Johnston Hotel in Richfield, Utah, where he earned part of his room and board by working as night clerk. From there he organized the dozens of San Juan River/Glen Canyon trips that were his main source of income during the summer.[10] He took pictures of the canyon lands during his explorations and gave illustrated lectures about them.

Georgie's Early Life

Georgie was a slim, athletic woman of medium height with piercing turquoise-blue eyes. She claimed to have been born and reared in Chicago, where she learned to swim in the cold water of Lake Michigan.[11] She was, in fact, born in Oklahoma and spent most of her childhood in Denver, Colorado. Her birth certificate shows that she was born Bessie DeRoss at Guymon, Oklahoma, November 13, 1910, to George W. DeRoss and (Mary) Tamor Fisher.[12] The 1920 census for Denver, Colorado, lists a George DeRoss, 45; wife Tamor DeRoss, 42; daughter Marie, 16; son Paul, 12; and a daughter Georgia, 9. Tomboy Bessie had apparently taken on her father's given name at an early age. The Denver city directories show nothing of them for the year 1921, but it lists the DeRoss family living there from 1922 through 1926. In 1927 there is no DeRoss mentioned in the Denver directory, but they were again listed as living there in 1928, 1929, and 1930.

Georgie's father, a tenant farmer and miner of French descent, worked at various sites in Oklahoma, Colorado, and New Mexico. He was away for long periods of time and sent little money home to his family. His wife, Tamor, worked as a laundress to support herself and the children. Georgie's parents had married December 4, 1898, at Stroud, Oklahoma (Tamor's home). They were divorced March 23, 1933, in Fremont County, Colorado. His grounds for divorce were that *she* deserted *him*.

According to Georgie, the family was quite poor but her mother had an upbeat philosophy. She told her children when you are at the bottom, everything has to be up. She admonished them never to cry because they would only be crying their own lives away.

She also taught them privacy, something Georgie would cherish for the rest of her life. They all lived in one big room, but Tamor made partitions of canvas so they each could have a territory to call their own. Within these spaces were a pad for a bed and enough hangers for their clothes. No one was allowed to intrude into the others' spaces. Tamor would not stand for any arguing, and when someone did, she would say, "If you can't be pleasant to one another, why, just go to your pad!"[13]

Georgie was a life-long vegetarian. This came about, she said, simply because she did not like meat. While she was growing up, the family only had meat once or twice a week. Even then, she would give her portion to her brother or sister and just eat the vegetables. She mostly ate cabbage, rice, tomatoes, and potatoes. Tomatoes, canned or raw, were her lifetime favorite food, closely followed by avocadoes.

While still in high school, Georgie met a handsome, all-American, six-foot, blond young man named Harold Clark. She married him in Denver on January 22, 1928. Her mother had hoped that she would finish school before getting married, but she understood Georgie had strong sex needs and could not, in that day and time, fulfill them outside of marriage. A daughter, Sommona Rose, was born to them in Denver on March 21, 1929.[14]

Georgie and Paul had been indifferent students, while their older sister, Marie, excelled in her studies. Marie obtained a teaching certificate and taught school in the Denver area for several years. Georgie worked at various jobs including cigarette girl in a night club and toiling in a rubber factory. She also learned how to operate a comptometer.[15]

As the Depression deepened, jobs became harder to find, so in about 1931 she and Harold left Sommona Rose with Georgie's mother and went to Florida to look for work. Finding no jobs there, they took a bus to New York City. In New York Georgie found work as a comptometer operator for Radio City; Harold was unable to find a job of any kind. Their favorite haunt was Central Park, where they became fascinated with bicyclists practicing for six-day bicycle races. Georgie easily made friends with the cyclists and they taught her how to ride.

On August 2, 1936, Georgie, always restless, set out with Harold for California on two racing bikes given to them by their new friends. The racing bikes had hard, narrow seats and Georgie said after the first day out she rode mostly standing up. After a few hundred miles their leg muscles became toughened, and it was easier going. They did not own a sleeping bag, so at night they would go a short distance away from the road and sleep on the ground. Occasionally they would work for a farmer for food and then sleep in his haystack. Most people outside of the big cities were friendly, so Georgie and Harold never felt threatened. Those were the days of the Depression and many displaced people were traveling West.

Georgie said the two of them left New York with just one week's salary from her job to get by on, so they did not have enough for the luxury of a bath. She knew most rooming houses had a bathroom in the hallway; when she spotted one she would walk in, find an open bathroom, take a bath, and change clothes. She never could get Harold to do it.

From Chicago on they traveled via Route 66. It was the first paved cross-country highway, stretching over two thousand miles from Chicago to Santa Monica, California, and it was the easiest way west.

When they arrived at Fontana, California, the two only had one dollar left. Upon seeing a sign, "Grape Pickers Wanted," they applied, claiming to be experienced pickers. They managed by watching how others did the job. After earning four dollars in two days, they headed for Los Angeles, and by the time they arrived, they were almost broke again. Georgie had a large diamond Harold's mother had given her as a wedding present. She found a pawn shop and hocked it so they would have something to live on until they found work.

Georgie claims she got a job within a week with a horse-racing bookie. But sensing the place might soon be raided, she quit that job after a few weeks, just before it was shut down by the police! She seemed always able to find work, even when jobs were scarce. In Los Angeles, she found employment as a comptometer operator once again.

Soon after Georgie and Harold settled in Los Angeles, her mother, sister, brother, and daughter joined them. Georgie recalled:

Over the next few years I grew restless and moved from Los Angeles to Chicago and back several times. About this time Harold and I went our separate ways. Husbands have always come second with me. Harold just didn't want to move around like I did, so we agreed to part. Later I filed for and obtained a divorce.[16]

The above stories certainly have some truth in them, but they are as yet undocumented. According to the divorce papers, Harold walked out on Georgie more than a year before the divorce, stating that he was tired of married life. Georgie was living in Chicago when she filed for divorce from Harold Clark in March 1941. At the divorce proceedings she claimed she and Harold had lived in Chicago for nine years, which, if true, meant she had been living there since at least 1932. (When they first moved to Chicago, Georgie's mother, daughter, and sister apparently went along. Her brother followed a couple of years later.)

During those early years in Los Angeles, according to Georgie, she joined the Sierra Club and did a lot of hiking, rock climbing, and skiing. Outdoor sports were not so popular then, and when she and her small group of enthusiasts would go cross-country skiing they would have practically all of the Sierra Nevada Mountains to themselves. One of the people she often hiked with was Elgin Pierce, who would later accompany her on her first rafting trip through Grand Canyon. She also organized a bicycle club called "Hollywood Wheelmen," and members would often pedal to San Diego or other coastal towns on weekends.

On February 6, 1942, she married James Ray White in Los Angeles. Whitey, as he was called, drove an oil tanker for Wade Transport. He was born in South Dakota in 1895 or 1896. At the time of his marriage, he stated his age as thirty-five. This was later amended by affidavit to correct his age at marriage to forty-six. His father was born in Russia and his mother in Norway. Some friends tried to warn Georgie that he was an alcoholic, but she naively thought he was a social drinker. At the time of their marriage, Georgie did not use the name Bessie, identifying herself instead as Georgie Helen Clark; she listed her birthplace as Chicago, Illinois. The reason for this deception is unknown. Sommona lived with Georgie from then on, and together they hiked the mountains around Los Angeles. They also did a lot of bicycling together.

Georgie Clark and James (Whitey) White at their marriage in 1938. *Cline Library, Northern Arizona University, Georgie Clark Collection, #91.13.2.*

Georgie's daughter, Sommona Rose Clark. *Courtesy of Don Briggs, by permission of Paul DeRoss, Jr.*

Georgie and daughter, Sommona Rose. *Courtesy of Don Briggs, by permission of Paul DeRoss, Jr.*

At the outbreak of World War II, Georgie took a job at Douglas Aircraft Corporation in the security department. Like all others who worked in a defense plant, she was forced to produce a birth certificate. She was listed as Bessie C. Clark on her I.D. card, but outside the defense plant she still used the name Georgie.

Her work there triggered an interest in aviation. She learned that the Army Air Force Ferry Command was looking for qualified woman pilots to deliver planes from the factory to destinations within the United States and decided to try for a position in that organization. To qualify for this training she needed a minimum of thirty-five hours of flying time.

Being fiercely independent, Georgie quit her job at Douglas Aircraft Corporation, took all of her savings out of the bank, and moved with Sommona Rose to Quartzsite, Arizona, where flying lessons were the cheapest.Whitey had his trucking job, and so he remained in Los Angeles.

Georgie's savings did not leave enough to pay rent after tuition and food, so she and Sommona unrolled their sleeping bags in a culvert near the airport. This posed no problem as they were used to roughing it on their hikes in the mountains. Sommona Rose was a big hit with the pilots, and between lessons with the students they gave her free airplane rides and some lessons. Georgie said Sommona learned to fly quicker than she did.[17]

After completing her course of training at Quartzsite, Georgie applied for ferry-pilot training. Her acceptance letter to the 318th AAF Flying Training Detachment at Sweetwater, Texas, is dated February 12, 1944. On it her name is listed as Georgie H. White. After her five hundred hours of training were completed, the war went on, but the Ferry Command was deactivated. Georgie wound up back in Los Angeles and resumed living with Whitey.

By this time Sommona was an attractive young lady of fifteen with a flair for art. A teacher had taken an interest in her and thought she would be eligible for a scholarship at a nearby college. Georgie thought Sommona was headed for a career as a commercial artist. Mother and daughter adored each other and spent most of their spare time together.

On June 23, 1944, shortly after returning from Sweetwater, Georgie and Sommona set out to pedal to Santa Barbara, a hundred miles north of L.A. They could not get anyone else to go with them, so they took off alone. Along the way Sommona Rose was struck by a drunk driver and killed. Georgie got the license number of the car and the driver was apprehended. She decided, however, not to press charges as this "would not bring back [her daughter]." Georgie was devastated. This was the most traumatic thing that had happened in her life. Whitey was afraid she would lose her mind.

Exploring with Harry Aleson

While Georgie was battling the depression from this tragedy, friends took her to a lecture by fellow Sierra Club member and explorer Harry Aleson. She was fascinated by his pictures of the canyon country and asked him to take her along on his next trip. Harry had been advertising for hikers to go with him on a trip that would begin several miles inside Grand Canyon. From there they would climb up the North Rim and hike across the Arizona Strip to St. George, Utah.

Georgie and Gerhard Bakker, a biologist from Los Angeles City College, were the only people to sign up for the forthcoming trip. An article in the *Boulder City News*, dated August 19, 1944, headlined: "Shivwits Hike Next Week, Biologist Mountaineer in Trio, Aleson Is Guide for Trip." The article read:

> A biologist and a woman mountaineer will be guided across the Shivwits Plateau during the remainder of August by Harry Aleson, Grand Canyon explorer and boatman. Mrs. Georgie White, member of the Sierra Club and Los Angeles mountaineer, and Gerhard Bakker, biology instructor of Los Angeles City College are the hikers Aleson will take on the long climb from the bottom of Grand Canyon to the top of Mount Dellenbaugh and thence to St. George, Utah.

They planned to take along still and movie cameras with both color and black-and-white film, and to "observe and study the terrain and animal life on the trip."

On August 20, 1944, the trio took a power boat across Lake Mead, past the Grand Wash Cliffs, to Quartermaster Canyon at Mile 235 where Harry maintained his tent camp. From there the party crossed over to the mouth of Burnt Springs Canyon where they began their climb out to the rim. The food they carried was mostly dehydrated, and their diet had been carefully worked out for the right amount of proteins, starches, fruits, and so forth. They took along blankets and two gallons of water each, expecting to replenish the water supply at water holes along the way. To begin with, each pack weighed about twenty-five pounds.

They hiked up Burnt Springs Canyon to where Twin Springs Canyon joined it. At that point it looked like Twin Springs Canyon would be the best route to the top, but as they neared the crest they found their way blocked by dry waterfalls 150 feet high in one branch of the canyon and 250 feet high in the other. Since Twin Springs Canyon proved to be impassable, they were forced to return to Burnt Springs Canyon. Georgie remembers:

> By the time we reached the top of Twin Springs Canyon the two men were almost ready to collapse. I don't mean to imply that I don't get tired, but somehow, since Sommona occupied my mind completely at this point, I just didn't seem to feel anything at all. We now worked our way back to Burnt Canyon, then painfully followed that canyon to the top. The last several thousand feet I wasn't really sure Harry and Gerhard were going to make it. Besides being tired, their feet were killing them. They had worn narrow leather boots that rubbed them badly. Every night after that they would take off their boots and together count their blisters. For desert hiking, that trip taught me, it is best to wear a type of boot or shoe with good ankle support but a canvas top.[18]

Upon reaching the canyon rim they headed due east toward Mount Dellenbaugh. While hiking through the heavy timber on the Shivwits Plateau they lost all sense of direction. No landmarks were visible and everything looked the same. One day they discovered they had traveled in a complete circle. After that they kept a close watch on the sun. Finding a brass survey marker helped them get back on course. They followed an old prospector's road into Oak Grove Springs, the third water they had found in five days. They also found a small cabin with a truck and other signs indicating the cabin was occupied. In due time Tom Cotton, his wife, and Reid Sorenson arrived from off the range. They had come from St. George in the spring to take care of water for range cattle at the Mathes Ranch and would return to town in late fall. The hikers were invited to stay for dinner. After dinner they had an evening's visit, slept over, and were treated to breakfast the next morning.[19]

Because of their blistered feet, the hikers chose not to take the extra day to hike to the top of Mount Dellenbaugh. Still, on the way across the plateau they had fine views of Mount Trumbull, Mount Logan, Mount Emma, Diamond Butte, Vermillion Cliffs, Hurricane Cliffs, the Virgin Mountains, and other sights.

On the cross-country hike one evening, while making a weed mattress pad for his bed at twilight, Gerhard Bakker captured a good-sized rattlesnake. He put the living snake in a muslin bag, ready to tote it out to California. For five days he carried the rattler in his backpack along with his other paraphernalia, occasionally moistening the cloth with his precious water.

Georgie said of this, "During the day's hiking the snake became accustomed to our movements and kept quiet. At night, however, that snake became supersensitive and every time I turned over it rattled. What an eerie noise *that* was."[20] Georgie was very sensitive to animals, including snakes, and wanted Gerhard to leave it there in its own environment, but he refused. In later years on the river, where she had control of the situation, she made absolutely sure that her passengers and boatmen left the animals, birds, reptiles, and even insects alone.

On the seventh day of hiking the group met Royal Blake and his two sons. Blake was a government hunter and trapper from St. George. They accepted a ride from him in the late afternoon, and the next morning rode into St. George. Georgie was not too pleased with the trapper. She recorded:

> On the seventh day, somewhere out on the desert, we met a hunter and trapper from Utah who offered us a ride to St. George. I didn't want anything to do with either him or his boys because I knew he was out there shooting wild horses. Harry and Gerhard, however, talked me into accepting the ride. I hated it. On the way back the boys spotted a beaver, stopped the truck, got out, and clubbed it to death. I know at that time a lot of people believed in killing animals. But I didn't. As far as I was concerned, that hunter and his family were just not nice people, and I was relieved to leave them in St. George.[21]

The trio reached St. George on August 30 and returned to Boulder City the next day. Gerhard Bakker left immediately for Los Angeles, but Georgie had not yet had enough of the canyon and river. It was balm to her grieving spirit, so she went across Lake Mead with Harry to recover the motorboat they had left at Quartermaster Canyon. On the way back the two stopped for the night at God's Pocket on the north shore of Lake Mead. Harry began tying up the

boat, and while moving a small log, he felt a hot sting in the ring finger of his left hand. In the bright moonlight he saw what he took to be
a scorpion scurrying away. Within half a minute the pain traveled up
his arm to the glands in his arm pits. He doped the wound with iodine
and made a tourniquet for the finger.

They immediately launched the boat and headed for Boulder.
On the run down the river and across Lake Mead Georgie ran the
boat while Harry gave directions. Harry's feet began to hurt, his arms
twitched, and his ears began to tingle. His legs became almost para-
lyzed, it was difficult to speak, and he thought for a while he would
pass out. Still he was able to give Georgie directions from points sil-
houetted against the shoreline.

After the seventh hour the pains began to moderate. At dawn
they landed the boat and, after a short nap, had breakfast. They then
crossed the rest of the lake on clear water and arrived in Boulder City
at about noon on Monday.[22]

Harry spent forty-eight feverish hours recovering from the sting,
and Georgie reluctantly returned to Los Angeles. Her lifelong love
affair with the Grand Canyon and the Colorado River had begun.

Georgie's relations with Whitey deteriorated as she spent more
and more time with Harry. By 1945 Harry had moved from Los
Angeles to Richfield, Utah. Georgie was involved in a candy-making
operation at that time, working ten to twelve hours per day. The candy
was manufactured by her sister, Marie, and packed by Georgie.[23]
Georgie sent candy to Harry from time to time and wrote frequent letters to him. Film was hard to come by in those war years and Georgie
bought film for Harry whenever she could locate what he needed.

In the spring of 1945, Georgie was in some kind of trouble. On
April 6 she wrote Harry and told of working long hours packing candy
for Easter. In the letter she mentions:

> I am in a mess & afraid to jump for fear I land in the fire. I
> knew the final separation would be bad, but dumbbell me, I
> walked right into this, will tell you later. In my wildest dreams
> this never came to my mind. I sure learn the hard way. Marie
> and Paul sure stand by. I'm very lucky to have them & so many
> good friends, at least when I look like the black sheep.[24]

It is not clear what this "mess" was about. On April 24 Georgie
wrote, "Had my trial on trouble I mention—dismissed case but it cost
me money and time. Have started divorce." In the same letter she

says, "I can get off in June [for the Grand Canyon swim]."[25] On May 1 she wrote, "Divorce is started. . . . Dog & cat are fine. Keeping them in garage till I get runway in. Went skiing last weekend—*well burnt and peeling now*. Hope to fly with C.A.P. this weekend." And in the same letter, "This sun really gives me spring fever & makes me think of you & Colo. River." Again on May 11 she mentioned that divorce papers had been served.

In an undated letter of about the same time Georgie writes, "The sun & warmth today makes me think of you and the Colo. River and that cold bath by (Your Home)," and, ". . . divorce started but I haven't appeared in court yet." Then, "Seems odd having a house to myself." She also mentions spending two days a week with the Civil Air Patrol. She closes by saying, "You desert rat, come to town & I'll tame you. Must close now and work, work, work. Your friend Geo." On June 20 Georgie sent Aleson one roll of 16 mm colored film and wrote that she could be away until after July fourth. She said she had to put out a carton of cigarettes to get it. There is no more mention of a divorce in subsequent letters, so apparently she and Whitey patched up their differences.

2 Rafting the Rapids, 1946–1947

For the first few months after her swim with Harry Aleson in 1945, no one could have talked Georgie into swimming that river again. She and Harry still went hiking in and around the Grand Canyon, checking out old mines and other interesting places. Georgie wrote:

> I knew there were a lot of questions about my relationship with Harry. After all, I was married and spending weeks and months out on the desert with another man. The truth was that after seeing Harry's pictures I became determined to explore the desert and the canyon country for myself. I couldn't hike alone (at least I didn't think I could at the time) and Harry was the only person who would go with me.
>
> After awhile I came to admire his determination and drive, but I was never romantically attracted to him, nor was our relationship physical. Harry simply needed someone to hike with him and be on hand in case of an emergency—so did I.[1]

As time passed Georgie and Harry began to look back and glorify the swim down the Colorado River of the year before. They had a tendency to forget the pain and remember only the good parts. By winter they had decided to tackle the river from farther up and to try a different method. They spent the winter months planning another expedition.

In 1867, two years before Major John Wesley Powell's epic voyage,[2] a prospector named James White (no relation to Georgie's husband) emerged from Grand Canyon on a log raft. He was emaciated, half starved, and claimed to have floated all the way through the Grand Canyon.[3]

Georgie and Harry thought it would be exciting to float a portion of the river on a wood raft as James White had done. They wanted to prove that James White had made a longer raft ride than many believed he had done. They also wanted to find out whether a river party could come out safely on a driftwood raft in case of a boat loss or wreck.

By 1946 the war was over and defense plants were cutting back sharply. Georgie tried to keep her options open whenever there was a possibility of an adventure with Harry. In March she wrote him: "Have been working at this and that, trying not to get tied down too much . . . " and "Have passed a lot of things by in the business line because it would mean keeping my nose to the grindstone. . . ."[4]

Harry was guiding regular trips through Glen Canyon by this time. Georgie could not afford to go on any of these trips as a paying passenger, but apparently went along on at least one as a helper. Harry wrote to her in late March saying, "Glad you can make all 3 trips. . . . You'll earn your river trip by working on the long hike and raft trip."[5]

In a later letter Georgie expresses hurt from some of his criticism. She writes:

> I did try to do my share of things on trip but at times your remarks made me wonder if I was more in the road than of good use. I really enjoyed the trip but your new ways puzzled me a great deal. Please remember on the raft trip, I have the nerve but no skill at all so I depend on you. I have a lot of faith in you. I do want to learn all things but feel badly when you make me feel silly & helpless if I don't do things (right) the first time. Remember 35 yrs is an old goat to be teaching things to. Just working in an office all my life didn't help any.[6]

Back into Grand Canyon

On June 18, 1946, Georgie met Harry in St. George, Utah. Harry had a wide range of publicity contacts through his lectures, and a Mr. Sheridan of *Life Magazine* telephoned him from Los Angeles about the upcoming trip. Sheridan told Harry that he might send a plane to make pictures of their log raft drift. During the day Harry had long-distance calls from Ruth Lusch of the Las Vegas Chamber of Commerce, from a reporter at the *Baltimore Sun,* and from a reporter at the *Las Vegas Review-Journal*. In the evening he called Elton Garrett at the *Boulder City News*. Then he worked on maps and bearings for the flight plan of an airplane that would check on them and wrote a letter to go with it.

On the afternoon of June 19, Georgie and Harry loaded their equipment into Royal Blake's pickup truck and headed south to rancher Slim Waring's cabin. After lunch Blake returned to St. George. Georgie and Harry climbed to the top of 6,750-foot-high Mount Dellenbaugh, where Harry took some movies. Upon returning they found Waring and his wife at home, then enjoyed dinner with them and spent the night in comfortable beds.

The next day they loaded their gear onto a pack mule and were led about four miles on horseback by Waring to a break in the canyon northeast of Castle Peak. At that place Waring pointed out a possible route down into the canyon and left them to proceed on foot. They struggled through thick brush with their heavy backpacks until they came to a faint trail down the canyon. Travel was difficult and they rationed the water from their two-quart canteens to one swallow per half hour. By evening they were very tired and their water was gone; they made a dry camp. Georgie slept on her sheet in the wash while Harry pitched his sheet on a big boulder. They used Navy life preservers as pillows.

The next morning they headed out early looking for water. By nine o'clock they were quite weakened from thirst, so they cut off the top of a barrel cactus and chewed on the pulp. It tasted terrible! Still, they took some with them and chewed on it as they hiked along. Soon they came to a sharp drop in the cliffs. After finding a route down, they noticed a number of wasps flying about, a signal that moisture was nearby. After digging holes by hand in the wet earth, a little brackish water began to seep in. When this had settled somewhat, they were able to get a few swallows of water. Then Harry dug a deeper hole while dozens of wasps buzzed around his face. While the water was settling they lowered their backpacks on lines down a second steep ledge.[7]

By noon they were able to make a lime juice/sugar water mixture from the brackish water. Sipping it slowly and experiencing no ill effects, they made cupful after cupful with lime and then with instant coffee. To restore their strength they alternately slept and drank most of the afternoon. Then they filled their canteens, packed up and were on their way again.

Within the next hour they came upon six potholes, all filled with water! Some even had tadpoles swimming in them. While Harry went on ahead through a narrow corkscrew passage and over a short limestone ledge, Georgie stayed behind and bathed in one of the pools. Then Harry returned to the pools and took a bath. The two then proceeded down the ledges. They each kept a mouthful of water between rest stops to force nose breathing in order to relieve their dry throats. At dusk they made a dry camp in a canyon they believed to be Parashant Wash. Harry searched ahead for water but found none.

They breakfasted next morning on cold instant coffee, conserving the water in their canteens for the descent ahead. The two would hike about twenty-five minutes, then rest ten. At a rest stop after several hours of hiking, Georgie could hear a faint sound but was not sure whether it was the wind on the high canyon walls or the roar of rapids. They were now deep in rugged Parashant Wash, which enters the Colorado River 198.5 miles below Lee's Ferry, Arizona. At the next rest stop she was sure she heard running water. They arrived at the river at about 9 A.M. As far down as they could see, two miles by Harry's estimate, was a continuous rapid.

Harry recorded, "What a glorious experience to see so much water in this parched desert area! After cooling down, we wade into the delicious running water. We make colored motion pictures of it."[8] In the next seven days they were to see plenty of the "delicious" waters. They alternately rested in the shade and swam until they were thoroughly refreshed. Then they began to gather driftwood logs for their raft.

According to Harry, at the mouth of Parashant Wash they found an old camp with ashes from a campfire. Under a ledge he discovered a box with three sticks of dynamite wrapped separately in three sacks. They also found an ancient Indian mescal pit. As they sat in the shade drinking cool water, a hot wind came up, blowing sand all around. The wind, blowing upstream, whipped spray from the tops of the waves, making the waves look formidable. A handful of water tossed in the air landed thirty-five feet away. While reading in the shade of a mesquite tree, Georgie was struck in the back of the head by a small stone that had been blown off a nearby ledge. Toward evening the wind subsided and they supped on Klein's dry soup. Harry commented that salt was very much appreciated. Just before dark a plane passed high overhead.

Harry says he was awakened at dawn the next morning by the odor of smoke. Georgie had a fire going and was cooking brown rice that had soaked overnight. For breakfast they had the rice with sugar, candy, and instant coffee. Harry took apart the dynamite box for the nails and boards and carved out three paddles from the boards. Among his equipment Harry listed a heavy hatchet, a combination folding hatchet and knife with belt, two U.S. Navy life preservers, two U.S. Air Corps life preservers, swim fins, various items of clothing, first aid materials, backpacks, and three magazines.

The two filled their backpacks for travel on the river, then built a test raft using cottonwood and juniper logs tied together with a light line. In a drift pile they found a three-inch by twelve-inch plank that was seven feet long which they used for a crosspiece. On it they placed one pack with a hatchet inside and set it adrift. Harry took pictures of it as it circled in a backwater. They tried four times over a period of two hours to get it into the main current, but to no avail. Finally they abandoned it, deciding it was too flimsy to ride through the rapids anyway.

Carrying their gear along the right bank past the worst of Parashant Rapid, they entered the river on an airfloat, a one-man rubber raft they had carried for emergencies, steering it with sweeps Harry had made from the dynamite box ends and a couple of driftwood sticks. The three-by-six-foot raft was barely able to keep them afloat in calm water; it capsized in rough water at the foot of the rapid at Mile 200, but they were able to hang onto it. They came out of the river and walked along the bank to calmer water, reentered for a short way, then portaged along the bank past some more rough water.

Georgie, however, gives an entirely different version of this experience. She claims they used the same wrist lock as the year before and swam down the river in their life jackets.[9] She does not mention the raft at all nor how they transported all their gear.

The pair camped on the right bank at Mile 204 at the mouth of a canyon. Water had seeped into their food cans, so they spread everything out to dry. They kept watching for the log raft to come by but did not see it. Next morning, June 25, they drifted on down the river, portaging around seven rough rapids, looking for logs suitable for building another raft. On Thursday morning they reached Kolb Rapid 205.5 miles below Lee's Ferry. They feared it would be almost impossible to ride, so they climbed about one half mile up the left bank to get around it. Drifting on down, alternately floating and portaging, they came to the mouth of Indian Canyon at Mile 206.4 and camped on the right bank. Along the way they saw only one log suitable for building a raft.

On Wednesday, June 26, after floating a few miles, they found logs to make another raft, marked it with two ax cuts, and set it adrift. After several tries to force it out into the current, this raft also remained in the eddy. That day they saw the Desert Skyways plane carrying Ted Swift, Ben Thompson, and William Belknap, Jr., flying high above. They made twenty-five-foot letters "OK" in the sand and waved sheets. The plane continued on without circling. Georgie and Harry reentered the river and drifted on through rapids for a mile or two before reaching Three Springs Canyon. It took hard work to get out of the river before being swept past its mouth. The swim fins came in handy here. They made camp on a small sand bar on the left side. Next morning they portaged past the big rapid below camp and reentered the river. There were still no logs in sight for a third raft.

Harry took some pictures, and then they drifted through another riffle and pulled in at the mouth of a canyon they took to be Trail Canyon at Mile 219. After a short rest they ate a five-ounce can of green beans and some coffee—all that remained of their food except for bouillon cubes. At dusk they were able to struggle to the left shore at the very head of Granite Springs Rapid. Leaving their packs on the bank, they immediately began groping their way in the dark down through the boulders two thirds of a mile to a food cache left there by Harry in February of 1944. They took tomato juice, grapefruit juice, citrus marmalade, soy beans, and peanut butter and fumbled their way back up to camp. When light came the peanut butter turned out to be mustard.

On their portage past the rapid they picked up enough canned food from the cache to last them to the next cache eighteen miles downstream. They reentered the river at the same place they had begun their forty-two-mile life preserver swim a year earlier. At this time they were two full days behind schedule.

The pair's rubber raft almost capsized just above Diamond Creek Rapids, Mile 225.7. They were surprised to find they could balance the small craft on six- to eight-foot waves. That night they camped on a silt bar.

While Georgie and Harry were resting in the shade of a mesquite tree at Diamond Creek to escape the blazing heat, several airplanes flew over. Harry signaled to the planes with mirrors and a bed sheet but was not spotted. At sundown they made a tough portage along the left bank, past the worst part of Diamond Creek Rapid. Then they went back on the river and ran several small rapids and one large one. Occasionally they would pull over to the bank and empty a half-barrel of water from their tiny raft. They camped that night at the mouth of Travertine Creek.

On Saturday morning, June 29, they took time to take motion pictures of the beautiful waterfalls a short way up the canyon. On the river again, they soon reached the brink of 232 Mile Rapid with its short, steep drop and big waves. Aleson recounts:

> We feel like we slide down 10 to 15 feet in a short second. The big waves fall back over us and flip the float upside-down. From the heavy waves I see Georgie hanging on the airfloat, and in the backwater. In 3 seconds we were 50 feet apart. As quickly we were out of sight. The roar drowns any effort to yell. In the next 3 miles are 9 to 12 rapids. On this day they are vicious, far worse than 48,000 sc. ft. 1945. Repeatedly, I am pulled under in waves and whirlpools. I took water in throat, my nostrils. I gasp for air, choke, cough out water—came near drowning 10 to 20 times in those terrible three miles. Between rapids I lay on the water gasping in agony, hoping and praying I may hold my breath long enough to live through the coming rapids. To swim out I know is out of the question. There was no panic or fear, but gratefulness for getting thru. As the next rapids came in sight, a backwater took me near the wall, and with great effort, I struggle to the rocky black granite wall.[10]

A heavy metal clasp had been torn from the case carrying Harry's precious motion picture camera and film, and it now hung by one shoulder strap. Feebly he opened the metal can and found water in it and in the camera. The tape-sealed film can appeared to be all right. Harry wondered how Georgie had fared, anxiously looking up and down the river for her. Finally he sighted her as she came down the current riding the airfloat. Having only a single paddle, she was unable to land where Harry was and was swept on past. Eventually she was able to land in a backwater below. Carrying his gear, Aleson climbed painfully along the granite wall, reaching her about two hours later.

They drifted on down, reaching another food cache, and uneventfully floated twenty-two miles to Quartermaster Canyon. It

Harry Aleson and Georgie White being picked up by the park cruiser on the upper end of Lake Mead, June 30, 1946. *Photo by Bill Belknap, Cline Library, Northern Arizona University, Georgie Clark Collection, #91.13.5.*

was hot and Aleson was "done in." Too late to make the trip out of the canyon before nightfall, they rested until the next day. On Sunday morning they met the Park Service boat above Emery (Columbine) Falls. It was piloted by Ray Poyser, who had made two trips up the river about eleven miles above Pierce Ferry the day before. Aboard were Ben Thompson, assistant National Park Service superintendent; Domal Jollev, chief ranger; Philip Van Cleeve; William Belknap, Jr.; and ten other passengers.

For the first time in more than a week Georgie and Harry were emerging from the confining mile-high walls of the lower Grand Canyon. "Never again!" said Harry, as he boarded the National Park Service boat. "Never again and I hope no man ever attempts to come down the Colorado River on a raft."

Despite Harry's vow of "never again," they both would do it often in the future. Georgie would do it for the rest of her life.

Georgie returned to her home in Los Angeles that Sunday night. In one of her many letters to Harry, Georgie wrote, "I think of you and the Colo. River often." In January 1947 she wrote, "I hate office work but it pays off the best."[11] She was doing "temp work" for an oil company to keep her options open. In April she wrote: "If I never had another trip I would still be grateful, your best friend, want to see you, and hear from you. I could never forget our trips on the rapids, few people have the companionship and thrill those trips were."[12]

Rafting Cataract Canyon

By 1946 war surplus stores were opening all over the country. Georgie and Harry shopped the stores in Los Angeles, where Georgie bought a ten-man raft and Harry bought a seven-man craft. There was no doubt in either of their minds they would tackle the river again. It was just a matter of how and when. On August 4, 1947, Georgie wrote Harry:

> When the rapids are mentioned I forget everything else, they cast a spell on me, let's ride them all—don't you think a large rubber boat can make it, or won't the passengers be willing. . . . Seems a long time since I have been on [the] river, it certainly grows on one & is always different.[13]

By October it was time for Aleson to end the season of hauling paying tourists, so he and Georgie picked this time to launch a raft trip through Cataract Canyon. Georgie wrote that she was still doing part-time office work, but planned to quit and start a candy-packaging business. She said that Whitey could take care of it while she was away. This was the first time she mentioned Whitey since writing about a divorce. In September she wrote that she had started her business. In her letter she said, "Be sure and write all time—am glad to hear from the only free person I know of."[14]

Georgie took a bus from Los Angeles to Richfield, Utah, where she met Harry. From there the two took another bus to Green River, Utah. According to Georgie the cold blast of a winter wind hit her when she got off the bus, and it seemed to go right through her lightweight jacket. She was soon shivering and her teeth chattering. Harry noticed this—he was cold too. "Maybe we shouldn't try it, Georgie," he said. "We could go back."

"No way," she told him. "I've come this far. I'm going the rest of the way."[15] So they launched their boat and headed down the river,

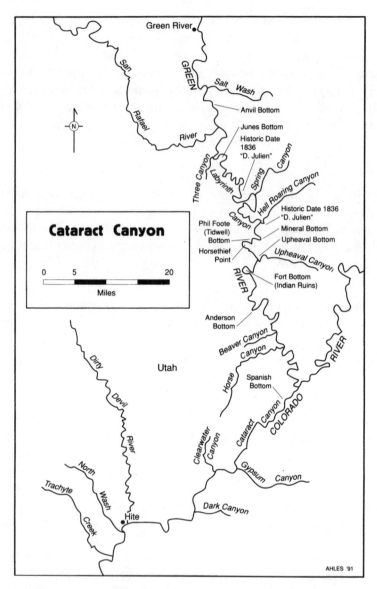

From Rough-Water Man: Elwyn Blake's Colorado River Expeditions, *by Richard E. Westwood. Copyright © 1992 by University of Nevada Press. Used with permission.*

and came upon spectacular views as they drifted through Labyrinth and Stillwater Canyons.

Aleson kept a journal of the trip.[16] It varies somewhat from Georgie's memories and gives more details. One morning they stopped at Keg Springs to examine a register there. Harry added "ALESON & G. WHITE 10–26–47" to the register of "ALESON & BADGER 7–17–47," "ALESON & B. LOPER 7–18," and "ALESON 7–19."

They stopped at Hell Roaring Canyon to take pictures of the D. Julien 1836 inscription. A good camping spot was found a mile and a half below. It was level, grassy, and near sheltering boulders. From Green River they had brought two and a half gallons of water for cooking and drinking and had refilled the canteen at the stream in Trin-Alcove. This water was now gone, so fruit juices took the place of drinking water. That night they settled river water to fill the canteen.

They passed around the Great Bend where an old Indian fort or watchtower stands. From their view it appeared to be almost impossible to climb the sheer ledge on which the fort stood, though many had done it. They stopped at Cliff House Canyon, hiked up it half a mile to the ruins then on for another mile to where they were blocked by a dry waterfall.

On October 30 they reached the confluence of the Green and Colorado Rivers. They landed for camp number eight on the left bank of the Colorado, a quarter-mile below the junction. After dinner they watched the changing tapestry of moonlight coming down the opposite wall.

On October 31 the pair was off into Cataract Canyon.[17] At 11 A.M. they went over a small riffle and half an hour later landed at the lower end of Spanish Bottom for lunch. They then hiked out to the Land of Standing Rocks to take photographs. After returning to the boat they made a short run to the head of Rapid No. 1 (Brown Betty) where they made camp. The weather was fine.

Georgie and Harry looked over No. 1 carefully. Then Harry hiked down to see No. 2 and No. 3, all nice rapids. They decided that Harry would run No. 1 in the morning while Georgie shot movies. Next morning he made a good run and tied up below to wait for her. They lined (towed the raft along the edge of) the upper two hundred feet of No. 2 to give Georgie some experience in that procedure.

During the next six days they would come to more than fifty rapids. At eighteen of these they lined the boat on the more difficult sections, and on four the cargo was portaged. Harry did not record any upsets. In the narrow, deep gorge where the sun seldom reached them and they were frequently doused with icy spray, they often stopped to build a fire, warm up, and dry their clothes.

By November 4 their food was running low. From three-quarters of a mile upstream, Harry recognized the mouth of Dark Canyon, where food had been cached, and soon they could hear the rapids. He could see the A-shaped pile of driftwood he had built on the left bank in July 1945. They landed at Dark Canyon Rapid to make camp number fourteen. For dinner they enjoyed hot cakes, sugar, coffee, tea, and the end of their candy. Harry noted, however, "Hervig's cache of food all gone. We had counted on food here."

The next morning they broke camp and began portaging equipment around Dark Canyon Rapid. The boat was lined down the left bank to just below the mouth of Dark Canyon Creek. They then reloaded the raft and were off down the river. They rode the balance of the rapid, and went on six miles and through six more rapids to Mille Crag Bend. There they saw a pole on the beach with a tin can on top. In it was a note from Arth Chaffin and Ralph Badger, who had come up from Hite on November 4, stayed overnight, and gone back the next day, leaving greetings for Harry and Georgie.

They arrived at Hite and hiked down to Arth Chaffin's ranch. Aaron Porter hauled the boat and equipment up to the ranch for them. They dined that night with Pearl and Mart Guymon and Linda Lou Watring.

Georgie described Hite as "a desolate place at the end of a narrow dirt road many miles from the highway." It was actually a beautiful green oasis in the desert, with famous melons and fruit trees that brought pickers all the way from Hanksville. Porter and his wife agreed to take Georgie and Harry out to Richfield, so the next morning they piled in the couple's old pickup truck and headed along the winding dirt road that led up North Wash. On a hill, after going about fourteen miles, the truck stalled. The battery was dead and the generator was not working. After talking it over, they all agreed that the Porters would camp overnight while Georgie and Harry hiked back to Hite Ranch for a spare battery. By the time they got to the ranch they were stumbling in the darkness.

On November 8 Mart Guymon and young Porter, with a cart and team, brought them back to the stalled pickup. From there on the trip was uneventful. They reached Torrey by midnight with a half-dead battery and, with a new battery installed in the truck, made it across the Wasatch Mountains in a blizzard, arriving at Richfield by noon. From here Georgie headed back to the warmth of Los Angeles.

This year (1997) is the fiftieth anniversary of that river trip by Georgie White and Harry Aleson. According to John Weisheit, who has researched it extensively, it was also "the first military surplus inflatable boat to be used on a river trip on the Green and Colorado rivers."[18] Many others would follow.

3 *From Passenger to Boatman,*
1948–1952

*I*n February 1948 Georgie wrote to Harry: "I am open to any and almost all trips. That is what I live for and one summer to the next certainly seems long. Does it to you?"[1]

Down the Escalante River

Over the next few months Georgie and Harry made plans to go down the Escalante River. They arrived at the small town of Escalante in southern Utah on May 24 and bought provisions for the trip. Both the town and river are named for Fray Silvestre Vélez de Escalante of the Domínguez-Escalante expedition of 1776. Oddly, Escalante neither saw nor came close to the river bearing his name. Major Powell also floated past its mouth on both his 1869 and 1871 explorations of the Colorado River unaware that it was a major tributary. A year later in 1872 the Thompson-Dellenbaugh survey party at first took it for the Dirty Devil, then realizing their error, took credit for its discovery. It proved to be the last river to be discovered in the contiguous United States.[2] Even at this time in 1948, very few Anglos had traveled down the Escalante.

By mid-afternoon Georgie and Harry had their raft inflated, afloat, and loaded in a narrow, shallow pool at the junction of Calf Creek and the Escalante River. They shoved off downstream, but before they had gone fifty feet, they were aground.[3]

They spent the rest of the day dragging and lifting the boat over rocks, sandbars, and riffles. Whenever it was possible to float, they would sit on opposite ends of the boat and guide it by pedaling with one foot over the side. The stream was lined with box elder and scrub oak. The pair estimated they had traveled four miles in four hours.

Pine Cr.

Sand Cr.

Boulder Cr.

Hite

■ Escalante

Escalante River

Colorado River

San Juan River

Utah

Colorado River

■ Lee's Ferry

Arizona

Cartography by Thomas Zajkowski, University of Utah

Glen Canyon and
the Escalante River

N

25   0   25   50 Miles

By mid-morning the next day they reached the mouth of Boulder Creek, about ten miles below Escalante. Aleson wrote, "At that time I was more certain that we would get through. There must have been ten times as much water in Boulder Creek as in the Escalante River."[4]

That afternoon they discovered a two-room Anasazi ruin on a high ledge where the canyon opened to form a half-mile-long valley. Throughout this area of the Southwest, the Anasazi had chosen some fairly lofty and scenic locations for their villages. Either from drought, enemies, or other unknown causes, the Anasazi culture disappeared around A.D. 1300. Georgie and Harry continued down the river, but travel became more difficult. It was a battle to get the raft over the rocky, shallow places and there were many fast chutes of white water. When portaging around these, they had to boost the boat bodily over rocks six to ten feet high. At one place the channel was only about two feet wide. To get the six-foot-wide boat through they unloaded it, stood it on edge, and slipped it through vertically on its beams; they had to portage their equipment many times.

On the fourth day they passed through miles of fast, narrow channels. In one place they crashed against a four-foot-high boulder. The gunwale went under, and the boat began to fill. They both jumped out and put the Philco portable radio and a box of valuables onto a nearby rock.

The boat swung about and an oar knocked a box off into the river. Harry yelled, "Hold the boat!" He then plunged for shore and bounded over and among boulders a couple of hundred feet downstream, where he dove into the river. He grabbed things as they floated by and flung them onto shore. In this way he was able to rescue backpacks, oars, bed rolls, and some other items.

After rescuing all the equipment he could find, Harry returned upstream and found Georgie standing waist-deep in the current, jamming the boat against the shore. Together they bailed the water out of the boat and ran it down to where they could reload the rescued articles. At the next good landing spot they spread the bedrolls and clothing out to dry and checked to see what had been lost. All of the movie film, both exposed and unexposed, was either lost or damaged. The camera motor and exposure meter were water-logged and dead. Papers, books, maps, and some clothing were all gone. Harry's wristwatch and three-fourths of their food were also missing.

When the bedding and clothes were dry, the two repacked, reloaded, and went on. Soon they began recovering other items along the riffles: clothing, socks, shirts, a blazer, a can of sausages, a box of crackers, a large canteen, an envelope of maps, and one blank sheet of diary booklet. About a mile below the mishap, Harry thought he saw the yellow box containing a hundred-foot roll of 16mm film. It turned out instead to be a large piece of unwrapped Tillamook cheese, which came in handy during the eight days ahead. The last recovery was a canoe paddle, which gave them two oars and two paddles.

By evening things finally began to look brighter. When the camera and exposure meter were dried out, both seemed to be all right. And of course the scenery was superb. They counted twelve arches, windows, or natural bridges. One spectacular bridge had an opening of about 150 by 200 feet. It was located about 700 feet up the orange-red canyon wall, and blue skies filled the huge opening. Centuries of wind and running water in the colorful rock formations had carved fins, domes, alcoves, arches, and natural bridges in shades of red, brown, gray, purple, and green. Hanging gardens of white and purple columbine flourished around seeps in the red rock. It gave Georgie a feeling of awe whenever she paused to look at the beauty of the landscape.

On the seventh day they came to Davis Gulch, where Harry recognized two rock cairns he had built in 1945. The pair was now on familiar ground. About eight miles farther on they came out into the Colorado River.

Coming down the Colorado, the two picked up spring water and registered at Hole-In-The-Rock.[5] They also registered at Music Temple,[6] and finally arrived at Lee's Ferry, Arizona, after eighty-eight miles on the flood-swollen Colorado. At Marble Canyon Lodge, Georgie was given the last cabin and Harry slept in the lodge with the Art Greene family. The next morning Georgie boarded the 10:30 A.M. Santa Fe Trailways bus for Flagstaff and Harry took a bus back to Richfield.

Georgie's next letter to Harry, written July 1, 1948, said she had passed the California real estate test, had a license, and was now working with her sister, Marie. She said they had sold one house so far.[7]

Hiking the Escalante Trail

During the last half of October, Georgie and Harry made a long hike that took them over a portion of the route taken by Domínguez and

Escalante in 1776. Harry had hoped to have several others accompany them, but, as had happened on other occasions, when it came time to start, it was down to the two of them. Aleson summarized the trip in a letter to Otis Marston:

> The last 15 days of October, Georgie White and I hiked an average of 12 and a half miles per day, in following the general route of Dominguez and Escalante. Started hike at Marble Canyon Lodge. Had two plane contacts, one on the day before crossing the river between Kane and Padre Creeks, and one on the day of crossing. We ended the hike in cold, rainy and foggy weather on the desert road to Rainbow Lodge, some miles from Inscription House Trading Post. Returned to Richfield early Nov.[8]

The River Goddesses

By 1950 there had been enough publicity about Georgie's hikes and boat trips with Harry Aleson that she was considered by some to be an experienced boatman. In 1950 Carl Junghaunatz, a German officer in World War II and now a movie producer in Hollywood, set out to make a film called *River Goddesses* featuring five young starlets and models.[9] One requirement was that they had to be good swimmers, as they would be on the Colorado River in Glen Canyon for about a month. Junghaunatz chartered the boats of Mexican Hat Expeditions for the trip.[10] He hired Georgie to row one of the boats and chaperon the young starlets. Elgin Pierce, Georgie's friend from the Sierra Club, was also hired as a boatman.

The party left Hite on September 5, 1950.[11] Three cataract boats and one San Juan boat were used. The San Juan boat had a six-foot-by-six-foot platform built over the stern deck to accommodate the professional photographer and his equipment as he shot the beautiful scenery along Glen Canyon as a backdrop for *River Goddesses*. Georgie rowed one of the cataract boats and Elgin Pierce rowed the San Juan boat used by the cinematographer. Members of the boat crew, then, were Jim and Bob Rigg of Mexican Hat Expeditions, Elgin, and Georgie. The starlets were Irish McCalla (later known for her role as television's "Sheena, Queen of the Jungle"), Irene Hettinga, Becky Barnes, Lee Moi Chu, and Martha Moody. The latter two were sorority sisters and on the swim team at a California college.

Georgie as boatman and chaperon for starlets in Glen Canyon, 1950. Left to right: Georgie, Jim Rigg, Irene Hettinga, Irish McCalla. *Courtesy of Irish McCalla.*

The party stopped at most every canyon or other place of interest to hike and take pictures. The river was low and the shoreline was very muddy. At the mouth of nearly every canyon they found cows bogged down in the mud. Much time was spent rescuing these animals. The cattle had gotten mired as they came down to the river for water. It was a messy job, but everyone pitched in to dig the critters out; even the models were down there with the crew digging in the mud and pushing and heaving on the cows! It was filthy, dirty, stinky work. McCalla said, "We'd draw straws to see who had to dig at the rear end. I lost twice, but we did that."

Due to the slow current on the river, the boats had to be rowed, and Georgie did her share. Bob Rigg declared:

> Georgie White was *one strong, tough lady!* She never missed a stroke. Georgie could pull a boat with the best of us, I'm sure. And she was a great, positive contributor to the entirety of the trip . . . she had a good knowledge of the water of the Glen Canyon. She knew how to handle a boat well and she could

row it as long and as many hours as anybody else. She was just a great gal and a very motivated one.

According to Rigg and McCalla, Director Junghaunatz fit the Prussian officer stereotype: stern, demanding, and superior. McCalla remembers he "openly said that women should be kept in concentration camps for breeding purposes only: that's all we were good for." He expected them to climb everything in sight, and he could be unbearable at times. When he gave an order, he expected obedience without question. As time went on, the party became united in their hatred of him. He did not scare Georgie, though; she was the only one he never yelled at more than once or twice.

Georgie taught the women to climb and kept them out of trouble. She was rather dictatorial at times, and would scold or yell at them if she saw they were getting into trouble, but the women accepted it from her because they soon learned she knew what she was talking about. If they were afraid to make a climb or some other equally challenging stunt they had been asked to do, Georgie would show them how to do it safely. If she thought it too dangerous, she would tell them not to do it. McCalla said:

> We all respected her. Because she obviously knew what she was doing, which our director didn't! And we'd say, "Hey, look. He wants us to do so-and-so and one of us is going to get killed!" And we always said, "But he throws a fit!" She wasn't afraid of him, you see. And she'd go up and tell him, "You can't do this and you'd get just as good a shot if you go over here and do so and so!" "Don't tell me how to do it!" he'd yell! And she'd just come back and she'd say, "Don't move, whatever he says, don't move unless he says go in that direction." So, Mother Georgie would take care of us.

At one point Martha Moody went down to the river in her pajamas to get some water and got bogged down to her knees in the mud. When she called for help, photographer Dave Evans replied, "Stay there Martha! We'll get some pictures!" He then took pictures of Irish on one end of a big stick with Martha hanging onto the other end, supposedly rescuing her. Afterward, Georgie came along and really rescued her. She had the muscle to pull her out of that mud.

The party visited all the historic places along the river: Moki Canyon, Hole-In-The-Rock, Music Temple, Rainbow Bridge. A plane would fly over once a week to check on them. They could hear it roaring down the canyon long before it passed overhead. If they were out of any vital supply, a pre-arranged signal would be left in the sand and during the next pass a package would be dropped.

McCalla credits the trip for causing Georgie to think about going commercial. She says:

> I don't know if she ever had the idea before, but I know during the trip, when one of us would fall down something or go off in the wrong direction, she'd rescue us and say, "I'm going to take people down the river because I can take anybody down, if I can get you dingalings through."

Bob Rigg observed that "Jim or Frank Wright or myself probably made a mistake by not inviting Georgie to be a part of Mexican Hat."

Georgie kept few records of her river runs and hikes; she just did them. She also tried to interest her husband Whitey in the sport. In a letter of January 2, 1951, to Otis Marston, Harry Aleson wrote, "This past year James D. [sic] White, her husband, made two San Juan [River] runs with us. So, I have had a boatman named Jim White."[12]

Hiking Accident

In 1951 Georgie listed two trips in her own boat, one from Mexican Hat to Lee's Ferry and one from Hite to Lee's Ferry. A planned expedition with Harry Aleson was called off after Georgie had a serious hiking accident. On August 28, 1951, Georgie's sister Marie wrote Harry:

> Georgie was quite seriously hurt in an accident the 18th. Will be in the hospital 2 weeks this coming Saturday. Skull fracture—bruises etc. . . . She would make the trip if she was able. . . . Doctor says it will be a *long* time before she is back to normal—says she has to be in bed at least 6 weeks and won't be able to work for at least 6 months.[13]

In an undated letter which Harry received on September 24, Georgie wrote:

> So this makes two weeks in hospital. . . . Had just started to work at Douglas. Will *never* be able to do that job again, but phooey didn't like it anyhow—too close. Have six weeks flat

on back to go (in hospital if they have their way but I'm objecting plenty).

Had finished rock climbing Red Buttes over beyond Bishop and was only *hiking* down over rock talus—It had started raining—snowing etc. when we were over on peak & now it made sort of a river—was close to drop-off hiking parallel when a lot of water came & and small boulder I was on just in a flash was off into space, about 30 ft. drop & of course you hit & just keep going for some time—(I almost flew). Managed to get on down to truck. Only one person with me— Of course that did more damage. Fractured bones on both side of head—cracked the middle one—cut just into side of right eye—cut above and below so see double, etc. With time they will be OK. They tell me mainly head injury—Body feels OK—chest hurt coming down but seems OK now. Lost lot of blood—ear bleed—nose bleed & you cough up lots of blood but am OK now. (Doc says I am built like a mule). My face took a terrific beating. It is just coming to life & so is not comfortable. The reason for staying in bed is because of blood clotting and so I *won't* have those horrible head pains when the bones heal. Am lucky that body is fine condition considering. Will be raring to go in Dec. I would and believe I could get up & go right now—don't believe in this rest and quiet stuff. I never could sleep over six hours as you know & don't do any better here.

If you can't read this—tear up & forget—I am writing flat & can't see it too well.[14]

Lee's Ferry to Lake Mead in Grand Canyon

In January 1952 Georgie was still unable to work, but apparently she was all right by March. She wrote Harry that she was going to Hite to meet Whitey who was coming off a San Juan River trip there. Although Georgie still made long hikes with Harry, she no longer made river trips with him.

Of all the outdoor people she knew in the Sierra Club, she thought a few of them might be interested in running the river with her. However, none of them showed any interest until the summer of 1952 when Elgin Pierce agreed to go with her through Grand Canyon.

Elgin Pierce and Georgie ready to leave Paria Riffle, July 11, 1952. *Photo by Bill Belknap, courtesy of Westwater Books.*

On the morning of July 11, 1952, Georgie and Elgin Pierce began the first trip that would take her all the way through Grand Canyon. At Lee's Ferry they met Mexican Hat Expeditions, headed by J. Frank Wright and Jim Rigg. Georgie and Elgin had no map of the river, so Rigg gave them one of the lower section.[15] He sat down with them and "went down the river, rapid by rapid, turn by turn, told her where to go, how to run this rapid, where to land, and told her where we normally camped or what to look out for and how to run it."[16]

Georgie wanted to be on the river ahead of the Mexican Hat party in case of an emergency, so, using her ten-man war surplus raft, they departed at 11:30 A.M. and passed under Navajo Bridge at noon. At 1 P.M. they heard a roar ahead, so they landed on the left side to look over Badger Creek Rapid.[17] Minutes later they took off, running down the rapid's tongue and then slightly left. To test how the boat would stand the water, Georgie pulled up the oars as soon as she got off the tongue and let it rip! Rigg was on the cliff above taking pictures.

Georgie and Elgin did not scout Soap Creek Rapid, but ran right down the tongue and again pulled up the oars. They ran Sheer Wall and House Rock Rapid, then camped on a sandbar. The next day they ran rapids and heavy riffles, then landed for lunch just below Vasey's Paradise.[18] Here, fountains of clear water gush from the red cliff, producing a lush growth of redbud trees, maidenhair fern, moss, and poison ivy. Half an hour later they were at Redwall Cavern, a giant cave in the left wall that has been carved over the ages by the river out of the red limestone cliff.[19] From a distance it looks like a small band shell; however, its sandy floor is large enough to hold a football field. By 3 P.M. they reached President Harding Rapid where they ran to the right of the huge midstream boulder. At 5 P.M. they camped on a sandbar below Nankoweap Canyon.

The next day, July 13, everything went well until they reached Hance Rapid in mid-afternoon. They first landed on the left to look it over. Before leaving Lee's Ferry, Jim Rigg had told them to run down the left side and stay away from the wall and the big reversal waves. Still, they had had such good luck so far, they figured their boat would take anything. Georgie said, "We really feel like the king of all we survey." So they ignored Rigg's advice and headed down the tongue along the right side. When they tried to pull left, the rapid took over. Thrashing waves tipped the boat violently and Elgin was thrown overboard. He grabbed onto an oar, but the rope holding it broke loose from the boat, so he abandoned the oar and swam to shore.

When the river current races down on a big rock upthrust in its path, it rushes around its edges and over its top. On the downstream side a concavity in the water is formed. The bigger the rock and the swifter the current tearing over it, the deeper the hole. All through Hance there were gigantic holes where slab-like rocks lay. Some seemed capable of swallowing a boxcar.

Georgie could not control the boat with only one oar, and it soon drifted over a submerged rock into a huge hole and flipped. Georgie wound up underneath the boat and had difficulty breathing. She hung on and soon worked her way out from under the craft, but could not climb onto it. She said the boat was "like a greased pig." In the next hole she was under the boat again. When she got out from under it the lost oar floated beside her. She grabbed it and hung on. She went under again as the boat went through a huge hole, but she still managed to hang onto the boat and the oar. When she finally reached calmer water, she threw the oar onto the bottom of the boat and made three tries at landing before finding something to hang onto on the left side. She wound up on a small ledge holding a rope to the boat to keep it from floating downstream.

Georgie's back muscles tired from holding the rope, and she was worried what might have happened to Elgin. She decided that if her strength gave out and the boat got away she would stay put until the Mexican Hat party came along and rescued her. Finally she heard a yell and spotted Elgin on a high rock where he had climbed to look for her. He went into the water and edged his way along the cliff until he ran out of handholds. Then he swam into the current. He saw Georgie sooner than he expected. He was lucky enough to hit the same backwater the boat was in and they were back together again. He went under the boat and got hold of another rope. There was hardly room for two of them to stand on this small ledge, but they could see a breakdown about fifty feet downstream where there was more room. They spliced the ropes together and Elgin swam down to the breakdown. Then Georgie jumped onto the upside-down boat and he pulled it in just as darkness fell. The two managed to get a food bag out before going to sleep on the rocks.

The next morning they hoisted the nose of the boat onto a rock to get the bags untied from beneath it. There was no room on the ledge to turn the boat over, but with the bags out they managed to turn it over in the water. They then reloaded and were on their way once more. They sailed through Sockdolager, hit a hole in Grapevine without mishap, and plowed through Zoroaster. They stopped at Phantom Ranch to swim, eat, and stay overnight.

Off again the next morning, the pair hit rough going above Horn Creek, were unable to stop, and ran it without scouting. They came to Granite Falls Rapid at 3:20 P.M. and made camp. Elgin got his first lining experience here, and they very nearly lost the boat. On July 16 they camped at Hermit Rapid, only one mile downstream, and lined the boat along the left side. They continued on for the next few days and on July 19 camped at Tuckup Canyon, Mile 164, where they remained until the following Monday so as not to get too far ahead of the Mexican Hat party.

At noon on July 21 Georgie and Elgin pulled in on the left at the head of Lava Falls, the most powerful of the Grand Canyon's rapids. Here they made camp and waited for Wright and the Rigg Brothers, who arrived on Thursday. All boats of both parties were lined and cargo portaged around the rapid, with the exception of the Riggs' power boat. Georgie and Elgin pitched in. Several photographs were taken of that operation. From Lava Falls on down, Georgie and Elgin tagged along with the Mexican Hat party. Bob Rigg says Elgin and Georgie sat on the raft facing each other with hands on the oars. On July 25 they all camped at Whitmore Wash.

Two days later Georgie and Elgin were invited to join the Mexican Hat group for an initiation of their passengers into the River Rat Society.[20] Tad Nichols, one of their boatmen, said of this ceremony:

> The basic way was to blindfold the inductee, have them follow you around with their hands on your shoulders and walk over some boulders and some rocks into the water and ask them what was most vivid in their mind, perhaps. You'd eventually end up at the river, you know, like at Diamond Creek, which we may have dammed up a little bit. We'd give them a bucket and have them bail, like they're in a rapid—they're still blindfolded—you know; "You're in the middle of Soap Creek" or "You're in the middle of whatever it might have been and you took on a lot of water on it." And they'd bail madly, generally trying to throw the water on *us*, as boatmen—and we did do this in the river a time or two. After this little exercise then they knelt down, still blindfolded, on a bucket upside down, put their hands on the bucket—all fours, as it were, and,

"Now, repeat after me, 'I know I'm weak, I know I'm blind, I know that I extend behind!' And, with that, they would get doused with buckets full of water and, swats with the oars, which were big oars, of course. You'd whomp them on the rear end as hard as you could, depending on which one is being initiated. That was basically "initiation."[21]

Georgie would later claim to have originated this ritual, but it had in fact been started by Norman Nevills many years earlier.

On July 28 Georgie and Elgin were up early, reluctant to see their last day on the river. After running the last of the rapids, Jim Rigg tied them to his motorboat and began towing them across Lake Mead. On the lake they met Jim Jordan and Bill Belknap, who took photographs of them and their boat.

They rode back with the Riggs to Art Greene's Marble Canyon Lodge, where they got their pickup truck and returned to Pierce Ferry to retrieve their boat. Georgie wrote, "How I hate to go back to work, eat, sleep, setup. Only good part is family, cat & Dog, which I missed. Can't have everything."[22]

Elgin, on the other hand, said, "Never again." It seems Georgie had long since fallen under the spell of the canyon, and she could not wait to go back. Georgie was not the first woman to float the length of Grand Canyon (Elzada Clover and Lois Jotter had done it as passengers of Norm Nevills in 1938), but she *was* the first woman to lead a boating party through it.

4 Taking Passengers through Grand Canyon, 1953

$\mathcal{I}$n the winter of 1952–1953, Harry Aleson organized a hiking trip that would attempt to follow the old wagon road made by rugged Mormon pioneers in the winter of 1879–1880 on their trek from Escalante to the town of Bluff, Utah.[1] By the time Georgie arrived at Richfield, Utah, on April 10, 1953, all who had signed up for the hike had dropped out except Harry. When asked if she wanted to call it off, Georgie replied, "I didn't come from L.A. for nothing."[2]

They left Richfield in a snowstorm on Saturday, April 11, and traveled for several hours in a Jeep with Dan Manning and Neal Magelby, both of Richfield. Georgie and Harry were dropped off at the top of Hole-In-The-Rock; after a little looking around, Manning and Magelby headed back to Richfield.

From this point in 1879, 250 Mormon pioneers from the Cedar City and Panguitch areas had blasted and prayed their way across this most isolated, wildly eroded "slickrock" wilderness in the dead of winter to settle the town of Bluff, Utah. Here at Hole-In-The-Rock, a narrow slit in the rim of Glen Canyon more than a thousand feet above the Colorado River, Georgie and Harry encountered the first signs of the powder-blasted, hand-built dugway made seventy-three years earlier.

Over time, erosion had taken its toll, and the trail was no longer passable even by mules. Mormon pioneers did *not* make the steps that Georgie and Harry found there; these were carved out later by Robert Brewster Stanton's men of the Hoskaninni Mining Company so that supplies could be carried down to the river by manpower and pack mules.[3]

Georgie and Harry put on their heavy packs for the scramble down the old dugway. Harry's pack was especially heavy at the start because it contained a small inflatable raft in addition to food and bedding. It took the pair an hour and ten minutes to work their way down to the river. They spent the rest of the day exploring an old Indian trail along the river. As it began to get dark they gathered wood for a fire to make supper. There was a wonderful spring of clear water at their campsite. The two were in bed by 9:30 P.M., and Georgie noted, "Stars are bright. No moon. Good fire. Bed fixed. We carry plastic light air mattress, so have fine sleeping arrangement."[4]

On Sunday morning Harry slept in. Georgie was up early, writing an account of the trip. She finally woke Harry an hour after sunup by splashing cold water in his face. After breakfast Harry showed Georgie how to use his camera. Then they packed their bags, inflated the boat, and took photos before crossing the river. Georgie said, "Boat is very light, round like a tub. Pocket on bottom to hold water & keep from tipping so easy—Life Line—English made for Royal Air Force—first I have seen like it."[5] After crossing the river, they deflated the boat and hid it and the oars behind a huge rock, where Harry would pick them up later. This lightened their packs for the climb ahead.

Over the next several days they looked for signs of the 1880 pioneer road. Here and there they found sections of hand-laid rock work. About four miles from the river, a long retaining wall had been built up a steep sand slope to gain the next bench. Then, in a place that would be heart-breaking to less-determined men and women, a steep-sloping, rock-work roadbed was built up among pinnacles and ramparts that guarded the higher plateau area.

Georgie and Harry climbed this, then lost all traces of the old road where it crossed a wide sand flat. Then, while scanning the countryside from a high knob of Navajo sandstone, they saw traces of hand-laid rock to the north. Picking up the road again, they followed it down steep pitches of sandstone slopes. They walked across Wilson Mesa in the deeply marked ruts made by wagon wheels so long ago. Hardly a bush had regrown.

While traveling the full length of the high mesa, they came across only two signs of other white men having been there since the pioneers. One was a brass cap set there in 1926 by a survey crew of the General Land Office, marking a quarter section corner. Within recent months a brilliant orange flag had been set beside the cap by helicopter by a USGS survey crew based sixty miles from Escalante. This was used to assist in triangulation and topographic surveys being carried out by that crew.

From the high mesa Georgie and Harry had grand views of the surrounding country. Nearby stood majestic, snow-covered Navajo Mountain. Its rugged, canyon-gashed northern slopes stood out in bold relief above the hidden confluence of the Colorado and San Juan rivers. Across the Colorado from Navajo Mountain stood fifty-mile-long Kaiparowits Plateau. Among other places they could identify was Sleeping Ute Mountain near Cortez, Colorado, 175 miles away. Two thousand feet below to the east flowed the San Juan River around the twelve-mile-long Great Bend. Harry noted, "Massive pinnacles in Monument Valley of Utah and Arizona stand out as though in the front yard."[6] The country was ruggedly beautiful. Georgie wrote, "Why did I leave a nice, safe job to do this & I do it every year. Just no accounting for human nature."[7]

On April 16 the two hikers crossed the heads of many canyons and came to a road leading to the abandoned Skelly Oil Company wildcat well and air strip. They camped there that night. Next day Arth and Della Chaffin drove in from Hite to meet the hikers. Traveling now by car, the group passed many more traces of the old road. At the top of colorful Clay Hills Pass on a large rounded boulder was the inscription "MAKE PEACE WITH GOD," carved in 1880 in bold letters. They noted at least twenty-six places where difficult road building had been done—switchback after switchback dug with shovels. That night after crossing the Colorado River on the Chaffin Ferry they arrived at Hite, where Georgie and Harry enjoyed a good meal and comfortable beds.

The next day, April 18, the pair hitchhiked back to Richfield. That night Georgie viewed Harry's "Green River to Lee's Ferry" movie. She was entranced by it; then it was back to Los Angeles.

First Share-the-Expense Trip

Georgie recorded a boat trip from Mexican Hat to Lee's Ferry in May and from Hite to Lee's Ferry in June. In July she led her first "share-the-expense" group through Grand Canyon. With her to begin this run were Charles B. Dustin, William I. Stewart, Irene McKeown, Georgie's brother, Paul DeRoss, and Gaylen S. "Lefty" Bryant of the *Los Angeles Times*. Esther Flemmer would join them at Phantom Ranch, where their group would be resupplied by mule train.

On July 9, 1953, the party gathered at Lee's Ferry, the only place for hundreds of miles upstream or down where the Colorado River could be reached from both sides without a descent into a forbidding canyon.

Georgie's two rafts were made ready and everyone was issued waterproof bags for their clothing and personal belongings. The next morning Whitey, who had hauled the rafts and supplies from Los Angeles, took the party from Greene's Motel at Marble Canyon back down to the river and waited to see them off. Whitey arranged to have groceries sent in at Phantom Ranch and Whitmore Wash. He then hired a driver to take the truck to Pierce Ferry and leave it for the haul back to Los Angeles. In the meantime he returned to his job as a tank truck driver in Los Angeles.

Georgie rowed one boat; her brother, Paul, rowed the other. They passed under Navajo Bridge, and by noon had reached Badger Creek Rapid, landed to look it over, ran through without incident, one after the other, and pulled in below for lunch. All rode the rapid except Dustin, who stayed on shore to photograph the run.

At 25 Mile Rapid the waves looked rough. Georgie thought an upset was possible, so the passengers stayed on shore to take pictures while Paul and Georgie took the boats through. It was rough going but they got through in fine shape and pulled in below. Those on shore got nice camera shots.

After running 25 Mile Rapid safely, their confidence was sky-high, so they did not stop to check Cave Springs Rapid a half-mile downstream. Georgie and Elgin Pierce had had no trouble there the year before. As Georgie said, "I always lead, knowing what to do if I upset, and it saves newer boatmen from difficulty."[8]

There was a huge submerged rock on the left with a big pour-over and Georgie went right over it into the hole below. The lashing tail waves caught the raft broadside, and over they went. Georgie hung onto the raft. Her immediate concern was for her woman passenger, Irene McKeown, whom she soon spotted floating along near the raft, holding her breath, eyes shut. Georgie hung onto the boat with one hand and grabbed Irene with the other. When Georgie told her that everything was all right, Irene soon regained her composure. She obeyed Georgie's instructions to hang onto the boat and move around with her to help get the boat in to shore. The current pushed them into the rocks in a cave-like overhang of the cliff. Georgie wanted to get a landing rope out to lash across the bottom of the boat so she and Irene could get on top and ride it on out to shore below, but before she could locate the rope she heard a yell. Bill Stewart had come overland to the shore above them, jumped in, and was swimming down with a rope. He tied it onto the boat and the three of them were able to turn the boat over. They then rowed down to the other boat and camped for the night.

Georgie noted, "Had blackberry brandy (carried for medicinal purposes), but on this occasion opened it. (All talked at once.) Very exciting and fun when it turns out OK—we will forget rest of trip in time, but never this." She observed further, "this particular rapid is safe, adventure to turn over in."[9] The following morning they visited beautiful Vasey's Paradise. They filled their water containers from clear springs gushing from the Redwall Limestone. Major Powell once wrote of this beautiful oasis:

> Riding down a short distance, a beautiful view is presented. The river turns sharply to the east and seems enclosed by a wall set with a million brilliant gems. What can it mean? Every eye is engaged, every one wonders. On coming nearer we find fountains bursting from the rock high overhead, and the spray in the sunshine forms the gems which bedeck the wall. Rocks below the fall are covered with mosses and ferns and many beautiful flowering plants. We name it Vasey's Paradise, in honor of the botanist who traveled with us last year.[10]

At Redwall Cavern the party stopped to explore and have lunch. Georgie chose to camp just upriver from Buck Farm Canyon at Mile 41. Bert Loper, the "Grand Old Man of the Colorado," had drowned in 24 1/2 Mile Rapid in 1949, two weeks shy of his eightieth birthday and during his second trip through Grand Canyon. His boat had been found near Mile 41, where it was pulled above the high-water line. Although greatly decomposed, the boat is still seen by river runners today.

The party stopped at Nankoweap Canyon for lunch. While there, they climbed up to inspect Anasazi granaries located under high cliffs several hundred feet above the river. There were many islands in Nankoweap Rapid, but the party threaded the two boats through without any problem. They made camp at Kwagunt Creek, Mile 56. Upon checking the rapid next morning, they decided to line it along the right shore. Kwagunt Creek, Canyon, Valley, and Butte were all named by Major Powell for a Paiute Indian named Kwagunt, also known as Indian Ben.[11]

The group next camped at Mile 65.5, Lava Canyon. Then they went through Unkar and 75 Mile (Nevill's) Rapids and came to Hance Rapid on July 15, arriving there early in the afternoon. Georgie remembered Hance Rapid very well from the previous year's upset. The rest of the day was spent lining the boats and carrying baggage to the foot of the rapid. Everybody worked hard at this and all were happy to make camp.

On July 16 it rained all day. Sockdolager Rapid came up fast and they looked it over from a high cliff on the left. Georgie held to the wall in order to miss the tongue and rough stuff, but got stuck on a submerged rock. William Stewart was able to pry her raft off with an oar, and they were soon on their way again.

Esther Flemmer met them at Phantom Ranch and would be with them for the balance of the trip. They enjoyed eating at the ranch, then were off again the next afternoon. They stopped for the night on a sandbar on the left opposite Trinity Creek. Georgie said, "Lefty always says I stop at bar but give none a drink."

At that camp Dustin found baling wire, oars, a blanket, an old, partially buried gunny sack, and a pick. He tried using the pick to pry the gunny sack loose. When this did not work he decided to open it at the top and see what was inside. Georgie noted, "The Lord had his arm around him. It was crystallized dynamite. Paul took and threw it in river. Felt sick from fumes."

Granite Falls Rapid was next, and it was split by an island. They landed and lined the rafts along the left bank. Paul was still sick from the dynamite fumes and was in a bad humor. They camped early at the head of Hermit Rapid. Hermit Creek was running a beautiful stream of good, clear drinking water, and they all bathed in it.

From Hermit Rapid they ran to Elves Chasm at Mile 116.5. Georgie pointed out a huge red arch in a corner turn just above this. They camped early to take life easy and enjoy the beautiful grotto and the fern-lined waterfalls. At Elves Chasm they signed the Park Service register and swam in the pool below the falls. Bedrock Rapid at Mile 130.5 was very rocky. Georgie said they had to ride the tongue because of rocks on both sides. Both boats made exciting runs with no mishap.

Georgie made an easy run at Dubendorff Rapid, although the channel was quite narrow. However, Paul said waves came completely over them. The party stopped at Tapeats Creek and pulled in below the rapid. They waded upstream, then climbed up the cliff to explore on the first rim. Then it was on to Deer Creek Falls, where they pulled in and made camp. After splashing in the pool at the foot of the 120-foot waterfall, they all hiked up the rocky cliffs and followed the stream into beautiful Surprise Valley.

On July 22 the group reluctantly left Deer Creek, stopping to take photos of some small Anasazi granary ruins a mile farther down on the left. They ran a number of rapids and stopped for lunch at the head of Upset Rapid. Colonel Claude H. Birdseye named this rapid when his head boatman, Emery Kolb, capsized a boat there on their survey trip of 1923.[12] Georgie had to stay on the tongue and, in the process of running the rapid, broke her first oar.

Georgie pulled in at the mouth of Havasu Creek. Paul was unable to make a landing, so they missed exploring this beautiful canyon stream and went on to camp at Mile 164, Tuckup Canyon. They stayed here an extra day to explore and swim in the natural pools. Georgie also wanted to wait for the Mexican Hat Expeditions group traveling behind them in order to see Martin Litton, an environmental reporter for the *Los Angeles Times*, who would be coming in at Lava Falls.

Still, on July 24 the group was on the river again. They stopped to hike up Stairway Canyon, and while they were gone the Mexican Hat group passed by. Georgie's group stopped again to explore another canyon, then went on to Lava Falls, where they caught up with the Mexican Hat bunch. Chet Bundy was there when they arrived and said Litton was on his way down the rugged trail from Toroweap on the North Rim. The Rigg brothers crossed to the right bank and picked up Litton. With him were two girls who would be finishing the trip with the Riggs to Pierce Ferry.

On this trip Georgie formulated a policy. She noted, "I take chances according to passengers. If they want excitement, we don't look at rapids. If they don't, we check, and on bad ones they can walk and be picked up on bottom. These people were out for everything." They even wanted to try Lava Falls, rocks and all, but Georgie thought better of it.

The next day they all helped the Rigg party line Lava Falls. Many photos were taken of this. Then the Mexican Hat crew helped Georgie's group line their boats. Below Lava they passed Rigg, as Georgie wanted to pick up supplies at Whitmore Wash. Chet Bundy and his two daughters were there to meet them, along with supplies that Whitey had trucked in to the Bundy ranch.

The next morning Chet Bundy, his two daughters, and Martin Litton left for the rim. Georgie's party had lunch at Spring Creek. Below Whitmore, Charles Dustin and Esther swam with their life jackets. They stopped at Granite Park to enjoy the natural beauty and the shade provided by some large cottonwood trees. This made a wonderful camp.

On July 27 Georgie's party ran down to Diamond Creek, where they landed at noon. Paul, Esther, and William hiked toward the mine that Harry Aleson and Georgie had explored on their river float of 1946, but they could not find it. Heavy rain had loosened rocks that fell and ruined an air mattress. Georgie had previously decided to take a cue from Mexican Hat Expeditions and initiate those who came with her. The Rigg party came in later that day and camped nearby. At their invitation, Georgie decided to wait until morning and combine the initiations. The Riggs volunteered to include Georgie's party in their initiations and let them share "Royal River Rat" pins. Those eligible were Irene, Paul, William, Lefty, and Charles. Esther would not be eligible until she ran the upper half of the canyon, which she hoped to do the next year.

When they reached smooth water near Separation Canyon, they knew the trip was coming to an end and the excitement was over. All of them would have some adjusting to do—learning to wear clothes again instead of the bathing suits all had worn on the trip. "No excitement, bills, phone, time clock, murder headlines, alarm clock, *Oh Me*," was Georgie's comment.

Whitey's friend had parked their old blue one-ton Chevy truck there for Georgie. The group deflated the rafts and got everything packed, then drove to the Canyon Motel in Boulder City, Nevada, for an overnight stay and a farewell dinner. Next morning they toured Hoover Dam before going their various ways. At home Georgie's final note was, "O me, back to work, the bitter after the sweet."

5 The Triple Rig Is Born, 1954

*B*y now Georgie's passion for Grand Canyon and running the rapids of the Colorado River was in full flower. Not only was there the excitement of running the rapids, but there was the magnificent scenery of Glen and Grand Canyons, and so many delightful places to stop and explore: Hole-In-The-Rock, Music Temple, Rainbow Bridge, Vasey's Paradise, Redwall Cavern, the Nankoweap ruins, the Little Colorado River, Deer Creek Falls, Havasu Creek, Elves Chasm, Tapeats Creek, and Thunder River, to name a few. Georgie wanted to share the canyon experience with as many others as possible and let them discover the beauty of these places for themselves, so she decided to make it a commercial venture. She worked hard, bought more equipment (including three ten-man war surplus rafts), and rounded up passengers for another trip through Grand Canyon.[1]

Whitey was along for this trip, his first through Grand Canyon. Among others who came were photographer Walter Blaylock, Esther Flemmer (again), Roger Bowling, and John M. Goddard, a well-known world traveler and one of the first three men on record to traverse the entire 4,200-mile length of the Nile River. Goddard would make a movie of the trip to be shown on a lecture tour as well as on television adventure programs.

All assembled at Lee's Ferry on the morning of July 10. There were thirteen cameras in the group and everyone wanted a shot of the launching. Georgie said, "Good thing I planned on time unlimited." At 1:45 P.M. they said farewell to civilization and Georgie led off down the river, followed by Whitey at the oars of one boat and Tom Corrigan rowing the third.

Since neither Whitey nor Tom had been through Grand Canyon rapids before, Georgie decided to take them through the first large rapid to point out the hazards and teach them how to handle the boats. So she piloted all three boats through Badger Creek Rapid.

On July 11 they were off early for Soap Creek. When they arrived they found it looking mean with a great many rocks, big waves, and threatening holes. After looking it over carefully, Georgie took the first boat through. It was a wild ride, but they made it safely. Georgie allowed Tom to row the second boat. They started off well enough, but Georgie's back seat instructions failed. Tom got too far over, hit a big explosion wave, and upset. Everyone managed to grab the safety rope of the overturned boat and hang on. They went over three small riffles with the boat whirling around in the fast current. The people hanging on made it impossible to have any control. Finally, with Blaylock's help, Georgie was able to climb onto the bottom of the boat. The oars had been tied loosely with nylon ropes especially for such an emergency and Georgie retrieved them and rowed the boat to shore.

They wound up about a mile downstream on the right side, but were able to walk back up to the last boat. Whitey said he would try to run the last boat through, but Georgie overruled him. Goddard wanted to go again, really daring the beast to do his best, so Georgie took him, Whitey, Paul Anderson, and Ed Laurence. Walt and Tom also wanted to try their luck again, but she decided that five was enough. Georgie got the number three raft to the foot of the rapid with no trouble. With all hands helping they were able to turn the foundered boat over easily without even untying the bags. The group continued on its merry way as though nothing had happened.

At Cave Springs Rapid, Grace fell overboard from Tom's boat, but she managed to grab onto the safety rope and was quickly pulled back in. They stopped at Vasey's Paradise for lunch. While the others were eating, Tom put on a show of rock climbing until the group got a little worried about him breaking a leg and yelled for him to quit. They told him they shot anyone who broke a leg in Grand Canyon. Before leaving, they explored Stanton's Cave and visited a human skeleton near the mouth of South Canyon. Someone had made off with the skull. "I won't warn the next person who rock climbs here, as we need a new skeleton," Georgie said.

On the fourth day, July 13, they passed many alcoves, visited Bert Loper's boat, and pulled up on the beach at the head of President

Harding Rapid for lunch. Here they indulged in lots of horseplay, singing, water fights, and mud baths. While there they hunted for the grave of David Quinley, a Boy Scout who had been lost in Glen Canyon. They located the grave and said a prayer for the boy. They then took photos, thinking his mother might like to see them. The place had become a sort of shrine to all canyon voyagers.

After President Harding Rapid they continued to Nankoweap Canyon, where they stopped for the night. Some made the half-mile scramble up the steep talus slope to see the Anasazi granary ruins with their breathtaking view down the canyon. Only Esther and Tom made it all the way; they were late getting back. The next morning Goddard, Walt, Ed, and Georgie climbed back to the ruins to take pictures, so the party got a late start. They found Kwagunt Rapid looking nasty, so Georgie piloted all three boats through. The group then stopped at the Little Colorado River to eat, play and swim. The blue-green water and white rocks made a beautiful and enjoyable playground.

While at the Little Colorado, they hiked upstream a short way to look at Ben Beamer's cabin and the old saddle, wood stirrups, and other implements found there. Ben Beamer had come to the mouth of the Little Colorado in the winter of 1890 or 1891 and converted an Anasazi ruin (one noted by Powell in 1869) into his own one-room cabin. He tried to support himself by prospecting and farming along the river bottom, but was unsuccessful due to the mineral-laden water.[2]

Georgie's group reluctantly departed, and in a few miles landed at Lava Canyon for an early camp. They were lucky to find a huge flat rock for a table. The wind was blowing sand everywhere, but they made it more livable by using a bucket brigade from the river to wet down the sand around camp.

The next day they ran through Lava Canyon (Chuar), Tanner, and Unkar Rapids. Tom hit a rock in Unkar, but no damage was done. At 75 Mile Rapid Georgie's boat got hung up on a rock. She had two non-swimmers on board and so did not want to risk an upset while freeing the boat. Goddard suggested swimming to shore with Grace, but Georgie vetoed that as being too risky. She also turned down a suggestion to cut the rope that held bags under the rock as she did not want to lose anything. Letting some air out of the seat inside did not work either, so she decided to stand on one edge and pull on a rope Goddard had placed through a ring on the opposite underside of the boat. It worked. The raft slid off without upsetting and all was well.

At Hance Rapid they unloaded and portaged everything overland, taking about half an hour for each load. Everyone helped carry the bags and equipment over the rocky shore. Ed proved to be a good slave driver. He kept everything moving by yelling, "Let's go, let's go, let's go!" And on every "let's go" the crew would heave forward with the boat. When everyone was gasping for breath he would call a halt for about a minute, then shout, "Let's not get set," then, "Ready, let's go, let's go!" Some thought his style pushy, but it did get the boats around in good time, and they looked so good sitting at the bottom of the rapid he was forgiven. All took their aching muscles to bed early.

The next day, July 16, they headed downriver to Phantom Ranch. When Georgie came to a rough, rocky, unnamed rapid below Mile 83 where the channel went between two big rocks, she pulled to one side and waited. Whitey soon appeared; his boat hit a big wave at just the wrong moment and over it went. Georgie pulled out promptly and hauled everyone to shore. Roger Bowling jumped onto the bank with the landing rope but did not have enough foothold to pull them in. Instead, the boats pulled *him* into the water. They now had another river rat to pull out. Soon Tom and others got a rope secured to a rock. Whitey came out mad and sputtering. He looked back at the rapid and said, "I run the big ones and spill on you, *you little bastard!*" So now the rapid had a name. From then on it would be known to Georgie's parties as "Whitey's Little Bastard."

The party arrived at the trail to Phantom Ranch at 3:30 P.M. At Phantom a man named Elmer Purtymun had left word that he wanted Georgie to put his boats (two ten-man rafts) back on the water and turn them loose so they would float down to Lake Mead. They had been left moored at the head of Granite Falls Rapid.

Georgie told the passengers they could walk around any of the rest of the rapids if they preferred to. She would be reminded of this on occasions later when she just did not stop.

Horn Creek Rapid was extremely rough, usually the case in low water. "The beast is rubbing its hands in glee on this one—so we fool him by portaging," Georgie reported. It was a rough portage over rocks as slick as glass. Everyone was tired, so they called it a day at Granite Falls Rapid, where they found Purtymun's boats moored and waiting.

On July 19 the party carried their own boats around the rapid, then placed Purtymun's rafts one on top of the other and shoved them into the current. The rafts picked a good channel on their own and went through the rapid in fine shape. They later got caught in a back-water, so Georgie's crew had to free them, but then they got stuck in rocks at the head of another rapid, so Georgie left them there to come down with the spring floods. (They actually came down in November.)

Elmer Purtymun was a grizzled character who had run Glen Canyon a few times and was trying to start a commercial river business. He had little idea of the nature of the river below Lee's Ferry and found that he lacked both the navigational skill and the courage to handle the risks he encountered there. He had abandoned his boats and customers below President Harding Rapid and climbed out of the canyon with his son and a single whisky bottle of water between them. He nearly died of dehydration and never returned to the river. Some of Purtymun's party had hiked out above Sockdolager and the rest left the river at Granite Rapid.

The next day Georgie's party went on to Boucher Rapid, where they were faced with another portage. Due to the extremely low water, there seemed to be no definite channel for a boat to pass. It was here Georgie decided to try a variation on an unsuccessful experiment she had tried earlier. Her idea had been to tie one raft on top of another so that their open cargo holds faced each other. If one flipped the other would always be right side up. According to Georgie, she had talked her brother Paul into trying this on a previous trip. She said they squeezed in between the two rafts and shoved off. Georgie described the ride this way: "We were on our way now, bouncing through those waves like a dancing cork. What a strange sensation that was! The cramped quarters and semi-darkness seemed to exaggerate every motion."

As they bounded along in the rapid a great deal of water splashed through the gap between the rafts. When the boats flipped it was essential for them to squirm around and turn over or their faces would be under six to eight inches of water. The discomfort was bad enough in moderate going, but when the raft was bouncing fiercely up and down over rough water with two thrashing people getting tangled in each other's arms and legs and in the luggage, Georgie realized she had spawned a real Rube Goldberg idea, nothing to try on paying passengers.[3]

Georgie's new idea was to tie the three boats together broadside—a triple rig. She believed that with the three ten-man rafts tied together side-by-side they would go through much rougher water without upsetting and the boats would balance each other in the big waves. She reasoned that the boats not affected by violent wave action would act as ballasts. Accordingly, the boats were tied loosely to each other by the handles. Georgie was already being referred to by some as "that crazy woman of the river," and some of her passengers looked at her now as if in agreement. Whitey shook his head; Walt was not so sure it would work either. The final craft looked ugly and unmanageable. An oarsman was seated on the side of each outside raft for steering, and they pushed off. They had a rough ride but did not upset, and it proved to be considerably easier than portaging. This type of boat, along with her larger pontoon triple-rig, came to be known as a "G-rig," the "G" standing for "Georgie."

After lunch they left the rafts tied together and passed over many rapids—Crystal, Tuna, Sapphire, Agate, Turquoise, Ruby, Serpentine, Bass, and Shinumo. Everybody loved it.

On July 23 they stopped for lunch just above Upset Rapid. Georgie had had no trouble here in the past, but suspected it would be rough in this low water. She did not walk down to look at the rapid because she did not want the crew to get frightened and she did not want to portage. Still tied together, they went sailing through the rapid broadside with Georgie leading, when suddenly her boat dropped into a huge hole and almost immediately slammed into a big wave that flipped it up and over onto the third boat. The middle boat was standing almost on edge, with the first and third boat folded together. This type of occurrence would later be referred to as a "Georgie sandwich." During this skirmish Alice went out of the middle boat but hung on until the others could pull her in. Goddard was thrown out of the first boat and said he was under the water almost too long. "It was exactly like being flushed down a gigantic toilet!"[4] But he soon caught the raft too and climbed right back in. Georgie dropped into the third boat feet first. The top of Whitey's hat was knocked off, but he still had the brim to wear. Paul lost the lenses of his glasses, but the rims were intact, so he still looked the same; he just could not see as well. The crew shoved the lead boat onto the middle one, then flipped it back over into the water. Georgie felt that all was well that ended well—to her, it just added excitement to the trip.

As they continued on their way the skies opened and poured rain. Georgie decided that Havasu Creek was probably in flood, and so abandoned plans to hike to the falls. They pushed on to camp at

Mile 160.7. Here they found a small stream of rainwater and good protection from the storm. The next day they traveled on and, due to the rain, passed up many canyons where Georgie's party had explored the year before. The cloudburst sent torrents of red mud and rocks hurtling into the canyon from side streams and instantaneously created spectacular thousand-foot waterfalls spilling over the cliffs.

Georgie was anxious to see Lava Falls this year as it was usually the fiercest rapid on the river. After landing above the falls, they saw that Lava Creek in Prospect Canyon was running in full flood. Huge boulders growled as they rolled along in the current. Georgie thought this must be how the prehistoric lava flows looked. The party could not cross the creek. "Just think—we would have missed this if we had explored canyons," Georgie noted. "This is once in a million this happens."

On Sunday, July 25, they portaged the cargo and lined the boats around Lava Falls. Georgie thought the boats could have ridden the rapid in safety, or at least as well as in Upset Rapid, but the vote was to portage. From there on they ran the boats separately, passing over several more exciting rapids, though none to match Lava Falls. About noon the party landed at Whitmore Wash, one day ahead of schedule, where Chet Bundy was to bring them fresh supplies.

Finally, on the evening of the second day, a flashlight appeared on the rim above. It was Bundy and his son coming down the trail with their pack animals. They got a royal welcome. In addition to groceries, Georgie had ordered in two new five-horsepower Johnson outboard motors and gasoline in order to save the long row across Lake Mead. The Bundys stayed overnight and left for the rim early the next morning to get the motors. With the motors and gas back down and packed in the boat, Bundy saw them off at 10 A.M.

Georgie liked this supply stop. It was a safety measure and made for lighter loads on portaging. Besides that, she liked Chet Bundy and his family. At 205 Mile (Kolb) Rapid they tied the rafts together again, "Not for safety but because it is more fun," according to Georgie.

The party arrived at Diamond Creek at noon the next day and at 3 P.M. began initiation ceremonies. Everyone had to be initiated except Georgie, so she used Paul's help and then gave him a special deal. Georgie maintained that when one had boated the upper canyons on the San Juan, Cataract, or Glen Canyon, he or she became a river rat. After going all the way through Grand Canyon, you were a Royal River Rat.

Georgie's group left Diamond Creek on Thursday, July 29, and stopped at Separation Canyon to attach the outboard motors. The next day, at the beach at Temple Bar, Marie waded out to meet them, clothes and all. With her was Georgie's dog. She had watched the dog keep cool by wading out in the water and drinking every so often and decided it was not such a bad idea. Georgie and Esther enjoyed a swim in the lake to celebrate the landing and others joined them for a water fight. Everyone helped roll up the boats and pack things into the truck. Soon they were on their way to Boulder City and the farewell dinner. This dinner party would become a tradition at the end of Georgie's trips.

In the 1950s, with cheap war surplus rafts readily available, more and more people began to run rivers. Implementing some of the things she had learned from Harry Aleson, Georgie helped the movement along by making movies of her trips and showing them throughout the winter season. Because she was a woman doing what was usually deemed to be the province of macho males, she convinced more and more people that river running was something that would be safe and exciting for them to do. Not only did this attract customers to her, but it benefitted other outfitters throughout the country. Running wild rivers would eventually become a significant part of the tourism industry nationally. In Grand Canyon alone, passengers increased from seventy in 1955 to over a thousand in 1966 and from there to sixteen thousand in 1972.

By the 1990s, river rafting would bring twenty-five million dollars annually to commercial outfitters, with many others going on private trips.

6 Branching Out to New Rivers, 1955

$\mathscr{J}$n 1955 Eisenhower was in the White House, Stalin was dead, and the Korean conflict was over. But things were hectic as ever for Georgie. Her schedule that year was quite ambitious. It called for two trips through Glen Canyon in April, a San Juan River and Glen Canyon trip in May, two Glen Canyon trips in June, and "The Mighty Grand Canyon" in July, about which she noted, "Only 216 people (as of 1954 figures) have made this trip."[1] She planned another Glen Canyon trip in August, also runs on the Middle Fork of the Salmon, the Big Salmon River, and Hell's Canyon of the Snake River in August and September. Motion pictures of previous trips were shown on request to groups and individuals to interest potential passengers.

This year Georgie also began to experiment further with three ten-man rafts tied together. These rafts were quite maneuverable with oars, but even more so with a small motor; and with the motor pushing the rafts, the trip was speeded up by several days. Linking the three rafts together was a real breakthrough, but was only for the more adventurous souls. She could now run all the rapids without portaging, though there was still the danger of one raft folding over onto the others. She wanted to be able to take families with children and older people.

Georgie's trips were not always full. On one trip in Glen Canyon, Marion Smith and her husband, Richard, were the only passengers. The crew was Georgie and Whitey. If no one else had shown up at all, Georgie would probably have gone anyway. In a letter to friends, Marion reported a most pleasant vacation. She wrote, "We came back with 6 rolls of movie films and 6 boxes of colored slides and that is the only way to do it justice."[2] A typical day would begin at daylight. Georgie and Whitey would already be up and getting breakfast. By the time the Smiths had their sleeping bags rolled up and their hair combed, breakfast would be ready.

As it happened, another party left at the same time as Georgie. Moki Mac Ellingson, another guide whom the Whites knew, had three dentists from Salt Lake City as passengers, and the two parties traveled more or less together. They camped each night near one another, which added considerably to the trip. An outboard motor was used on Georgie's raft since the Smiths only had seven days to make 163 miles. Each day they would visit a side canyon, sometimes two, and points of interest along the river. Each canyon was completely different and utterly fascinating. Marion wrote, "One canyon, called Labyrinth, had been cut so deep and so narrowly that one had to turn sideways in a couple of places to walk up it. Its walls were undulating rock, textured by the erosion done by water." The Whites prepared all the meals for their boat, and after dinner they would join the dentists around a common campfire and sing awhile. Marion said, "The Whites—Georgie, especially, is a fascinating personality—and also Moki Mac—the other guide."

One of the special places they visited was Rainbow Bridge. The six-mile hike up the stream was delightful, with ferns, flowering redbud trees, towering, dark-stained rock formations, and all sizes and shapes of pools. Another place that impressed them was "Hole-In-The-Rock," because they could not imagine that wagons could be taken down such a steep and narrow improvised pathway. They marveled at the little more than six-foot-wide crack through which the wagons had to pass.

Another place they visited was the Crossing of the Fathers (El Vado de los Padres). Marion told her friends, "I really think that I saw more scenery in less time and space on this trip than I've seen in many trips all put together before." The Smiths took many more trips with Georgie, and Dick would later become one of her boatmen.[3]

Georgie's Big Boat

Georgie was inventive and imaginative. She continued to make changes and improvements in her equipment and method of operation until they satisfied her. Several years earlier, she had seen newsreel shots of the Army Corps of Engineers making pontoon bridges out of elongated oval pontoons. She recalls:

I discovered several of these in a Los Angeles surplus yard, and the more I looked at them, the more I felt they might just be the answer. I could lash three together to make one huge raft. I also decided that in the oval interior of each of these rafts I would place a long inflated tube [sponson] that I called a sausage. This would give me tremendous floatation. It would take large waves and big water without difficulty and give me the safest boat on the river.[4]

On July 4, 1955, Georgie arrived at Lee's Ferry to put her idea to the test. She had one twenty-seven-foot pontoon and two twenty-two-foot pontoons on either side of it—all three tied together with nylon rope. One ten-horsepower outboard motor was mounted on the rear of the middle pontoon. Two other motors were carried for emergency use. On this trip she also had a smaller triple rig of three ten-man rafts and a single ten-man raft that would be hand rowed. The single raft was to be used for a thrill boat, but it would be protected by the big boat, which would be stationed below each rapid to come to the rescue in case of an upset. They took plenty of extra oars, shear pins, and propellers.[5] The Grand Canyon entourage included Whitey, Georgies brother, Paul, and twenty-six others, mostly from California but also from as far away as Illinois—Georgie's fame was spreading, and in the years to come her passengers would come from across the country and from abroad.

Margaret Gorman arrived on July 2. She would act as cook's helper as partial payment of her fare. She would ride on the triple rig on which Rich Chambers and Fred Eiseman (her future husband) were oarsmen.

Passenger Helen Kendall brought along a portable typewriter and made an extensive record of the trip.[6] Helen reported that at Marble Canyon Lodge "some Navajos came in and sat at some of the tables. A man dressed in white talked to them in their own language. He turned out to be the Reverend 'Shine' Smith, a free-lance Presbyterian minister among the Navajos." Later, when they were ready to launch, the Navajos, one of them an old medicine man with a white mustache, and Reverend Smith came down to the boats. Helen Kendall wrote:

> The Indians gave us the Navajo Blessing and tossed cornmeal on the water. Of course I would be in the water at that time and found out about it when it was almost over and didn't hear

the words. Rev. Shine said a few words, too. Georgie and Whitey shook hands with the Indians and thanked them and pictures were taken. Some of the others shook hands with them, too. Paul's young wife of about three months is a Mormon, so she said a Mormon prayer for us, too. So we started out with a lot of well-wishers.[7]

The party left Lee's Ferry on July 5, 1955, with twenty-seven people on board, the largest party by far to go through the Grand Canyon up to that time. Georgie ran the motor on the big boat, and it would be the first time she ran the canyon without rowing. This would be her third trip through Grand Canyon with paying passengers. Paul DeRoss ran the single boat, but his new bride, Mavis, did not like the rapids all that well, and she rode on the big boat with Georgie. She said frequent prayers for Paul's safety. Fred B. Eiseman, Jr., chairman of the science department of John Burroughs School in St. Louis, and Floyd W. Henney, an engineer for the Los Angeles County Flood Control Authority, manned the smaller triple rig. Georgie always referred to Eiseman as "Eisenhower." Whitey went along to take care of repairs and keep an eye on the passengers. Georgie noted:

> We carry no watches on this trip, and don't want the passengers to carry any. Just whenever we get ready to leave [in the] morning it is 8 A.M. If we are hungry it is noon. If we look over a rapid and the sun is midway and no one wants to get wet we just call it even and say it is 4 P.M. I plan no camping spots as I like to camp when the crowd as a whole wants to. This puts us on different spots each year.[8]

At the first camp, just below Badger Creek Rapid, a full moon flooded the upper wall of the canyon, and the Big Dipper and a few stars were showing. It was a lovely night.

The big boat exceeded Georgie's expectations and took all the rapids with ease. Georgie always took the lead and sometimes had to wait for the boats that were being hand rowed. Kendall reported that:

> Three Coleman 2–burner gasoline stoves are used. The third one is usually used for heating dishwater. After lunch we wash our dishes with water and sand in the river, then dip it in hot soap suds, then in hot clear water. Some use only one bowl,

eating one thing at a time. I managed to get a cup for coffee. A spoon, or maybe a fork added to this, completes our eating utensils. For supper we always have soup heavy with canned vegetables, not always the same kind, then meat of some kind and, last, fruit of some kind and coffee, tea, cocoa or milk. When dishes are washed, we put them back into the bag which we took them out of before eating. The bag of dishes are always placed by the "table" and we get out what we want.[9]

They picked up park ranger Dan Davis on a sandbar just above Tanner Rapid on July 10.[10] That brought the party to twenty-eight. Davis, a tall, lean man, had been transferred to the park in 1953. At that time there was no Park Service activity on the river, mainly because "river running" had not yet been commercialized. He was interested in the canyon, and the National Park Service finally decided they needed someone in charge of it. So, beginning in 1954, he lived most of the year at Phantom Ranch in a little stone house just off the beach. He would work ten days at Phantom, then return home to his family who lived up on the South Rim.

Davis recalled that the superintendent of Grand Canyon National Park in 1927 had been Miner Raymond Tillotson. Tillotson had been superintendent when park rangers Glen E. Sturdevant and Fred Johnson drowned while trying to cross the river above Horn Creek in some type of fold-boat that they had carried down the trail from the South Rim. One of the rangers drowned even though wearing a life preserver, proof of the awful power of whirlpools. The preserver did bring his body to the surface; that of the other ranger was never found. After that tragedy Tillotson forbade anyone from the National Park Service from going on the river. Even after Tillotson left Grand Canyon for Santa Fe to become regional director of the National Park Service, he had Grand Canyon under his jurisdiction and would not allow any of the park people to go on a river trip. Tillotson died about the time Davis was transferred to Grand Canyon, and the order was rescinded.

Davis had the title of "inner canyon ranger" at that time, and it just happened that Georgie was the next boat operator to put out an invitation for someone from the Park Service to go with them. Davis had hiked down the Tanner Trail to meet Georgie, as that was the nearest access to the beginning of Grand Canyon. The eastern boundary was at Nankoweap Canyon prior to 1975. Today, Grand

Canyon National Park begins at Lee's Ferry, which is at the upper end of Marble Canyon.

Dan Davis rode on the big boat with Georgie the first day in order to get oriented and learn from Georgie what the trip was all about. Afterward he rode on the triple rig and often relieved Fred Eiseman or Floyd Henney at the oars, as he wanted to get some rowing experience. He was absolutely overwhelmed with the view of the canyon from the river.

While going through Tanner Rapid on the big boat, passenger Doc Ferguson was washed overboard. He managed to grab onto the safety rope until he could be pulled in. He said, "I talked to the old man while under the water!"[11]

Snakes Have Right of Way

When they stopped for lunch that day, one of the ladies nearly stepped on a rattlesnake. At Georgie's insistence, the snake was prodded under the only bush on that rather small sand bar. They ate lunch within a few feet of it. Dan Davis reported, "No concern need be shown for the destruction of wildlife by Mrs. White's river party as she is almost fanatical in protection of animals, etc., very much against even fishing, which of course is legal."

On July 11 all three boats ran Hance Rapid, although it was very low and rocky. As usual, Georgie went first in the big boat so as to be in a position to rescue any passengers who might come floating through, or to take care of any other mishap. Cameras were poised on shore to watch Paul upset, but he fooled them and did a beautiful job in the single boat. Joel Sayre, a passenger and writer for *Sports Illustrated*, wrote:

> Again and again we were on the outermost edge of disaster, and time after time he would pull us away in an eyelash finish—bobbing and weaving, dodging and ducking, now with short, deft strokes of his oars, now with full-bodied pulls on them with all his might. The grand finale was his knifing us between the biggest rock and the deepest hole in the rapid.[12]

Those on shore booed when Paul did not upset. It was the first time all passengers had ridden over Hance Rapid. Georgie got the handle knocked off her motor, damaged her prop, and sheared a pin. The boats were all filled with water and required a lot of bailing. Rich Chambers grew to love the rapids so much that he would ride the first boat through and then race back up over the shore rocks in time to catch a ride on the last one.

Paul's luck was not as good when he reached "Whitey's Little Bastard," where Georgie's husband had upset the year before. Maybe he was overconfident after having made it through Hance. This time the bow of his raft went straight down into the hole and flipped over lengthwise. Joel Sayre described it this way:

> A little way ahead and just to our left, I saw, oh, my, what a hole! Everybody saw it, of course, but it had hypnotic attraction for me, that hole did: its sides were slick and glistened in the sun and they went down and down and down. I could hardly take my eyes away.
>
> Paul would have got past, I'll always believe, if a wave, not much of one, hadn't hit us from the right with a sort of sneak punch and pushed us slowly, slowly, hole-ward—despite all Paul's frantic efforts to row away from it. The interim decision was like those few moments of ringing silence when you're going under at the start of anesthesia, before the black closes around your consciousness. I did not see Eunice at all, but I saw Rich's big body flying through the air and I saw Paul going down the hole. He went down back first. His eyes were closed, his face was contorted, and his limbs were drawn towards his trunk as though by some muscular convulsion. He looked like a man who had been shot the second before. Shot dead. Then I was under water.[13]

Joel, Eunice Tjaden, and Rich Chambers were thrown clear, but Paul wound up under the boat in an air pocket with his legs tangled up in a rope. They did not find him until they got the raft to shore and turned it over, but all were rescued unharmed.

By this time some of the passengers had dubbed Georgie's big boat the "Queen Mary." Six new passengers came in at Phantom Ranch and nine went out, so the party was cut to twenty-six. When they reached Horn Creek Rapid and looked it over they found huge holes scattered so as to make it impossible to avoid them all, and also tremendous explosion waves. It all looked so ferocious that Paul refused to take the single raft through. Therefore they loaded it on top of the middle pontoon of the "Queen Mary" and secured it with lines. Now they had a "poop deck," and would have it for a while. As Georgie took the big boat through Horn, she seemed to hit every hole. Even the decked raft was under water at times, but no trouble was encountered because everyone obeyed Georgie's instructions to hang on tight.

The raft twisted and bounced so much Georgie decided it was too dangerous for the smaller triple rig. So she pulled in below the rapid, climbed back to the top, and told those who were to have ridden on the triple rig they would have to walk to the foot of the rapid. The triple rig was then set free without boatmen. The single boat had been unloaded from the "Queen Mary," and Paul, Floyd, and Fred rowed out to meet the empty boat at the foot of the rapid. Fred and Floyd jumped on board and rowed it back to join the others on shore. Georgie said they would probably always do this in low water. From then on Paul rode atop his single-rig poop deck much of the way. He said it was the first chance he had to see Grand Canyon. Previous to this he had spent all of his time at the oars and watching the water.

The group pulled in on the right at Bedrock Rapid to check it over, play around on the rocks awhile, and take photographs. Georgie tried to go to the right of the large outcrop in midstream, but the powerful current drew her to the left instead. She wound up in a huge whirlpool that kept the big raft circling continuously. Floyd and Fred ran tight to the right against the rocks, never hitting the tongue, and sailed through in wonderful shape. They pulled in below and returned to join in the fun. Eventually they were able to get a line to the circling big boat and held it while motion pictures were taken. The motor had to be removed from the back to make room to get the boat through, so oars had to be used. With Eunice Tjaden and Georgie rowing on one side and Paul and Whitey on the other, and with the line from shore, they finally got the raft out of the eddy and into fast water. Afterward they all had a toast to a lot of fun. On Georgie's film of the trip, she claimed everyone was just relaxing, when it was very clear they were hanging onto the lines to keep the big boat from continuing its endless circling. She said she took the left side route around Bedrock intentionally; in fact, of course, she just lost control.

The group camped early at Tapeats Creek, where they bathed in the clear water and rested for the next day's hike to Thunder River, the shortest river in the United States, and the only one that is a tributary to a creek. Paul led the way. Whitey stayed in camp, and he said that Frank Wright had passed while they were hiking but did not wave or stop.

Dispute at Deer Creek

Wright's party, which had stopped at Deer Creek Falls ahead of Georgie's, was hiking when Georgie's group pulled up. In the Wright party were twelve people in four boats, one boatman and two passengers per boat.

Georgie's group camped at the far end of the sandbar. It was too late for photographs of the falls, so they decided to stay until morning. Wright, however, came in and asked Dan Davis to get them to move. Davis told Wright that he was a guest and had no authority to make Georgie move.

Wright's party was small and he had sold the trip on the basis that they would not see other people, so to see this big mob camped nearby naturally upset him. Georgie told him she was running all the rapids and gave him the time she expected to be running the rest of them so that he could get there at a different time.

The two outfits each ran a completely different type of trip. Georgie was making something possible for ordinary folks at a very reasonable price. A full three-week trip was three hundred dollars. Mexican Hat charged a thousand. The people who went with Mexican Hat were mere passengers; everything was done for them and food was first class. Georgie's passengers, on the other hand, were expected to be part of the crew, whether it was the cooking, rowing, or whatever. Mexican Hat Expeditions provided luxury; Georgie provided involvement. The Mexican hat crew even hauled their passengers' sleeping bags out of the boats and made their beds for them, and did all the cooking and other chores. Dan Davis notes, "The women would be dressed like they were going to a tennis match or something, not the scroungy stuff the rest of us wore. Mexican Hat was called the Brooks Brothers Outfit by Georgie's people."

On July 18, after hiking to the Labyrinth and taking showers in the falls for pictures, Georgie's group left Deer Creek. When they reached Upset Rapid, Wright's group had just finished lining, so they camped under the ledges there for the night in order to stay out of his way. While they ran Lava Falls, Wright's party was portaging and lining. Georgie still carried the one-man raft as a poop deck, and the triple rig made it without trouble. Twenty-one people rode on the big boat, and photos were taken of their passage.

The Bundys

At Whitmore Wash, Chet Bundy swam out to meet the group. He had packed down groceries and gasoline for Georgie. With Bundy were his wife, Jenny; his brother; his eight-year-old daughter, Bonnie, riding her pet burro; and Toroweap ranger John Riffie. Dan Davis left

The Bundy family at Lake Mead. Left to right: Bonnie, Jenny, Chet. *Courtesy of Bob Atherton.*

End of Grand Canyon trip, July 26, 1955, the largest party to that time to traverse Grand Canyon. Also Georgie's first time using the "big boat." Front boat, left to right: Fred Eiseman, Margaret Gorman (later Mrs. Eiseman), Joel Sayre, Bill Nicholson, Alcie Andrews (later Mrs. Hendrickson), Dick Hendrickson, Bob Atherton, Marti McCoy, Floyd Henning. Rear boat, left to right: Georgie White, Eunice Tjaden, Doc Frederick, Ken Bertossi, Chet Bundy, Roger Bowling, Freda Walbrecht (at front and right of Bowling), Mrs. Bundy (behind and to right of Bowling), James R. (Whitey) White with Bonnie Bundy, Marge Gall, Hazel Eldinger, Mavis DeRoss (blonde), Helen Kendall (wearing hat), Paul DeRoss (seated), Orville Franzen, Carl Bucholz. (No name available for man in front of Bonnie Bundy). *Photo by Bill Belknap, courtesy of Bob Atherton and Westwater Books.*

the group here, as this was technically out of Grand Canyon National Park at the time. In addition, Riffie informed Davis of a forest fire in the vicinity of Mount Trumbull where his help was needed.

Bonnie Bundy was a beautiful little girl. She had hoped to go on the rest of the trip with Georgie but had been told by her parents that she could not unless Georgie gave her approval. She was tickled pink when Georgie said she could go. This made her the youngest person up to that time to ride through that portion of the Colorado River gorge. Chet's brother took the pack animals back to the rim while Chet, Jenny, and Bonnie accompanied Georgie for the balance of the trip.

At Diamond Creek the eighteen people who had made the entire trip for the first time were initiated into the Order of Royal River Rats. On July 25 the group landed at Temple Bar, where Marie and a bus were waiting. William Belknap, Jr., who had a photography shop in Boulder City, took pictures with the passengers' personal cameras as well as his own. Then they went to Boulder City by bus for a farewell dinner.

Exploring the Salmon and Snake Rivers

Georgie capped off the boating season of 1955 by exploring rivers that were new to her, the Salmon and Snake in Idaho. Her party of eleven met at Johnson's Flying Service field in McCall, Idaho, on August 22. From there, personnel and equipment (boats and all) were flown to Indian Landing on the Middle Fork of the Salmon in two old Ford Tri-motor planes. The people in one plane took photos of the other carrying the equipment because of its unusual appearance. Upon landing they all helped roll the boats over a small hill and down to the river.

Georgie's group this time used three single ten-man neoprene landing barges, hand rowed. The water was low and, in contrast to the silt-laden Colorado River, very clear. Georgie soon noted that "holes" in this river meant deep, clear pools where trout abound, instead of dangerous craters caused by water plunging over boulders. The water was too cold for swimming, and warm clothing was in order.[14]

There were no deep side canyons such as on the Colorado, but many gentle mountain creeks emptied into the Salmon. And, contrary to conditions on the Colorado, there were hunting and fishing lodges along the way. The McCall Lodge and Flying B Lodge were accessible by DC-3 airplane, and film, fishing tackle, and even ice cream could be purchased.

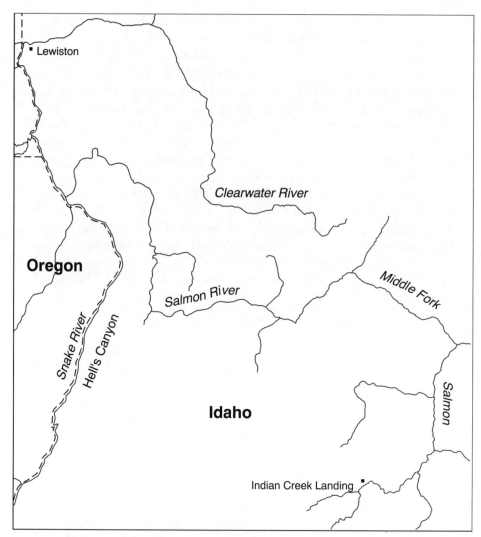

Lewiston

Clearwater River

Oregon

Salmon River

Middle Fork

Snake River

Hell's Canyon

Idaho

Salmon

Indian Creek Landing

Cartography by Thomas Zajkowski, University of Utah

Salmon and Snake Rivers

30   0   30   60 Miles

N

The party saw abundant wildlife, including otter, ducks, and geese, but very few deer, elk, or bear, which were reported to abound in the higher mountains. Georgie said, "The only spot that resembles a rapid is called Grouse Rapid which is a chute of water dropping about 4 feet. This is just a rocky fast run." On the second night they camped by a hot spring where everyone enjoyed a warm bath.

After traveling six days and about one hundred miles, they came to the confluence with the Big Salmon, or "River of No Return." Here, three people left the party and one joined. On entering the Big Salmon, they tied the three rafts together side-by-side and attached a ten-horsepower outboard motor. Marybelle Filer wrote afterward about Georgie in the *Idaho County Free Press*:

> Next morning I hopped down to see the take-off and was greatly bemused to note the captain of marvelous physique attired in a black two-piece play suit, red jacket, and atop her blond head was perched a conical straw hat that resembled an inverted ice cream cone. Draped around the silly feminine hat was [a] red rope, such as we use on the Christmas tree. The hat was securely fastened under chin.
>
> For an awful moment I was assailed by doubt as to how much captaincy such femininity could command. All doubt was dispelled as between quiet orders to [her] helper, she led me to her craft and displayed her grub system. Each day's rations for nine people was packed into a waterproof bag, for which she had some special name that sounded like "KKK." The diet was well balanced including cereals, fruits, juices, pancakes, vegetables and canned breads. What was left over from dinner and breakfast was served for lunch. Each bag was numbered so that when they beached, all they need unload was that particular day's ration along with one other main bag which contained much-used staples such as sugar, salt, milk, shortening, and powdered coffee.[15]

Here on the Big Salmon they saw eagles, ducks, and geese every day; foxes, coyotes, elk, deer, and sheep occassionally; one black bear; and numerous small animals. They passed many ranches and hunting lodges where people lived year-round. There was a landing strip at each lodge. The people were exceedingly friendly and kept the group well supplied with vegetables and fruit. Georgie in turn acted as a delivery service, taking articles from a lady named Zaunmiller to her neighbor, Marybelle Filer, farther downstream. The people were extremely proud of their country, and Idaho was their favorite topic of conversation.

On the fourth day out the group came to another hot spring, but this one was boiling—too hot to bathe in—so they used it for a wash tub by dipping their clothes in it with a long stick. This portion of the trip took nine days and ended seven miles from Riggins, Idaho. Georgie noted that there were no rapids but many large riffles with slow water in between. From Riggins the party disbanded, and Georgie shipped her equipment to Robinette, Oregon, for the trip through Hell's Canyon of the Snake River.

Hell's Canyon

Hugging the borders of northeastern Oregon and western Idaho, Hell's Canyon is the deepest gorge in North America, plunging 7,913 feet from the top of He Devil Mountain to the mouth of Granite Creek. The landscape of Hell's Canyon is a study in contrast, from the steep desert-like lower slopes and sandbars edging the river to the rugged peaks and alpine lakes of the majestic Seven Devils Mountains towering almost eight thousand feet above. Traces of human existence in Hell's Canyon date back as far as eight thousand years—from pre-historic Native American tribes to Chief Joseph's band of Nez Perce Indians to 1860s gold miners and the late 1800s homesteaders.

At Robinette, Georgie's new party was amazed to find a real old-time general store. Name almost any article and the owner could pull it out. There were drugs, clothing, plumbing supplies, hardware, groceries, and a marvelous arrowhead collection. They spent hours looking through the store-museum and were entertained in the evening by a local man who showed them pictures of the river and surrounding country.

The next day Georgie met Blaine Stubblefield, a famous river runner in that part of the country. He was friendly, cooperative, and helpful. Stubblefield added to their pleasure by joining them with his own boat and nine passengers, floating downriver to the first rapid. He had wanted to see how Georgie's rig and setup would run the rapid. Georgie said his thirty-foot boat rode the rapids well but was quite difficult to transport overland at the end of the trip. Georgie was running the same setup as she had on the Big Salmon, three seven-teen-foot landing barges lashed together with nylon rope and a ten-horsepower outboard motor mounted on the middle one.

While the Stubblefield party watched, Georgie ran Kinney Creek Rapid with no trouble at all and pulled in below. Since a road followed along the river at that point, Stubblefield and his entire party decided to ride down the river with Georgie for a mile or two and walk back. Now, with nineteen people aboard, every seating spot was taken. Georgie decided to initiate them by going through the long heavy rapid below Kinney Creek. They had a hilarious ride and Georgie pulled in at the head of Squaw Creek Rapid to unload the extra passengers and let them take photos of her running it.

Georgie's group proceeded with an exciting roller coaster ride down the rock-studded cataract, and then pulled to shore for lunch. Afterwards, Stubblefield decided to ride with them for another mile to Buck Creek Rapid. This rapid took some study as it was reputed to have upset most of the boats that tried it. As they dropped over the precipice into the foaming white water they were completely submerged, but came out cheering.

Georgie said she was enthralled with the mountain scenery, and spent so much time looking at it that she hit rocks and sheared two pins. They encountered four other large rapids, many riffles, and a great deal of slow water. The five-day, 145–mile trip ended at Lewiston, Idaho, in a rainstorm.

It is interesting to note that photographs of Georgie's rafts up to and including 1955 had the name "J. R. White" painted on the side, indicating that Whitey was at least a partner in the business. In 1956 the lettering was "GEO. WHITE," and from 1957 on the name had changed to "GEORGIE—WOMAN OF THE RIVER."

Georgie's Royal River Rats

THRU GRAND CANYON

[LIFE MEMBER]

This is to certify that_____
is a member of the ROYAL RIVER RATS, an exclusive
society of persons who have demonstrated their sterling
character, iron nerve and good fellowship in running the
WHITE WATER of the MIGHTY GRAND CANYON
OF THE COLORADO RIVER with Georgie •••••

Signed___*Georgie*___
Woman of the River.

Date_____

Certificate of membership in Georgie's Royal River Rats. *Cline Library, Northern Arizona University, Georgie Clark Collection.*

7 Controversies, 1956

Beginning in 1956 Georgie left her fall and winter months open for film lectures covering her more spectacular adventures. The following is an information release put out by Georgie in March 1956:

Biographical Information on Georgie White, "Woman of the Rivers"

Mrs. Georgie Helen White, little publicized for many years despite her numerous achievements, is a modest, but effervescent, easy-talking woman who only now is approaching the threshold of a hobby-turned-career, river running.

One of the nation's foremost woman adventurers, she has done more in a few short years to make this country's most dangerous rivers and canyons accessible to the average citizen than any other person living, man or woman.

Now in her early 40's she is a self-made sportswoman whose love of the outdoors has led her from pier plunges into Lake Michigan as a child in a North Chicago tenement district to personal conquest of the western United States' ruggedest rivers, including the mighty Grand Canyon of the Colorado River.

Mrs. White not only has guided groups of adventurers through the Colorado's most treacherous rapids and falls in military surplus rubber life rafts, but also has braved death itself in swimming 185 miles down the Grand Canyon. In doing so she became one of the first two persons ever to swim it. The other person, Harry Aleson, accompanied her in 1946.[1]

Marston Challenges Georgie on the Facts

Georgie's relationship with Otis "Dock" Marston was at this time becoming strained. Marston had received his training on the Colorado with Norman Nevills, making at least one trip a year with him from 1943 through 1948. At first Marston went as a paying passenger, and later as a ten-dollar-a-day boatman, even though he was quite wealthy. He became so enamored with the river that he began to collect diaries of Colorado River runners and all the facts he could obtain. He became a fanatical historian of the Colorado River, dogged boatmen for the true facts about their voyages, and kept a record of all those who ran Grand Canyon. He and Georgie had been on friendly terms for several years, and she would give him copies of her trip logs and passenger lists.

But Marston began to notice that Georgie had a tendency to leave out any bad things that occurred on her trips; in her lectures or in interviews with reporters and television appearances, she tended to exaggerate and embellish her earlier exploits such as her swims, hikes, and boat trips with Harry Aleson. Marston would check with Aleson or anyone else he could correspond with trying to ascertain the true facts. Then he would confront Georgie with the discrepancies.

Harry told Marston that every river trip Georgie took from 1944 through 1949 was as his passenger. Also, as indicated in the news release above, she claimed that the Grand Canyon trips with Aleson in 1945 and 1946 were both swims and that the total mileage covered was 185 miles. Georgie wrote Marston May 3, 1956, "My swims of 1945 and 1946 was [sic] for fun not records . . . I don't care for detail and don't care if it is recorded or not. They should be called floats anyway, as they are not really swims with a life preserver on."

Later, through correspondence with Harry Aleson, Marston would point out to Georgie that the 1945 swim actually covered fourteen miles of the river course and a total of forty-two on the river and on Lake Mead. He also pointed out that the Army Air Cruiser trip of 1946 had covered only thirty-seven miles on the river and thirty-three on the lake for a total of seventy miles. This added up to fifty-one miles on the river and sixty-one on the lake for a total of 112 miles instead of 185.[2] As Marston continually confronted her with these discrepancies, their relationship became more strained. And she didn't bother to change her story. Later, Georgie would claim to many people that she swam by herself, all alone, from Phantom Ranch to the head of Lake Mead. She also told her passengers that she boated through Grand Canyon all alone or accompanied by her brother for almost ten years. This was definitely untrue.

Georgie was first of all an adventurer, entertainer, motivator, and a storyteller who seldom let the truth get in the way of a good story. She was ignorant of both the geology and history of the Grand Canyon. She had a domineering character that led people either to fierce loyalty to her or intense dislike.

In 1955 two young life insurance salesmen named John Dagget and Bill Beer swam the Colorado—the whole length through Grand Canyon. Each filled two "large, black, watertight rubber boxes with sleeping gear, flashlights, cameras, first-aid kits, and food for twenty-five days."[3] They wore shorts over the bottom half of long underwear, rubber shirts, Mae West life jackets, and rubber swim fins.

Georgie said she ran into them on one of her trips and spoke to them. She made mention to someone that they boasted to her that they were going to tell everybody they swam every rapid, for their book, when in fact they did not. Otis Marston got word of this and wrote Georgie a letter asking question upon question about the entire incident. Georgie disagreed with Marston. She was a private person— thought he asked too many questions. She wrote, "Mr. Beer is writing the book. . . . I really like the boys and, if they can make money on book, more power to them." Their philosophy seemed to be pretty close to her own. She added further, "If in the book they say they swam every rapid why not accept it? . . . Please don't ask me to type details on this. If I had been along that would be different . . . I talked mostly to one on phone. I am sorry if I opened my big mouth when I shouldn't have." In a letter to Harry Aleson she said, "Marston asked me in detail about Beer and other swimmer talk. I don't care to say anything that they don't put in book. If I said anything to you please forget it."

Criticism

Rivalries were beginning to develop among river runners. When one woman who had booked a trip for Frank Wright learned that Georgie had a farewell party scheduled at the same hotel on the same night as Wright's, she canceled theirs and moved it to another lodge. Boatmen who had never seen Georgie run were severely critical of her. On a television show she had been labeled the "Woman of the River." They now referred to her as "that crazy woman of the river." Marston and some of his cronies referred to her derisively as "the woman" or "she." Those running wooden boats thought it unsportsmanlike to use the big rafts and pontoons to conquer the rapids as they said there was no incentive to miss rocks or holes. Some even questioned the safety of Georgie's boats. But the number of passenger miles that had been run since the war in pontoons and rafts with minimum accidents spoke loudly for their safety. Georgie was not discouraged by all this. She went ahead taking more passengers through the canyons than anyone else at that time.

1956 Cataract Canyon Run

On June 4, 1956, Georgie left Green River, Utah, with a party of seventeen, the largest group yet to run Cataract Canyon. They were equipped with Georgie's big boat, using thirty-three-foot-long pontoons, plus one set of the smaller triple rigs. The river was running at about 59,000 cubic feet per second (cfs) near the peak of spring runoff.

Evidence of mining activity was everywhere. All along the Green River they saw bulldozed roads used by uranium miners. In some sections there was a road on each side of the river, and every hundred yards or so, markers indicated uranium claims by various individuals or companies. The group stopped occasionally to visit with miners and prospectors.[4] In more than one place a cable had been stretched across the river and had to be avoided. At one place they saw about fifty feet of rock cores lined up where core drilling had taken place.

After entering Cataract Canyon, Georgie pulled into an eddy for picture taking with the big boat, and even with the outboard motor it took more than an hour to get back into the main current. The boat went round and round along with various pieces of driftwood. The huge waves continually pushed the raft back into the eddy and at one time ran it up against the rocks with quite a resounding thud. Only the heavy neoprene construction of the pontoons prevented a puncture. Finally, with the help of two oarsmen at the bow, they managed to get into the main current and pass the barrier of rocks below.

In a later rapid, Helen Kendall, once again traveling with Georgie, said the big boat went through like a submarine, "The water went over me and even up my nose. . . Couldn't hang on better if I were woven into the ropes."[5] In that big water, besides being swamped in the waves most of the time, the triple rig folded up a couple of times. When they went down into one hole, one of the side boats flipped over the middle one. Two people were thrown over on top of one person sitting in the middle section as it folded. Happily, no injuries resulted.

Often they were struggling through rapids with the boats totally filled with water. As a result Georgie said she would never take anything but her biggest raft down Cataract thereafter. However, the very next year, one of extreme high water, she brought a set of small triple rigged boats. Frank Wright of Mexican Hat Expeditions had become so disgusted with the trouble he encountered in Cataract in 1953 that he discontinued running it. The combination of rocks and rough water was really tough on wooden boats.[6]

On the last day Georgie's group stopped at White Canyon Trading Post. Candy was five cents a bar. Soft drinks right off the ice were fifteen cents per can, and a large bar of Ivory soap cost eighteen cents.

Georgie's Philosophy

In July 1956, just before Georgie embarked on another Grand Canyon trip, one of her would-be passengers fell ill in Flagstaff, Arizona, and had to go to a hospital. She later learned that the man had died. In a letter to Marston she wrote, "How little we know of what happens tomorrow. The further I go the more I know I am right in living *today. Yesterday is gone, tomorrow* may never come."[7]

At this time the park superintendent wanted Dan Davis to go down the river again, this time as a boatman, as he wanted Davis to get some experience along that line. There was a possibility that the Park Service would begin boating for rescue purposes, there being some rafts available at Phantom Ranch. So Dan teamed up with Fred Eiseman as an oarsman on the triple rig. Fred's friend, Margaret Gorman, was a passenger on the triple rig.

Also just prior to the trip, on June 30, 1956, a United Airlines DC-7 and a Trans World Airlines Super Constellation tragically collided over Grand Canyon. The two planes crashed into its depths, killing all 128 people aboard. On July 9, as Georgie's party approached the Little Colorado River, they saw pieces of one of the aircraft in the river. They could see more gleaming bits lodged upon the rocky lower walls of the canyon. The bulk of the wreckage had landed high up on Chuar and Temple Buttes. Some of Georgie's group climbed two or three hundred feet to photograph the DC-7s horizontal stabilizer, two pieces of elevator, and other pieces that lay scattered about. (In the 1980s the Park Service removed all wreckage so river runners would discontinue climbing the fragile buttes.) By this time rescue workers had removed the bodies of the dead by helicopter. Dan Davis had been ordered to pick up the extra rubber body bags left by rangers during the rescue work.

At Horn Creek Rapid there was some excitement with the triple rig. Dan Davis wrote:

> The hole in Horn which you have no choice of avoiding with the neoprene about got us: flipped one raft over on the middle one and pinned two passengers under it with their heads under water. I had to push it over by myself to get them out while still in rough water and it's a wonder I didn't get tossed out. No one got hurt, but, had they been caught between two rubber bags of gasoline or other solid bags, they could have easily got crushed.[8]

On July 25, Georgie's sister, Marie, met them at the take-out site. She had a big sign on the side of the bus which read, "River Rats Never Die, They Just Smell That Way."

Enter Orville Miller

Georgie ran the Grand again in August. On that trip she met Orville Miller, who would later become one of her most trusted boatmen, though her first impression of him was not that great. Orville was a professor of pharmacology at the University of Southern California and a member of the Sierra Club. He came into contact with Georgie as she showed her movies at Sierra Club meetings in Los Angeles after her first three or four trips through Grand Canyon.

He noted the portaging of the rapids and could see that it was a lot of hard work in very hot conditions. This did not appeal to Orville, but when she started putting the triple rigs together and going through all the rapids, he became interested. So he signed up for the last summer trip in 1956, which she advertised as a "Low Water Trip." She wanted to find out if she could go through the canyon with the big boat in August when the river was at its lowest. The water level was around 3,000 cfs at the start and dropped down to 2,500 cfs or even less. The trip was advertised as being for strong hikers only, as they might have to abandon everything in the canyon and hike out.

Because Orville was teaching summer school, he could not begin the trip at Lee's Ferry. Therefore, he arranged to join the group at Phantom Ranch. A couple he knew through the Sierra Club were also going in at Phantom. They all left Los Angeles on Friday evening, drove all night to the North Rim, and began the hike down to the river.

While hiking down the North Kaibab Trail, the woman began to lag behind. Orville became worried about her, as they still had eight miles to go and were going to be late for supper. He put her pack on top of his own for those final eight miles, allowing her to keep up. They managed to reach Phantom Ranch shortly before dinner.[9]

Georgie first saw Orville in the dining room waiting for dinner. He had fallen asleep with his mouth hanging wide open. In addition, he was wearing khaki-colored clothes that looked rather dirty to her. She had been hoping to get somebody "worthwhile" who could help her with the boats, and she thought from his appearance Orville was a lost cause.

For this low-water trip Georgie had mimeographed material about possible escape routes. Every afternoon they would go over the maps for the next day so that if they got separated on the river they would know whether to go downriver or upriver to get out of the canyon.

Orville was used to running around the mountains; he had taken a rock-climbing class with the Seattle Mountaineers and was in good physical condition. Despite her earlier doubts, he proved very helpful to Georgie by assisting others up the rocks on the hikes. At Elves Chasm they went up a side canyon to check a report of a large arch. Georgie and some others were much better hikers than several women who Orville stayed behind to help. They fell so far behind that they finally met Georgie on her way back down to start dinner. Orville did not like the idea of slowly working his way back down with the women, so he asked Georgie, "Can I go back with you?" She said, "Sure, here take my camera, carry my camera." Then she took off at a run down the canyon. She would run partway down a big rock and then jump ten to twenty feet into the sand; Orville stayed right with her. She was trying her best to run away and leave him, but she could not. After that, she had a new respect for him and they became good friends. The stragglers made it back in time for dinner.

Orville was very impressed with Georgie. "Here was this woman," he said, "doing this really amazing sort of trip. This was *real adventure* out in the wild country . . . once I got on the river with her, at first, I began to think that Georgie controlled the river. She told it what to do!" It took him some years to learn that Georgie instead had a very high respect for the river and what it could do to *her*, if she got careless.

On this trip the water was extremely low at Bedrock Rapid, where the normal route is around the right side of the rock mass that splits the channel. This time, they could have waded out to it on the right side. As in 1955, they were forced to go around to the left, the river's main channel. Here the current was bouncing off the canyon wall. The boat wound up in the huge whirlpool. They kept circling, but on roughly the eighteenth turn they were finally able to break free. They joked about how people would find them "years from now, these 16 skeletons . . . going around and around in this eddy."

In the left channel of Bedrock Rapid, the river hits a wall and makes a right turn behind the big rock, going through a narrow passageway between the midstream bedrock island and the canyon wall. In that low water the space between the rock walls was several feet shorter in any direction than Georgie's boat. Georgie was never one to lose her cool in a tight situation—she simply let the air out of the end cells of the pontoons so they would crumple up and the boat could squeeze through. When she made it through Orville thought, "Georgie is capable of anything. There is nothing she can't do!"[10]

Navajo Christmas Party

A new dimension was added to Georgie's life upon meeting Shine Smith. Big, six-foot-tall Hugh Dickson Smith had come to the Navajo Reservation as a Presbyterian missionary in 1917 after serving four adventurous years in Texas, where he was known as "Cowboy Preacher Smith." He learned the Navajo language and, over the next four years, became acquainted with the hard life and injustices endured by the Indians. Because of his love for the people (the *Dineh*, as the Navajos refer to their nation), he helped them in every way he could.[11]

In 1921 Smith withdrew from organized mission work because his heart and imagination were too big for its limited scope. He felt he could accomplish far more by teaching Christianity to the Indians without any petty restrictions. He took Christianity to them by his deeds, not merely printed words in a book. Clothing the naked, feeding the starving, and helping the sick became his sole objectives. He fought those who would exploit the Navajos and battled with every weapon possible to obtain justice for them.

The lot of the children was the hardest for Smith. He pushed himself beyond ordinary endurance on their behalf. He helped and saved the lives of so many one winter that the Navajos began to say, "He brings hope and life like the sun shining on Mother Earth." Within a short time he was being called "Sunshine Smith," later contracted to "Shine." Volumes could be written about his experiences with the Indians. He solicited goods and money from far and wide to help them. Early in his self-imposed ministry he had begun holding Christmas parties on the reservation. Food, bedding, and clothing from donated sources would be divided among the families, along with candy and toys for the children. Soon after Georgie met Shine, she became involved in the Christmas party project. The site of the party was a bare red bluff overlooking the Little Colorado River and the Painted Desert, a spot on the reservation surrounded by a large population of Navajos. On Christmas Eve and Christmas day, some eight thousand (mostly Navajo) Indians received more than one hundred tons of food, clothing, and toys. Many individuals acted as collecting agents for other donors to this remarkable cause. Among them were Georgie White and her friends, who accounted for a big share of the total. Their donations were trucked gratis from Los Angeles to Flagstaff by Navajo Freight Lines.

Georgie's old employer, Douglas Aircraft Corporation, donated money for the purchase of flour and lard. One of Georgie's former passengers, Walter Blaylock, brought a truckload of groceries, clothing, and thirty-five cases of baby food all the way from Twin Falls, Idaho.

For entertainment on Christmas Eve, the Navajos sang ceremonial chants and danced the *Yeibechai* until dawn. In the 1956 celebration the Moencopi Village Hopi Indian Concert Band played appropriate music for the occasion and Bandmaster Heber Dan gave several cornet solos. Adolph Maloney's wife gave the story of Jesus over the public address system in Navajo, and Buck Rogers, Sr., and his wife sang "Silent Night" and other religious songs to their guitar accompaniment.

Georgie had a special spot in her heart for the children. She sent word to her Boulder City friends: "If you or your friends have any old toys or warm clothes for children, save them and I'll pick them up on the way through." She made a special appeal for candy as she knew that, like all children, the Navajo kids dearly loved it. At that cold time of year it provided warmth and food as well as luxury. Georgie personally hauled the candy and as many of the toys as her truck would carry to the Christmas party. She took along a Santa Claus suit to help pass out the candy and toys to the younger children.

8 Glen Canyon Dam and a Clash of Personalities, 1957–1958

$\mathcal{J}$n April 1956 President Dwight David Eisenhower signed a bill that would forever alter the character of the Colorado River between Cataract Canyon and Lake Mead. By that legislation the Bureau of Reclamation was authorized to build Glen Canyon Dam fifteen miles upstream from Lee's Ferry between the dark-stained orange walls of Navajo sandstone. Controlled flows below the dam would eliminate the scouring floods of springtime and the deposition of new sand on the beaches alongside the river, but beautiful Glen Canyon would be buried under a lake.

When completed, the seven-hundred-foot-high dam would create a lake with double the shoreline of Lake Mead and be seventy-six miles longer. Conservationists had pushed for the dam in Glen Canyon as an alternative to one proposed for Dinosaur National Monument, a decision most of them would soon regret.

Scaling of canyon walls at the dam site began in August 1956. By the 1957 boating season, a coffer dam and diversion tunnel were in place and boaters had to leave the river at Kane Creek (above the dam site) rather than at Lee's Ferry. This would be the takeout point until 1963 when the dam was completed and the reservoir began to fill.

Although Georgie had taken many Sierra Club members through Glen Canyon, their fiery leader, David Brower, had never made the trip. However, his series of trips through the canyon during the construction period left him aghast at what was about to be lost. His experience led him to edit a lavish book entitled *The Place No One Knew*. This in turn gave further impetus to the environmental movement that had been kicked off with the Echo Park controversy of the late 1940s and early 1950s.[1]

Today the river in Grand Canyon is controlled by Glen Canyon Dam. "Its flow is regulated, usually through power-producing turbines; its temperature is constantly cold; and its namesake, the reddish-colored silt that once choked its flow, has been replaced by flourishing green algae."[2]

Construction of the dam had a profound effect on Georgie's trip schedules. When the reservoir began to fill in 1963, Georgie ceased running Glen Canyon. When it reached full pool in 1980, drowning out more than half of the rapids in Cataract Canyon, she abandoned that stretch of river as well.

Georgie's attitude toward the dam was rather philosophical, observing in essence that as long as people keep having babies they are going to have to have more water.

Dick McCallum's Adventures with Georgie

Dick McCallum graduated from North Hollywood High School in 1957. He was seventeen. One night on television he saw a movie of Georgie running the Grand Canyon. It really caught his interest, and he tracked her down in the Los Angeles area. McCallum found out how to get on a trip with her and began saving three hundred dollars, the price of her sixteen-day trip.

McCallum was enthralled with the canyon and enjoyed the camaraderie of the group. He rode in the triple rig the entire trip, learned how to row, and jumped at the chance to replace Eddy Gooch as an oarsman when Eddy had to leave at Whitmore Wash. Chet Bundy, one of Georgie's favorite people, was the other boatman on the triple rig.

Georgie took a liking to Dick McCallum and asked him to stick around that summer. He stayed with her from then until 1964, when he and Ron Smith went into business for themselves.[3]

McCallum thought of Georgie as a special person in that she was a collector of people—people she could help direct into something else. Many of her passengers and boatmen became her "river family" and went on trips with her over and over. He said that Georgie would put a lot of responsibility on those who worked for her, then sit back and watch how they performed, though she stood by in case they got into something that was too deep for them.

McCallum would usually meet Georgie at Moab, Utah, in May to begin the season with trips through Cataract and Glen Canyons. In

Moab he'd met Mitch Williams, who had an airplane. Mitch would pick up Georgie's people at Hite and fly them back to the Moab airport, where they would retrieve their cars and return to their homes.

Mitch had not met Georgie before making his first flight to pick up her passengers at Hite. When he got to the airstrip that first time, the truck was already there and being loaded. Mitch walked up and said, "Where's Georgie?" Some of the passengers pointed up on top of the truck where Georgie was arranging equipment as it was being passed up to her. Mitch said:

> I looked up there, and all Georgie had on was a little old narrow black bra and these little black panties. And she'd worn a great big hole in the cheek of each side. There must have been four inches across each one of those holes. And she was all bent over working on something; when I looked up, that was the view I got. That was my first look at Georgie. And what a view it was.[4]

McCallum said that occasionally things would ruffle Georgie's composure so much she would bow out. She did not have a lot of patience for obnoxious people. One trip they had a group of Boy Scouts from Beverly Hills for a float down Glen Canyon, and it started out terribly. The kids had brought a change of clothes for every day, much of which was left behind at Hite. The Scouts had gotten a special deal on a river trip because they said they wanted to hike and climb. As it turned out, about all they really liked to do was have water and mud fights.

By the third day Georgie was growing disenchanted with the whole bunch. Therefore, when one of the youngsters developed an eye infection and was homesick, Georgie said, "This kid needs to get out and go to the doctor. I think, Dick, I'd better go along with the Scoutmaster to make sure this all works out. You and Ron can stay here and run the trip." She took one of the boats and left McCallum and Ron Smith, the other boatman, and one troop leader to herd the thirty Scouts for the rest of the trip.

Apparently these were not the regular brand of Boy Scouts. McCallum, Smith, and the remaining Scout leader did everything they could think of to entertain the boys. When they reached Aztec Canyon for the hike up to Rainbow Bridge, a distance of six miles, they were *sure* all the boys would go on the hike. But only five or six of them did. The boys got so out of control that the morning after staying at Aztec Canyon Dick and Ron awoke to find the last troop leader gone. He had hitched a ride out with Art Greene, who had come up in his air boat.

McCallum and Smith had all the kids, no leader, no Georgie, and no idea what to do with them. The next day at Cathedral Canyon, Dick said, "Hey! We're going hiking. Anybody want to come along?" He found no takers, so he and Ron went hiking by themselves. They hiked all day long and came back just about dark. To their joy and surprise they found Georgie and the troop leader waiting in camp. They had come up in a powerboat and brought ice cream and other goodies. Dick and Ron felt they were saved at last. Dick McCallum said, "I loved Georgie . . . but she could test you sometimes . . . to see what you were made of."

Journalists in Cataract

Two writers went on a Cataract Canyon trip with Georgie in 1957. Randall Henderson, a refined gentleman of sixty-nine, was editor and publisher of *Desert Magazine* and doing research for a story about Georgie. He spent a lot of time talking to her or, more often, listening to her.[5]

White-haired Joel Sayre was writing another story about Georgie for *Sports Illustrated*. He had a book with him by Wallace Stegner titled *Mormon Country*, which he read to them when conversation lagged.

This time Georgie had a motor on the big boat, and it carried the bulk of the passengers and the baggage. About this time in her operations, Georgie introduced her "lunch table." It consisted of a four-foot-wide plastic wading pool. To prepare lunch she inflated the tubular rim of the pool, placed it on the ground, and filled it with an assortment of cold meats, cheese, jam, honey, fruit, fruit juice, and canned bread. This arrangement kept things from tipping over into the sand on uneven ground. One member of the party dubbed it "Cataract Canyon smorgasbord."

Henderson described Georgie in this manner: ". . . has the smooth legs of a teenager . . . light blue, expressionless eyes . . . appears hard as a rock on first encounter . . . a soft heart . . . a sucker for all wild life, even hating to step on ants . . . a genius at handling people in her rough way."

By 1957 Georgie was boating rivers of the Southwest and Northwest full-time except for the winter months, when she spent her

Lunchtime along the Colorado River, Arizona. Georgie used a plastic wading pool as a table until the Park Service forced her to go to the more conventional type used by other outfitters. *Photo by Josef Muench, courtesy of Dan Cassidy, Five Quail Books-West.*

time repairing equipment, attending boat shows, and lecturing about her trips. Her sister, Marie, took care of the office work, correspondence involved in booking trips, and keeping in contact with passengers. Whitey took care of the shore duty by trucking in the boats and supplies for the start of each trip, inflating the rafts, and helping Georgie with the critical job of roping them together. He also met the parties at takeout and trucked the equipment to the next trip start.

High Water in Grand Canyon

The Colorado River had a high water year in 1957. The U.S. Geological Survey gauged the river upstream from the mouth of Bright Angel Creek at 124,000 cfs on June 13. The flow did not drop below 85,000 cfs from June 7 through July 7, and it ran at flood level until the end of July. Georgie's first run of Grand Canyon for the year began near the peak flow, on June 17.[6] Fred Eiseman wrote of this:

After an unbelievably wild ride through Cataract Canyon in early June, we left Lee's Ferry just about at the flood crest. Georgie was operating her recently-invented motorized monstrosity of bridge pontoons. But I always rowed one of her not-yet-perfected contraptions consisting of three 10-man rafts tied side by side, with two oarsmen separated by three boat widths. We tried to keep the boats lined up so that one oar was downstream and one upstream, but the flow this day soon made it apparent that there wasn't a great deal we could do to control our course, fate, destiny or survival. The river was totally in charge.

I have never felt such power in a river as that summer. Of course I have never been flushed down a toilet, but I can imagine now what it must be like.[7]

The big water moved the boats along at a much faster velocity than normal, and passengers complained when they found themselves sped down to Phantom Ranch in two and one-half days instead of five. This caused a long layover at the ranch to await passengers hiking in to join the trip at Phantom.

As the party progressed downstream, the shoreline became unrecognizable. All the familiar beaches were under water, and the tops of trees lined the banks. At Boulder Narrows water was pouring *over* the gigantic rock that usually split the channel there.

At 25 Mile Rapid, Georgie's rig started down first as usual to wait for the little boats that followed. Following Georgie, the triple rig was flung against the left wall of the canyon with great force, causing a long rip in the neoprene of one of the outside rafts. A whole section deflated directly under boatman Ed Gooch who was suddenly sitting in choppy water up to his waist. It seemed funny at first, until the crew realized they could no longer maneuver the rig as they swirled on down through what seemed the longest, meanest rapid they had ever encountered.

Sensing possible trouble, Georgie had pulled in downstream to wait. When she saw their predicament, she pulled out into the current to intercept the crippled rig. She ordered all of the women off it and conscripted some strong young men to help bring the rig to shore. It swirled away with only men on board and was soon out of sight. That was the last those on the big boat saw of them until the next day.

The high water came down the canyon as if in a flume. This did not allow for many eddies to escape into (or get caught in, depending on one's point of view). The little boats shot past Georgie's camp like a runaway truck, but at last the triple-rig caught an eddy where one "strong passenger put the bowline in his teeth, jumped off and swam to shore to snag the line around a rock."[8]

The little boats did not carry food. Georgie found them and the crew the next day, a few miles down the river. By that time they had the rip patched and the raft reinflated. They were hungry but ready to take on whatever adventure the river had to offer.

At Vasey's Paradise water gushed from the cliffs directly into the river, and all the redbud trees were under water. When the group reached Redwall Cavern, they realized the immensity of the flood: There was no cavern visible! The only identifying mark was a small recess of a few feet where the overhang begins. Small rapids were drowned out; larger ones had tremendous waves.

At Bedrock Rapid Georgie ran into temporary problems. When the two rigs arrived, they stopped above the rapid on the right bank to ponder potential problems that might occur in getting past the big island in mid-river. The strong, swift current seemed to lead directly to the center of the massive rock. There was plenty of water on the right side for Georgie's big boat, the most prudent route. So Georgie set off in the big boat confident and purposeful while the triple rig crew stood on the right bank to watch.

Georgie headed down the right side, but almost immediately the powerful current took over. The big boat headed straight for the center of the big rock and smashed into it. The shock of those on shore was instantly relieved when the raft pushed off without losing any passengers. But then it swung around to the left side and disappeared behind the rock. They became concerned when her raft did not soon appear downstream.

To their surprise Georgie's raft finally reappeared heading upstream along the left bank. Then it swung around and went back downstream behind the rock island. It was caught in the huge whirlpool always awaiting the hapless rafter forced to run the left side of Bedrock Rapid.

Those watching from shore finally realized that they had to try to come to the rescue. They made a safe run down the right fork of the rapid and managed to find a place to land on the left bank below the island. From there they scrambled over treacherous ledges to get up to where Georgie's crew (still going in circles) could throw out ropes to those on the bank. While holding the lines fiercely so that the raft was held snug against the bank, the rescuers helped the passengers off the raft. The raft was then lined down to the chute and coaxed through.

Everyone scrambled along the ledges to reboard. As usual with Georgie's passengers, they took this adventure in stride and soon were back floating down the Colorado with very knowing looks as they recalled Georgie's well-known comment, "The average can't imagine!"[9]

At the entrance to the area of the inner gorge known as Granite Narrows, the canyon walls are only seventy-six feet apart, the narrowest point along the Colorado River in Grand Canyon. Here Georgie's party experienced some of the most dangerous kind of water, full of cross currents, boils, and whirlpools. Not long after getting into this section of the canyon, Georgie's motor quit and the boat began drifting toward the canyon wall; this did not unduly perturb them after so many past encounters. They felt secure until the raft on the right ran up on the canyon wall on a boil. The middle raft seemed to buckle; due to the high water it had caught on top of a huge ledge of rocks. When the water ran off the wall, the raft on the left dropped straight down, as if on a hinge. It all happened so fast that most of those on the left pontoon were taken completely unaware. They were not even holding on. Before they could recover they were thrown into the river.

There was a whirlpool beside the raft, and the ledge on which the middle pontoon was lodged held them in one spot. Passenger Albert H. Blum wrote, "Immediately after I was thrown into the river I heard a terrific crash and it seemed to me as if the rafts had turned over. I felt I had had it, as the British say. I could feel the rubber raft over my head."[10] Later, those on the raft said they saw the top of his head come to the surface, and then he was sucked under again. When it seemed he could hold his breath no longer, Albert came to the surface and was close enough to grab a rope hanging from the raft. Despite the drag of the whirlpool he was able to hang on, and ultimately two of the men pulled him out. He could offer them little help as by that time he was totally exhausted.

Eight people had been washed overboard. Blum said, "Ironically enough it happened on my birthday; believe me, that is one birthday I shall never forget." Marshal Bond was also sucked under and thought he'd never get out. He lost his movie camera and ruined his still camera, which was tied around his neck. Others had comparable experiences. Chester Kelley was separated from the bunch and got caught in a large whirlpool quite a distance from the rafts. With unerring accuracy Georgie threw a rope to him. He was able to grab it and was pulled free. They christened him "Whirlpool Kelley" because he'd been sucked down by that whirlpool and was the last to be rescued.

The Heiniger Fiasco

In April 1958 Georgie did a charter trip in Grand Canyon that brought out the darker side of her personality. Ernst Heiniger was a Swiss motion picture photographer, a top producer of Disney's nature films. He already had one Oscar to his credit and would earn another later for his film of the Grand Canyon. He lived at the South Rim for over a year while working on the film, and Dan Davis worked for him almost every weekend. Dan was his employee on the river trip.

What Heiniger wanted and needed for his motion picture project was a stable platform that would allow him to make photographs of the river and canyon. Georgie had the largest and most stable craft on the river, so Dan hired her to do the job for Heiniger.

Heiniger wanted to shoot film of the flowing water—his movie was to have no people or boats in it. Therefore, he mounted his camera on the front end of the middle pontoon. He just wanted to pan pictures of water and the shoreline going by as he went down the river on the calm stretches between rapids.

Jeanne Heiniger had pleaded with her husband to make the trip without her. She was terrified of the river and wanted only to get the trip over with. She was not even able to swim, and had not the least desire to run rapids or view breathtaking sheer canyon walls. He encouraged her, however, saying it would be the "adventure of a lifetime." So although she was dead set against the whole idea, Jeanne found herself on the river.[11] This was the first tension brought to the trip.

Heiniger and his wife were accustomed to high living, used to the best cuisine served with the finest of wines. Dan Davis was well aware of Georgie's menus and warned Heiniger about her normal meals ahead of time. Heiniger, therefore, gave her five hundred dollars extra with the understanding that it was for better food. Georgie said the extra money was given because she had to hire an extra truck driver, as Whitey had taken a San Juan group she had scheduled. She did upgrade her food quality somewhat, but not nearly to what Heiniger expected.

On the first night out from Lee's Ferry, Georgie warmed up some canned vegetables and canned tamales, and that was dinner.[12] This did not sit well with Heiniger. This was the first night out of Lee's Ferry, where she could have had steaks and all the trimmings. The next night she served corned beef hash and a can of mixed vegetables, and Heiniger blew his stack. He accused her of robbing and cheating him on the food. Georgie retorted with, "You s.o.b., I wish I'd got fresh meat and you'd got sick and died."

At that, Jeanne reportedly said to Ernst, "It is certainly a shame to go through such beautiful scenery with such common persons."

Georgie responded, "You Hollywood s.o.b. The last photographer I took down was a s.o.b., too."

Jeanne then told her husband, "Don't even talk to such common people." And the Heinigers and Georgie never spoke directly to each other from that day on. Whenever Heiniger wanted anything, he would say to Davis, "Tell that woman to land here," or whatever he wanted. Georgie would be five feet away and hear every word of it. So Davis would turn to her and say, "Georgie, Mr. Heiniger would like to land here," or whatever he had asked.

Then Georgie would usually say, "Tell that man that I can't land here because we've already passed it!"[13] Georgie would have to plan her landings ahead of time because spur-of-the-moment landings were almost impossible and were dangerous to attempt.

When the group arrived at Phantom Ranch, Heiniger ordered down a lot of "good" food. From then on Georgie and her helper, Jack Kelso, would cook and eat their own meals. At that point the work load was such that Dan knew he needed help. He hired Hubert Lauzon, a maintenance man at the park. Davis and Lauzon did all the cooking for Heiniger and his wife. They would have to find firewood for heating a Dutch oven in order to prepare special delicacies such as pie and pineapple upside-down cakes. Davis wrote that after getting up at 4:30 A.M. and carrying fifty pounds of movie equipment up to the top of a granite peak and back six times a day, while serving constantly as peacemaker between Georgie and the Heinigers, and then returning to camp about dark, he was not in the mood for cooking pineapple upside-down cake.

To make matters worse, Georgie was continually making fun of them. At one time Davis and Lauzon were setting up camp in an area where there was practically no firewood. They had to climb all over the cliffs to get enough little sticks for their fire. They were just getting ready to start their fire when Georgie and Kelso came up and set up for their primitive dinner less than ten feet away. Heiniger made Davis and Lauzon move the sticks to another place that Heiniger selected far enough away from Georgie so he could not hear her. And Georgie called out, "You fellows are gonna wear out those sticks movin' around!"

Heiniger would just turn purple at things like that. Dan Davis wrote:

> The above incident was just one of many where I lost all self respect and did things that all the money in the world couldn't hire me to do but the situation was so tense that both Lauzon and I both felt that the only way we'd ever get out was to bend over backwards to both factions, especially in the case of Jeanne who we both thought was on the verge of a complete mental collapse as she was scared most of the time, depressed and brooding and would go for a day without saying a word, just sitting and staring—and that would have been all we needed.

The most frequent causes of their battles were Heiniger's last-minute requests to make a stop. When Georgie would pass the spot by, there was no question in his mind she was doing it on purpose. Each time there would be a violent clash of tempers. Davis knew enough about the river to know that it was really difficult landing at some of these places. He says he even told Heiniger ahead of time that because of the high water conditions, she would not be able to land at certain places, such as Travertine Falls and Havasu Creek.

A couple of times they pulled Lauzon into the water after he had jumped off and tried to snag the rope around a rock or tree because Georgie could not make the landing. In many places there was just nothing to tie onto. She *really* tried every time Heiniger said, "Land here," if there was the slightest chance she could make it, but where it was obvious she couldn't, she just said so and went on.

Jeanne and Heiniger would not camp or eat within earshot of Georgie, whose voice had a remarkable carrying capacity. This made for some difficult situations, as many of the camps were on small sand-bars, where Heiniger wanted pictures rather than comfortable camps. Davis said that some nights when he was dead tired and had to work into the night to fix fancy food for the Heinigers, he would gladly have settled for "Georgie Stew": a can of chicken or beef covered with canned vegetables.

Heiniger had made a sizeable down payment to Georgie before the trip started, and the balance was due at the end. When they arrived at Temple Bar, he wrote out a check for the balance, somewhere between one and two thousand dollars. Georgie refused to take the check. She said she wanted cash. Whitey had not yet arrived with the truck to pick up Georgie's boats, and Davis knew Whitey was quite a brawler and could get pretty "ornery." Dan figured that if Whitey got there while this was going on, there would be a fight, because Whitey would have had quite a bit to drink when he arrived with the trucks.

Heiniger was big, strong, and taller than Whitey. Davis thought Heiniger would have probably killed him. So all Davis wanted was to get out of there before Whitey showed up. Davis said, "I was poor as hell, but in order to get out of there I had to endorse that check as that I would make it good if Heiniger cancelled the check." He said he did not have twenty dollars in the bank, let alone two thousand.

Davis summed up the trip by concluding that the fault was about fifty-fifty between Georgie and Heiniger. After the trip he talked to each of them separately, but neither would concede that the other might have been partially correct on occasions. Both blamed Davis for a portion of it, mainly for exposing them to one another and lining up the trip. He said, "Both started out as good friends of mine, now I have no idea if either of them are and if they aren't—I haven't lost much."

Oddly enough, after all of the recriminations and tensions, Jeanne Heiniger was quoted as saying:

> We drifted out on the clear waters of Lake Mead just eighteen days after the start of our run. There was a momentary feeling of elation, but, ironically, even before we reached Las Vegas, we all longed to be back on the River again—to hear her deep, deafening roar—to ride one of the high waves![14]

9 Exploring Mexican Rivers, 1958–1959

Always looking for new rivers to explore, Georgie had for some time been considering a trip in Mexico. The first such expedition was finally set for the fall of 1958. The party would include Lillian Lasch, Paul Kelly, Marshall Bond, Jr., Frank Rich, Jr., and Orville Miller. They had planned to explore the Rio Papigochico Aros, but that didn't pan out, as the river and surrounding area were inundated by a tropical storm.

On the flight into Mexico the party encountered continuous torrential rains. On all sides were nothing but clouds. When they finally dropped low enough to see the countryside, the group found the entire terrain flooded. They would later find roads washed out, telephones out of commission, telegraph wires down, and people marooned on high spots hoping desperately for help. More than thirty thousand people were believed to have been left temporarily homeless.

The pilot tried desperately to maneuver out of the storm, flying up several valleys only to be forced back the same way he had come. Fuel was getting low and they were looking for a known emergency landing field. When they finally located it, it was one big lake with the runways completely inundated.

There was only one alternative—the paved highway, very straight and narrow, a mere ribbon. But the pilot, Brad Pearson, did a superb job. He landed in the center of the highway with a foot to spare on each side of the wheels. With the little remaining gas they taxied along the road until brought to a standstill where the road was washed out. A nearby sign indicated "Hermosillo, 75 miles."

Rich, Bond, and Miller started walking down the road in search of help; the others remained with the plane. They felt secure in the fact that Paul Kelly could speak some Spanish. Soon after, a truck came along and wanted to get past the plane. They maneuvered it enough for the truck to pass under one wing. The driver spoke English and was going to Hermosillo. Paul decided to go with him and pick up the other three en route if he could find them. This left three non-Spanish-speaking guards for the plane. Soon two policemen arrived and indicated they would help guard the plane. A truckload of workmen then arrived to repair the washed out road. From the looks of that road gang, the three were glad to have policemen standing by!

In the late afternoon the three were overjoyed to see the truck, with Paul and a barrel of gas, coming down the highway. Miller, Rich, and Bond had remained in Hermosillo to lighten the take-off load of the plane. Georgie noted, "Have you ever tried standing on the wing of a plane, trying to pour gas into a tiny tank inlet, using a large pail and the wind blowing a forty mile gale? Try it some time."[1] Fifteen minutes after take-off they landed in Hermosillo, and were soon joined by the rest of the party, glad to be back together again.

Early the next morning they returned to the airport determined to check the Aros River. The storm, however, had not abated. Their alternate river was the Rio Grande de Santiago, nearly a thousand miles to the southeast in the central part of Mexico. If they were going to explore any river at this time, that would have to be it.

They flew low over the Santiago to check it out as much as possible before landing in Guadalajara. Georgie said, "The canyon looked rugged, but not impassable, so we skipped over a loop or two, which the river made, without looking at it. This came close to being a serious mistake."

After landing the party at Guadalajara, the pilot immediately started back to Nogales, intending to return with the boats as soon as possible. Because of bad weather, though, he could not return for four days. During that time the crew talked to a hotel owner, Señor Barrato, who assured them they needed a licensed guide, if only to get the licenses necessary to enter the river. The American consul, a Mr. Johnson, confirmed this. So they hired a guide to obtain the permits but did not take him on the trip.

Since the Rio de Santiago was a federal river, the group needed a federal license. They also needed a military pass to use the road, which was blocked by a huge log chain. A power dam was being constructed on the river at that point, and they had no idea of river conditions below. They also had to have a pass from the Tourist Bureau with a government stamp on it to assure them passage through the many villages along the way.

When the plane arrived with food and the boats, the party lost no time getting them loaded on a truck. They headed for the small village of Santa Rosa thirty-five miles away, the put-in point on the river.

The Santiago River looked fast and interesting, but Georgie worried a little because the pilot had only been able to get two rafts into the plane. She felt that three rafts tied together gave marvelous balance; with only two, she judged that safety was reduced by half.

At Santa Rosa they soon had an audience. The natives helped inflate the boats, sat on them, punched them, felt the motor, and indicated they thought the whole idea was wonderful. They stayed most of the night even though it flashed lightning, thundered, and poured rain. Georgie's crew had to move camp in the middle of the night as the river quickly rose. The next day work on the dam was cancelled. In broken English one fellow said, "We can work any day, but there has never been a group of any kind try to run this river and we must see how it is done." One man said there were alligators farther down the river. The crew hoped fervently that they would not be hungry enough to eat black rubber boats.

By 10:30 A.M. they were ready to take off. The water was fast, about twelve miles per hour, and they made good time. The first day they ran some spectacular rapids and did a lot of bailing. Below the first rapid they came to a small settlement where the people only spoke Spanish. The male children were mostly naked, but all of the girls wore clothing. Some of the adults were barefoot in spite of numerous snakes; others wore heavy-soled sandals. The party gave them gifts of cigarettes and candy and tried conversing with them in poor Spanish. Farther on they came upon a crude ferry. A pulley and cable had been strung across the river and a boat hooked to it. They observed a native hauling a mule across the river in the boat.

Midway through the trip the group was conscious of an increasing roar from downstream. The water ahead disappeared abruptly, and they could not see any splashing beyond the drop-off. Standing at the motor, Georgie said she could see the water down the river. They were in the middle of the river going ahead when some men on shore shouted, "Presa!"

When Orville and Paul recognized the word for "dam," they each grabbed oars and dug in to assist Georgie in getting the boat to shore. Georgie had taken only a light five-horsepower motor, figuring they might have to abandon both it and the boats and hike out. Lillian balanced on the front of the raft to jump ashore and moor it. By dint of the motor and some hard rowing, they made it to a banana patch several hundred feet above the dam.

Sure enough, there was a thirty-foot-high dam across the river. The natives told them that a German fellow had built it in 1907 for power in connection with his silver mine. It was completely unknown to the Department of Water and Power at Guadalajara, who had asked the party to mail their notes of the river back to them. There was no doubt about having to portage this one!

The crew was fortunate to find several men working at a silver mine nearby. A few pesos soon made them willing helpers. These men were adept with machetes and quickly had a narrow trail straight up the canyon wall, past the dam, and straight down again. The boats were deflated and rolled up lengthwise so that eight people could lock arms in pairs and carry them. Lillian Lasch said it looked like a giant sixteen-legged caterpillar crawling up the trail. Mules were used to carry some of the rubber bags of supplies.

All of the men here carried guns and machetes. The party surmised that they were guarding the silver taken from the mine. It was the only place on the trip where they encountered Mexicans carrying guns.

One hour below the dam brought them to a village called Paco Delia Yerca, Hostotepaguillo, in the state of Jalisco. They were surprised by many things about the town besides its name. First, they were greeted with Coca Cola that had been brought in through miles of jungle. Goats and other animals ran loose everywhere. Thatched huts were built on stilts, affording the natives a dry bed at night and the animals shade during the day. The people baked delicious hard rolls in huge, round-topped outdoor brick ovens, and corn raised in small patches high up on the hills was a staple of their diet. The men were excellent swimmers, using an unusual frog-like stroke. Most of them worked in the silver mines. The young girls were pretty and poised, perhaps a habit formed by carrying urns of water on their heads.

The jungle air was full of beautiful yellow butterflies and swarms of not so beautiful mosquitos. The jungle was alive with birds, including magpies, colorful parrots, and one vulture. They saw a huge, black, eight-foot snake hanging from a tree.

As they progressed down the river it widened, with tropical islands in midstream. The flooding Huynamota River joined the Santiago, which grew ever wider with many sandbars, large rocks, and islands. The party was confused as to which channel to take, as they all looked alike. In the distance they could see palm trees and banana plantations.

As the party traveled on they saw many iguanas sleeping on tree limbs overhanging the water. Flocks of roseate spoonbills dotted the shore, and birds of every description filled the air. This and a glorious sunset made a tropical picture to behold.

A train whistle brought the crew members out of their individual reveries and signaled that the end of the trip was near. It led them to the railroad and highway bridges they were looking for. Given directions by a Mexican from atop a bridge, they made their way to the village of Santiago Ixcuintla and landed at the foot of a street—the river was so high that the regular boat landing was under water. They floated right into the main street and landed at the "Street of the Señoritas" about 8 P.M. Their arrival appeared to disrupt evening business.

The mud was ankle deep, but they rolled up the boats as best they could. This was no place to camp. They located a police officer who spoke English, and when Georgie showed him the letter from the government office in Guadalajara he helped them watch over their equipment and located a truck for them to rent. They piled everything into the truck and made the all-night ride back to the airport at Guadalajara on top of the muddy boats.

Green River

In 1959 Georgie had a full schedule of rivers to run. She claimed in a newspaper article that "her itinerary for the season, which began in March, are 18 rivers." And, "The log this year will include 3,000 miles of river jaunts, about her yearly average."[2]

On May 11 she began an expedition at Green River, Wyoming, to retrace the John Wesley Powell expedition of 1869, this being the ninetieth anniversary of Powell's trip. Construction of the Flaming Gorge Dam had begun, and Georgie's party would be the last boat group allowed to pass through the dam site.

The party of fourteen included seventy-eight-year-old Tallulah Elston of Carmel, California; Helen Kendall, with her trusty typewriter;

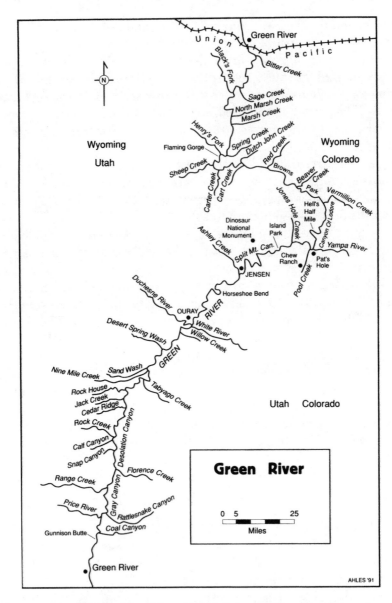

From Rough-Water Man: Elwyn Blake's Colorado River Expeditions, *by Richard E. Westwood. Copyright © 1992 by University of Nevada Press. Used with permission.*

and L. C. B. McCullough. The river was so low Georgie was unable to use a motor for most of the way for fear of hitting sandbars or rocks.

L. C. B. McCullough, a passenger on several of Georgie's trips, remained her friend for the rest of her life. While on this trip he began to create what was probably the first mile-by-mile guide to the Green and Colorado River system.

In a response letter to Dock Marston, Helen Kendall described this trip:

> What do you mean, how does she run Ashley Falls? We were lucky to get through without walking. The water was so low that all those rocks were from four feet up out of the water and some of the air had to be let out to get 17 foot boats thru a 14 foot channel. Floated down to it, the men jumped out onto a rock and eased the nose over, then jumped back in again. It may have been a falls to Ashley but at first look it resembled a dam to me. Didn't find Ashley's name but found the others and Nevills. From then on the water was so low that had there been any less water it would have been dusty.[3]

In Lodore Canyon one of the rafts caught on a sharp rock and was irreparably ripped. Ken Sleight, another outfitter who had embarked into Lodore Canyon a short time ahead of Georgie, knew and liked Georgie. At the end of his trip, while he was loading up his gear at Jensen, Utah, Georgie's outfit came limping in. As they visited, Georgie mentioned she was going to have another raft brought by truck from her warehouse in Richfield before heading into Desolation Canyon. The river was flat between Jensen and Desolation Canyon, and she could get by with only two boats to that point. To save her the trouble, Ken offered the use of his raft. It was black and hers were painted silver, but it would float just the same. Georgie accepted his offer; Ken brought back his empty boat and joined her party at the head of Desolation Canyon for the run to Green River, Utah.[4] On June 1 Georgie's entourage was increased to forty-five for the run from Green River, Utah, to Hite through Cataract Canyon.

Accident at Elves Chasm

Georgie was making another Grand Canyon run on June 12 when an unfortunate accident occurred. On a side trip to Elves Chasm, a passenger, Vernon Reade, climbed a high ledge to help some women who were trapped there. Just before reaching the women he slipped and fell to the rocks below.

Luckily, two physicians were in the party. They eased Reade's pains with medication and made splints and a stretcher to get him back to the raft. The ride through Lava Falls was extremely painful for him. At Whitmore Wash Chet Bundy hiked out to the Tuweep Ranger Station, where he awakened Ranger Riffie and asked him to call Nellis Air Force Base for a helicopter. They came to Whitmore Wash and flew the injured Reade out to a hospital in Las Vegas.[5] X-ray examination showed an eggshell and basal fracture of the skull and two compression fractures of the spine. He also had a broken hand. Georgie's reaction to all of this was to pretend it hadn't happened.

Rio Grijalva

Georgie said she planned to traverse an unexplored river or unexplored section of a known river each year. The one she chose next was little-known Rio de Chiapas in Mexico, also called the Grijalva. In 1959 Georgie made a second trip down the Rio Grande de Santiago. Then in August of that year she led a group on the uncharted Grijalva River.[6] Halfway along its course, in the vicinity of Tuxtla Gutierrez, the river plunges into a narrow, tortuous gorge with nearly vertical cliffs two thousand feet high. The gorge is called El Sumidero, "The Place where Water Flows into the Rocks." Georgie planned to enter the river at El Sumidero.

According to Georgie, this write-up appeared in a Mexico newspaper: "Nine American adventurers, including two women, have embarked upon a rapids shooting expedition into the never conquered Sumidero Canyon in the jungles of Chiapas state near the Guatemala border." The article continued:

> The canyon has taken the lives of at least six persons. Last year it frustrated a Mexican army charting expedition aided by helicopters, radios and other modern equipment when the vanguard of six officers and men lost their boats and had to be rescued from an island on which they were stranded.
>
> Francisco Fernandez, a Spaniard, disappeared in the canyon two months ago. He was the last known explorer to attempt to become the first man through the narrow canyon alive.[7]

For equipment Georgie brought along three rafts which were to be lashed together to make a triple rig. With two motors, plenty of oars, and waterproof rubber bags to hold food and other equipment, they had a raft capable of plunging entirely under water without loss of luggage or personnel.

The river party departed from a park-like beach just south of the Pan-American Highway bridge. Marshall Bond, Jr., saw them off, then watched for them from the rim with field glasses. As they entered the canyon, the current narrowed and picked up speed. A roar from around the first bend convinced them to pull to shore and scout ahead on foot. They picked their way over great boulders at the river's edge and around the bend. All were impressed by the strange beauty of the towering walls and the dense jungle growth. They were fascinated by the thunderous roar from downstream.

As they climbed the last boulder the group froze as a unit. Georgie later wrote, "In the distance of one hundred yards or less the water was transformed from a lazy river into a tongue that sped into a boiling smashing roaring maelstrom of white water the likes of which I had never seen or even visualized before." They were so awed they could not take their eyes away from the spectacle. The sheer power of the great crashing waves and deep holes seemed to numb them. By mutual consent the party decided they had gone far enough. Part of the group hiked over the rim through the jungle to get help. The rest struggled to haul the boat and luggage over big shore rocks to a place where they could start towing the boat upstream.

Undaunted, the party reentered the Rio Grijalva below El Sumidero Canyon near the village of Chicoasen. On this leg of the journey, Bond accompanied the party. They ran several rapids that furnished some excitement. Then the canyon became more and more rocky and narrowed down to a miniature El Sumidero. Here they came to a rapid that looked as bad or worse than any in Grand Canyon. Below the rapid the river was studded with rocks for several miles. It made them wish there was another way out, but they could neither retreat nor portage around this ugly trap.

The next morning they tied everything down tightly and headed into the rapid. Midway, an explosion wave spun the boats around and sent them sliding onto a huge submerged boulder. Georgie raised the motor as high as she could to protect it, but it smashed into the rock anyway. It was a sickly sight dangling from the end of the boat, grating back and forth on the rock. The middle raft was now on the rock and the two outside ones thrashed back and forth in the waves on either side.

Then the boats seemed to pull apart, and one of the side boats literally sank out of sight. Only the heads of Orville and Phil were visible as they tried to ply the oars. After that the current gradually pulled the boat around and off the rock. It was still intact but badly battered. All three sections of the raft were full of water, and bags were hanging willy-nilly by their ties.

Extricating themselves, the crew eventually drifted into calmer water where they were able to make shore by using the oars. Inventory of the damage showed that the boats had come loose from the rock when two of the seats were torn loose by the strain. Georgie was able to retie the rafts, but the motor was damaged beyond repair—the spare she carried replaced it.

With the worst of the rapids behind them, they were now able to enjoy the sights along the river. Orville was the first to spot a crocodile, an eight-footer, sunning itself on the sand, thereby winning five pesos from the rest of the party. The crocodile looked almost like a log until it plunged into the water. Then just its eyes and nostrils showed. There were iguanas and all manner of colorful bird life along the river and in the jungle bordering it. As they neared villages, no more crocodiles were seen, as the natives killed them for food.

At a camp further downriver it rained so hard they could hold out a cup and it would fill up in a few moments. A native farmer saw their plight and invited them to share his home, although it was already crowded with his wife and five children. The home was a three-room affair with dirt floor and galvanized roof. Various animals, including three dogs and four pigs, were shooed outside and the floor swept clean before the party was invited to spread out their air mattresses. The pigs could not understand all this and kept trying to get back in. There was a small homemade altar on one side of the main room. It was adorned by flowers, a single lighted candle, a crucifix, a picture of Jesus, and six pictures of Saint George and the dragon.

Before the party got to sleep, six neighbors arrived and were served a meal of tortillas and stew. One of the men had a crude violin, which he began to play. The weird concert reached a grand crescendo with the pounding of rain on the roof and the banging of pigs at the door. Applause and encores continued until the musician was exhausted. The celebration went on until the host blew out the candle and retired to his room. The party later referred to this fondly as the "Pig Motel."

Along the way, the men's feet began to bother them. It began with the toes rubbed raw and healing very slowly, making it painful to walk. They called it jungle rot. Only Georgie and Ivan Summers escaped this painful condition.

At the small village of San Manuel they met a jungle dentist. He wanted to visit the next village, so he locked up his business and begged a ride with them. He was in such a hurry to leave that he forgot to remove his short-sleeved, white dentists coat. The village he wanted to visit was about a mile and a half from the river and they later found out that he had never been there. Georgie and Summers decided to go with him, hoping to be able to get more gasoline. The dentist climbed trees in his white suit and eventually located the village; Georgie and Ivan returned to camp with their can of gas.

The party was surprised to find a dam under construction on the lower river. There was an airfield here, and three who needed to get back to their jobs departed for home. Georgie and the rest continued on and exited the river at Villa Hermosa.

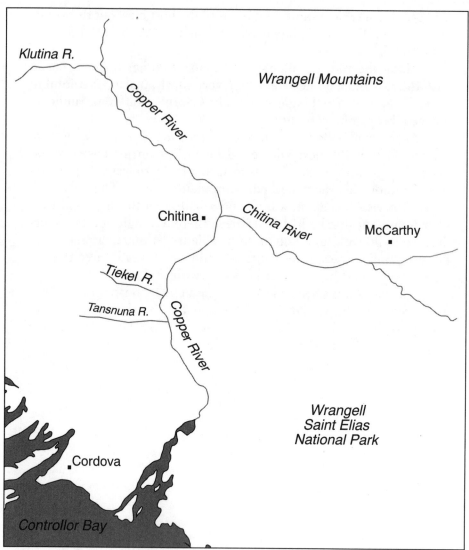

Cartography by Thomas Zakowski, University of Utah

Copper and Chitina Rivers
Alaska

N

| 50 | 0 | 50 | 100 | Miles |

10 Dead Man in Cataract and Other New Experiences, 1960–1961

On May 22, 1960, Albert Q. Quist of Salt Lake City was leading a two-boat, twelve-member party through Cataract Canyon. About noon, after running three rapids, one of the twenty-four-foot rafts slammed into a rock and hung up there, pitching four of the men into the river. Quist and his son, Clair, made it safely to shore about three-quarters of a mile below, but the other two men, Leon Peterson and Keith Howard Hoover, both of Provo, Utah, could not be located and were presumed to be drowned.[1]

Two weeks later Georgie embarked at Green River for a trip through Cataract Canyon with a party of thirty-five. She was asked to watch for the missing pair. Among Georgie's passengers was Father John Finbarr Hayes, a twenty-eight-year-old Catholic priest, who had gone through Grand Canyon with her the year before.

Georgie was leading the party in her big boat when they came to placid water below Dark Canyon. It was Sunday, about nine o'clock in the morning. The party had been on the alert for the bodies of the two lost men, and as they drifted along Georgie spotted something unusual in a mass of floating driftwood. She knew instinctively what it was even though the man's body was arched over with only the top curve of his back above the water. Both his head and his feet were submerged.

In a calm voice she summoned two people back to where she was and told them what she had discovered and what they were to do. Then she said, "I want all the women and children at the back of the boat."[2]

Georgie told those she had summoned to take oars and snag the body, and she would take it in to shore. When they had done this

Georgie gently steered the boat over to a sand bank. There was a doctor on the trip, but he knew the man was already dead because of a large gash in the back of his head, making it clear that, if he had drowned, it would have been after he had been rendered unconscious by the severe blow to the head.

The man wore cut-off pants, hiking boots, and a life jacket. The kapok life preserver, designed to keep the head and chest up, was *under* him, completely water-logged. He had thinning hair, and his skin was chalk-white. The body was decomposing and gave off a sickening odor. Georgie quickly decided they would have to bury the man. They had nothing to dig with except oars, so the grave in the sand was only about four feet deep.

To Georgie all people on her trips were equals. Recalling the incident, Father Hayes said:

> It was the first, the last, and the only time that Georgie ever called me "Father". We were all always very comfortable and informal on the river. She said to me:
>
> "Father, would you say some prayers after we bury the body, before we close the grave?["] Well, all I had was a breviary. And a breviary was a priest's prayer book, in Latin! . . . And the breviary doesn't contain a funeral service, but I knew enough about where to look to be able to come up with some suitable prayers for the burial, in the Psalms, particularly. But what was difficult about it was the breviary was all in Latin! There wasn't a single word in English in the breviary. This was 1959 or '60, before the Catholic Church changed in its prayer in this country, from Latin to English. So I sat over, under a little shade tree, going through the breviary, first of all trying to find what I would say at a . . . under these most extraordinary circumstances, and then, when it was time, got up and translated in my head a sentence at a time and said it in English. And kept it . . . I felt a need to keep it as—the breviary, after all, was a specifically Roman Catholic and clergy prayer book—and this man was a Mormon! And so I had to, out of respect for that, you know, make the prayer service efficiently generic and not . . . I certainly couldn't be saying this specifically Catholic-type thing.[3]

The burial took place on a high sandbar at the mouth of Sheep's Canyon, near a marker established by the Kolb brothers on the

U.S.G.S. expedition of April 1921. When the grave was closed, a cross of driftwood was placed on it bearing the names of both Peterson and Hoover with an "or" between them, as they did not know which of the victims they had found. Georgie wrote down a description of the man's clothing (in which he was buried) and took a camera, shoe, and pocket knife from the body to aid in identification.

Upon completion of the trip Georgie reported the discovery to San Juan County Sheriff Seth S. Wright. She established tentative identification by calling Dr. Dick H. Johnson, a member of the boating party from which Peterson and Hoover were separated. He said the description of the personal effects indicated they belonged to Leon Peterson.

The Peterson family wanted to recover the body for a proper Mormon burial. So on the evening of Monday, June 6, a party of three headed by Noel M. Taylor left Provo for Hite with a four-wheel-drive truck and a motor boat. Others in the party were Kent Heaps and Wilburn Couch. After recovering the body, they stopped in Hanksville for gas. Barbara Ekker reported that all "were quite ill from their experience."[4]

Because Georgie was such a unique person and entertaining talker, she was often asked to be a guest on television talk shows. While on the Groucho Marx show, she related the story of finding the dead man in Cataract Canyon and burying him there. Marx then said, "It sounds like you need to take an undertaker along."

"No," Georgie responded, "just a shovel." The crowd roared. She was soon hustled off stage. She assumed that Marx thought she was trying to upstage him.

Drinking River Water

Marge Petheram was a passenger on a trip through Grand Canyon in early July. She described Georgie thus: "She's a rangy, rugged, 49–year-old woman with a rascally twinkle in her eye and up to no end of mischief. She keeps the group hopping and they love it, while on shore, that is. When the boat is in motion she tends strictly to business and man—can she ever handle that barge!"[5]

With Georgie's example and that of several passengers who were repeat customers, Marge observed that "everyone must have let his hair down far beyond its normal length because horseplay was the standard procedure and more fun than a picnic. It was sort of like being a kid again." With the midday sun bearing down on them, it could become unbearably hot. The experienced members had an answer for this—after shouting, "Put away your cameras," a mad water fight would begin, utilizing the plastic bailing buckets. It was both cooling and fun.

Drinking the silt-laden river water was a surprisingly good experience for Marge. She was very reluctant to start, though, and waited until every drop of clear water was gone from her canteen before taking the first sip. Amazingly, she found it to be rather tasty. She was told that at the time there was very little contamination in the stream and the high volume of mountain-born water diluted it to the point where it carried less bacteria than most tap water.

Alaska

Georgie had heard that the rivers of Alaska contained some huge rapids, and she wanted to find out if this was true. She consulted with her photographer friend, Josef Muench, who had been conducting "Thru the Lens" tours in Alaska and Canada teaching clients how to photograph the scenery. He told her, "Georgie, the only river I think you will like is the Copper River near Cordova, Alaska."[6]

She then wrote letters for information on the Copper River, and arrangements were made for eleven passengers to meet at the Windsor Hotel in Cordova the last week of August. Georgie noted, "A length of rope permanently attached to the window competes with our modern fire escape."[7] Among Georgie's crew was boatman Dick McCallum.

From Cordova the party flew to the abandoned mining town of McCarthy, where they danced that night in the deserted saloon to the tune of a Victrola and a tub used as a drum. Others played poker at the gaming tables.

The following day the party flew to Jake's Bar on the Chitina River, a tributary of the Copper River. Georgie wrote:

> Practically everyone I met in Alaska felt it was necessary to carry guns when in the brush. Of course I have never carried a gun myself. Because I don't believe in guns and don't want animals harmed in any way, I won't let anyone else carry a gun on my trips. Before we left to go on this trip, I had quite an argument with an Alaskan who wanted to run the Copper River with me. Finally, with great apprehension, he left his rifle at home.[8]

Dick McCallum told the author that the Alaskan did indeed carry a rifle on the trip, so Georgie again demonstrates a convenient memory.

During the first morning one of the women called for a rest stop. When Georgie pulled to shore two women climbed out and disappeared behind some bushes. Suddenly one of them started screaming, "Bear! Bear!" and bolted back, pulling up her pants as she ran. A huge brown bear reared up on its hind legs to view the commotion. Georgie said that was the only close call they had on the trip.

The party pulled to shore at the junction of the Copper and Chitina Rivers and hiked to the small town of Chitina for an overnight stay. There they made an acquaintance with an Athabascan Indian woman named Susan who did a tribal dance to entertain them.

Georgie had been told of numerous huge rapids in the Copper River; however, the only one that gave them a real challenge was Abercrombie Rapid. Six days after leaving McCarthy, they came to a bridge fifty miles from Cordova where a bus from the Windsor Hotel was waiting for them. A big banner draped along one side read, "Welcome River Rats."

Georgie commented that because of the spectacular scenery and the unique experience in McCarthy, the trip was well worth it. She said, however, that the rapids just did not stack up to those in Grand Canyon.

Before leaving Alaska the party flew to Seward on the Kenai Peninsula and ran about sixty miles of the Kenai River. When they were ready to leave for home, the weather turned bad and the plane Georgie had chartered could not come in for several days because of low clouds and swirling rain. When one of the locals heard Georgie grumbling about being behind schedule, he told her, "Georgie, it is better in this country to be down here wishing you were up there, than up there wishing you were down here."[9]

Dick McCallum stayed in Alaska longer than he planned. As a boatman for Georgie, his expenses had all been paid. At the airport, as the party was getting ready to leave, Georgie told him, "Well, Dick, I've been meaning to talk to you about this. We didn't do quite as well this summer. I spent all my money up here, Dick. So I don't know how I'm gonna get you home." Delays and higher than expected costs in Alaska had left her without enough money to buy McCallum a ticket home. He said he had to get a job up there and earn enough money to fly home, as he did not have any money either.[10]

Jet Boats Upriver

In 1960 Jon Hamilton, a New Zealander who had invented some jet boat engines, headed a group that would test these engines on an upriver run of Grand Canyon. Before making the upriver run they first ran it downriver to become acquainted with the river and to make caches of gasoline and other supplies. At Lee's Ferry they met up with Georgie. Joyce Hamilton wrote:

> Four boats were now ready for launching. We were waiting for Slim to put in an appearance with his winch, a hang-over and a dozen cans of beer, when a truck drove up in a cloud of dust. It came to a halt and out of it leapt the sprightly figure of Georgie White. We knew in an instant that it was Georgie, although until now she had been known to us by reputation only.
>
> Georgie wasted no time on the scenery. She'd been here before. She went immediately to the back of the truck and with the help of her husband Whitey, proceeded to roll three massive bundles down the bank to the water's edge. They were rubber pontoons. Inflated they were enormous, and the three lashed side by side made a floating platform thirty feet long and almost as many wide. The middle pontoon was placed several feet in advance of the other two, and on it, mounted aft, was an outboard motor . . . .
>
> Georgie showed much interest in the jet boats and their method of propulsion. Nevertheless she prophesied doom for the upriver attempt.
>
> "You won't get up Vulcan [Lava Falls], even in jet boats," she said, and Whitey backed her up emphatically.
>
> "If you get one o' them back to Lee's Ferry, I'll eat it!" he said, and we thought he looked capable of doing so. With his broad muscular build, and heavy jaw, he looked a force to be reckoned with . . . .
>
> On closer acquaintance, however, we came to understand Whitey better and to appreciate him for what he is. One evening with Jon and me as his sole audience, and a few whiskeys to warm him, Whitey shed his rugged calyx and blossomed into a man with a cult. Georgie was his God. His self appointed mission in life was the upholding and enhancement of Georgie's reputation as "The Woman of the River".

"She's the greatest river-runner of all time," he said, developing his theme. And we could not but feel admiration for this woman who runs not only the Colorado but whose activities extend from the Snake and Salmon Rivers in the North to the Aros Canyon in Mexico.[11]

Dock Marston was an important member of the upriver group, along with his son, Garth. Another member of the crew was Bill Belknap, the photographer from Boulder City, Nevada. They later met Georgie and her large party during their upriver run. Joyce Hamilton described the meeting:

It was 3:20 P.M. before the yellow boat was pronounced seaworthy once more. They levered her back into the water and Fireball attacked the rapid and made a beautiful run to the top. *Dock* and *Wee Red* followed up without any difficulty and they left Dubendorf behind them and moved on up river. Bedrock Rapid presented an ideal "Kiwi-course" up one side and they covered the next fifteen miles without incident. The first discomforting signs of the black Archaean rock began to appear in the walls. They were approaching Elves' Chasm. The side canyon and beach came into view as they cruised round the great loop in the river, and to them, after the desolation of the canyon behind them, Elves' Chasm looked like Fifth Avenue at closing time. There were people everywhere, crowds of people, milling around at the bottom of the Grand Canyon! They rubbed their eyes in disbelief and saw the huge inflated neoprene rafts with "The Woman of the River" emblazoned on their sides. They had run into Georgie White and her happy band of "river-rats" bound for Lake Mead. This was certainly the first time ever that two river parties travelling in opposite directions had met midway through the Grand Canyon.

To Georgie and her tourists the sudden appearance of four boats coming up-stream was even more unexpected. Georgie knew of course that the attempt was being made, but she had heard that story a dozen times before and nothing had ever come of it. She had not troubled to prepare her passengers for the possibility of actually meeting an up-stream expedition. When the boats drew in alongside the great rubber rafts and Dock and his team leapt ashore to exchange

Georgie's big G-rig in Lava Falls, 1960. *Cline Library, Northern Arizona University, Georgie Clark Collection, #91.13.47.*

greetings, the tourists were entranced. Georgie, however, could not conceal her surprise, nor Dock his satisfaction. Georgie had been convinced that no boat would ever succeed in making the journey "against the grain". To her this was almost a sacrilege, a disparagement of the formidable reputation of "her" river. It was almost with a stamp of her foot that she accosted Dock with the allegation,

"You lined the boats up Vulcan."

"We didn't," Dock said bristling.

"You did."

"You couldn't line boats up-stream through Vulcan."

"*I* could!" said Georgie, and for a moment these two, who knew the river better than anyone else, stood regarding each other with antagonism. Then Dock laughed. But Jon for one was almost convinced that Georgie could—single-handed, if she really tried!

An interested crowd gathered around the boats. The principal characters in this historic meeting were lined up for photographs. It was 5:20 P.M. when Dock called a halt to the cheerful exchange of stories and experiences by announcing that the up-river party must now be on its way. They left Georgie and her happy band already preparing their camp for the night, and headed on up-river, as if fifty miles before dark would be no effort.[12]

Hamilton and his party completed a successful run upriver to Lee's Ferry. They did, however, lose one of the three boats, the "Wee Yellow," in Grapevine Rapid.

Rio Balsas

In the fall of 1960 Georgie decided to tackle Mexico's longest river, the Rio Balsas.[13] One man on the trip was Orville Miller. Besides the fun of the trip, he was also in search of new plant species that could be used for medicinal purposes. On these Mexican expeditions the passengers paid for their own transportation, food, and other personal necessities.

Georgie had scouted the upper Balsas area previously and knew they could get onto the river by means of a tributary that crossed the Pan American Highway. Their truck driver headed for the spot Georgie had in mind, and they arrived about midnight.

By the time the party was ready to leave the next day, they had an audience of about sixty people perched on rocks, ledges, and bridges. The river was a narrow, fast-moving, mud-colored stream with many sand waves, bordered by a thick growth of trees. It was necessary to proceed in single boats rather than lashing them together in a triple rig as they had intended. Fortunately, they encountered no rapids the first day.

The group stopped to give trinkets to the villagers along the way. At one place they were entertained by huge butterflies with six-inch wingspans; they were attracted to the yellow bailing buckets. The party did not understand how information was passed along, but their group seemed to be expected at every community along the way. Whereas the natives had watched them from a distance up to this point, the people in the small village of San Juan de Los Rios were friendly and seemed delighted to mingle with them. This village was located where the Atoyac and Mixteca Rivers formed the Rio Balsas.

Georgie's party handed out jewelry and religious icons in exchange for a tour of the village. The houses were constructed of bricks made of clay and wattle. Dirt floors, yards, and streets were swept clean and in each yard was a granary in which corn was stored.

Along the river were fence-like structures of poles, called *milpas*, extending into the shallow reaches of the stream. In times of high water the poles would catch drifting tree limbs, which would in turn catch silt. This made rich soil for growing corn in the spring once the water receded.

Embarking on the Balsas, the party now had the three rafts lashed together. The water was slow and placid at first but soon narrowed to one third of its original width and formed a fast chute between steep walls. After several days the party arrived at the village of Coacalco. They were greeted by four boys with hollow gourds, called *boombas*, tied to their stomachs. The boys floated high on the water with these gourds. The group also observed a raft consisting of a platform built on top of and attached to a solid layer of the gourds. Later they learned that large quantities of merchandise could be floated on the river with these rafts, which were steered by swimmers alongside.

When the sun came out for the first time, everyone got badly burned. Swarms of mosquitos seemed to thrive on the brand of repellent they had brought. One of the passengers wrote, "In simple fairness to the manufacturers, I must say that you can kill a Balsas mosquito with their preparations. If you hold him carefully and pour enough of the stuff on him, he will drown."

At Tuxtula, where the Acapulco Highway crosses the river, they landed for the last time and packed up for the trip home.

Grand Canyon Record

The next year, in May 1961, Georgie made another run through Grand Canyon. According to the records kept by Otis "Dock" Marston, this group of twenty-five were roughly the 460th through 485th persons to transit Grand Canyon, making them among the first five hundred. Of these, Georgie had taken more passengers through Grand Canyon than any other outfitter.

Getting supplies to Georgie was not always easy, and sometimes mishaps occurred. In order to supply Georgie and other boatmen with gasoline at Whitmore Wash, Chet Bundy had strung a hose from a barrel at the rim down to the river. If the supply valve at the top was opened when the outlet at the bottom was closed, pressure could build up so high the line would break. Therefore, Bundy would have one of his children stay on top and open the valve when he gave a signal from down at the river eighteen hundred feet below.

Bundy was scheduled to meet Georgie's group with gas and supplies during the July 1961 trip. He left his young daughter, Bonnie, at the top to turn on the gas when he got down with the cans to fill. He then took his little boys, Mark and Eddie, to help with the two pack horses getting supplies down the steep trail. He had done this many times before without encountering any serious problems. This time, though, he was late getting started and pushed along faster than usual. He led one pack horse and Mark led the other one. Eddie had a light pack and followed behind Mark.

All went well until they reached the steepest and most dangerous part of the trail. Bundy looked back and saw that the pack bags had come loose and were slipping down on the horse's neck, so he stopped to retie them. Suddenly the horse felt the bags sliding onto its neck and spooked. It jumped and knocked Bundy off the trail, then went bucking and running down the tortuous path. When the horse came to a sharp turn the pack caught on a projecting rock and pulled the horse off the trail. The horse—pack and all—went tumbling helter-skelter down the ledge and lodged some fifty feet below. A large rock followed the horse and pinned one of its legs to the ground. Bundy said it was only because of his fear he found the strength to roll the rock off so the horse could get up. It was a miracle that the horse's leg was not broken. It had beaten its head so hard trying to get up that it injured an eye socket. Bundy managed to get the horse back on its feet and up to the trail, but the packs were a mess, the contents all broken and mixed up. Although the horse survived, it was never able to work that trail again.

Meanwhile, little Mark and Eddie were horrified, not knowing what had happened to their father. Bundy went back to where they were and sent the two boys down the trail with the other horse while he collected what he could of the wreckage. When the boys reached the last stretch of the trail, their horse began to flinch because its pack had loosened and was sliding up its neck. The two were able to quiet him down, then Eddie held the lead rope tightly while Mark ran back up the trail to get his dad. Bundy then ran down to fix the pack.

Throughout this ordeal Bonnie was waiting for the call to turn on the gas. She knew something had gone wrong. When Bundy finally got the packs down and called for her to turn on the gas, none came down. Something was wrong with the gas line. He could not make Bonnie hear him telling her to shut off the gas until he got halfway up the trail. By then it was the hottest part of the day and Bundy was ready to collapse from the heat and exertion. He found a break in the gas line, repaired it, and was finally able to fill Georgie's cans. At first he thought he had lost half a barrel of gas, but it turned out to be only six or seven gallons, for which he was thankful. He was more thankful that his children were unhurt.[14]

In 1961 Georgie had sixty-seven-year-old Sylvia Tone as a passenger in Glen Canyon. Sylvia had recently had a mastectomy and did not have much strength in one arm. She doubted she could hold on tightly enough, but Georgie said, "I'll fix it so you can." Georgie got an automobile seat belt and fastened it to the raft. Buckled in this way, Sylvia made it through safely. Thereafter, Georgie used seat belts as a means of securing at-risk passengers.[15]

One day Georgie found Sylvia crying over the recent loss of her husband. She put her arms around Sylvia and told her about losing her own daughter. They were close friends from then on. Sylvia would eventually go on fifteen trips with Georgie and become like a mother to her. Of all the letters Georgie wrote, the only ones she signed, "With Love," were to Sylvia Tone.

11 Runaway Rafts, 1962

$\mathcal{A}$t the end of a Glen Canyon trip in May of 1962, Georgie made a difficult landing on a silt and mud bar at Kane Creek. They arrived one day early because dam construction and high water had backed the river into the mouths of some of the canyons they planned to visit. Whitey was late arriving and had been drinking heavily. He and Georgie had an argument, and it almost became a fist fight. It was a disagreeable ending to a fine trip. Georgie told Tony (Sylvia Tone), "Running the rapids in Grand Canyon is no problem, but Whitey is."[1]

On May 14, 1962, Georgie left Lee's Ferry for another Grand Canyon trip. Shine Smith was there to see them off, along with an elderly Navajo medicine man named Many Songs, who blessed the boats. L. C. B. "Mac" McCullough said, "We think he may have cursed them [the boats], the way we had trouble."

On the evening of May 22 Georgie landed on the sandbar at Tapeats Creek. The party's second set of boats landed there as well. But an oarlock on the third boat broke as they were attempting to land, and it was swept a mile further downstream before the crew could bring it ashore. They decided there was daylight enough left to tow the boat back up to Georgie's camp. So young Art Gallenson stayed on board to fend it off the rocks while the rest of the group pulled on ropes from the shore. Gallenson wrote:

> The men tried to pull the boat but the current was a bit stiff and so the outside nose line was tied down. Immediately the nose of that boat dove under the current and the boat filled with water. Seeing this, someone untied the nose line and the

Reverend "Shine" Smith and Navajo medicine man preparing to bless Georgie's boats at Lee's Ferry. *Courtesy of L. C. B. McCullough.*

boats started down stream. On the other nose line (inside boats) were six men, but the outside boat was too heavy and actually drug them into the water. Well, they had to let go and there yours truly stood on top of the drifting boat with the little thought of going through Lava about twelve at night. Well, I jumped (like an ass) and came out on the other side of the river in the Granite Narrows.[2]

Harvey Troutman and others climbed high on the cliffs to see if they could discover what had happened to Gallenson. They finally spotted him and the boats, each in a different eddy. As they watched, the boats disappeared and Art was swept into the rapid. The men tried to follow, but scrambling along the cliff was difficult. Then a passenger began wigwagging in Morse Code. One of the men watched with binoculars and relayed the dots and dashes to another who wrote them down. In the meantime, one of the men ran back and told them that Art had been spotted on a sandbar on the other side of the river. The message turned out to be "Art alive on left shore. Waiting for pick up."

Everybody started making suggestions and giving advice, but Georgie would not be panicked. She explained to the group that there was a mean canyon and rapids ahead of Art. Trying to pick him up that late in the day would mean endangering other lives, as the remaining boats would be heavily overloaded. She would not take a chance on sending even the one little boat to try to rescue Art. He broke Georgie's first rule, which was: "In any emergency, never leave the boats. If you are washed overboard, try to hang onto the boat rather than swim to shore."

They were a pretty glum bunch. Everybody was trying to tell Georgie what to do. She finally said, "Everybody around here is too excited. Now calm down. If anyone should be excited, it's me. Art is all right." She reiterated that Art was seen walking and had taken off his wet life preserver and clothes to dry them on the rocks, which was the right thing to do. She said, "He may get hungry, but he will have to spend the night there."[3]

Next day a small crew of experienced men took the little boats and were able to pick up Art. Later in the day, as they rounded a bend, three or four people shouted at once, "The little boats!" The empty little boat was peacefully circling around and around in a backwater. One of the three dangling ropes had snagged on a rock and held the boat as if moored. Upon examination, they found not one thing missing or harmed. Finding the triple rig saved Georgie a great deal of embarrassment and possible adverse publicity. Members of the party had been concerned about the worry it would cause loved ones if one of her empty boats was found floating in Lake Mead. The extra people were transferred to the little boat, and the rope was cut to set it free.

Cataract

After the Grand Canyon trip Marjorie Steurt joined Georgie in Moab for a run through Cataract Canyon. In her journal under date of June 7 Steurt wrote:

> Off at 7:30 and immediately in the rapids. Nothing like them in Grand Canyon. Easy at first, then came the Mile Long Canyon, solid rapids. Amazing. These weren't white horses, they were rampaging dinosaurs. Huge waves dashed at us from all directions. Soaked and hanging on for life, a great hole opened up in front of us. We dropped into the hole, then dived into the volume of water towering over it, which completely submerged us. When we came out another huge wave was waiting and still another. I have never taken such a battering in my life.[4]

The third boat stood on its side ready to drop on them, but another wave slapped it back in the water. No baggage fell out, but it moved into weird positions. One bag flew across a woman's neck. A neighbor saw it and was able to free one hand and pull it back just in time, as her face was turning purple.

The triple rig, rowed by Chet Bundy and his son Lamar, had a worse time of it. Chet said there were four miles of continual rapids, out of one and into another, scarcely catching their breath between. Two or three times an outer raft flipped over the middle one. Each time it threw everything, people and all, overboard or onto the middle raft. Chet and two other men were thrown overboard once and had a rough time getting back to the raft. They were dragged for a mile or two through the surging, icy water before others could pull them back in. The Bundys lost their river bags once but recovered them further down.

In early August Georgie took a group of forty-two Boy Scouts and scoutmasters through Glen Canyon. This troop must have behaved better than the earlier one, as Georgie stayed with them all the way. This trip, according to Georgie, made more than fifty times she had toured this beautiful canyon.[5]

Visit by "Sambo" at Virgin Canyon, Lake Mead, May 29, 1962. Georgie's dog was a passenger on many trips until the Park Service put a stop to it. *Courtesy of L. C. B. McCullough.*

12 Exploring Canadian Rivers, 1963

*E*arly in June 1963 Georgie made a trip through Cataract Canyon. There were thirty-seven passengers in all, plus Georgie and her dog, Sambo, who made a number of raft trips with her before the Park Service decided dogs should not be allowed on the river.[1]

Delphine Mohrline was riding on the little boat when they came to Satan's Gut. She saw the rapid at close range and began to wonder whether it was not a waterfall instead. The drop looked tremendous. She said:

> Over we went into this trough about 12 feet deep—the front side came up to meet the backside, we were all lifted off our seats and slammed back down again, twisting and turning, and wondering if our fingers were going to be able to keep holding on. Art and I knocked heads together, even though we were sitting 4 feet apart in different sections of the boat. He said he had been a steeplejack in earlier years and didn't think the rapids of the Colorado could offer anything more exciting than that. Wonder if he still holds that opinion.

The passengers agreed that this was the ride they came for. One's oar broke in two, leaving him helpless until, with much dexterity, another untied a spare and handed it to him while they were still in the rapid. The boat took on so much water they bailed frequently to keep from being swamped. Delphine noted, "The vultures along the bank should have gotten some exciting pictures of that ride. We learned it was called Satan's Gut."

One passenger said, "If that is Satan's Gut, the whole river must be his intestines."

Big Bend of the Columbia River

In July and August of 1963 Georgie's craving to explore new rivers took her north once again, this time to Canada. She first tackled the Big Bend of the Columbia.[2]

On July 6 at Fort Steele, B.C., her party of eight men and eight women set up camp on a plateau high above the muddy-green Kootenay River. On July 8 the party crammed into a truck and rode fifteen miles to where the boats were moored. People had said the rapids of the Big Bend could not be run. Georgie was unfamiliar with the Columbia but confident she could run it with her equipment.

On the river they passed between thickly wooded hills with vistas of towering, glacier-creviced mountains. Finally, they came to Death Rapid, classed by many as impossible for boats of any kind. It proved to be less bothersome to Georgie than many of the rapids in Grand Canyon.

Bob Atherton, a passenger from Georgie's history-making 1955 Grand Canyon trip, had brought along a folding kayak. On the last day he decided to launch it and run some rapids by himself. He expected to follow behind Georgie, but she was not in the habit of waiting around for anyone. By the time he was ready to go, the big boat had disappeared around a bend. As he was running the rapid, the kayak dived into a hole and upset, leaving him to flounder through the rest of the rapid in his life jacket. Looking back, he saw the kayak standing on end stuck between two rocks. Bob left it there and climbed out to the road that paralleled the river. From there he hitched a ride to where Georgie's party was de-rigging. He later said that nobody had missed him except his wife![3] At least for Bob, running the Big Bend was an experience never to be forgotten.

Hell's Gate

From Revelstoke on the Columbia Georgie went to the Fraser River at Lillooet, 130 miles north of Vancouver, B.C. The river ran mostly through cultivated countryside and Indian reservations, so the group had no trouble finding camping sites. The rapids were fun until they came to Hell's Gate. The build-up for Hell's Gate was terrific—everyone told them they could not make it. They were even told of an Indian who was paid five dollars per head to fish out the bodies. Some

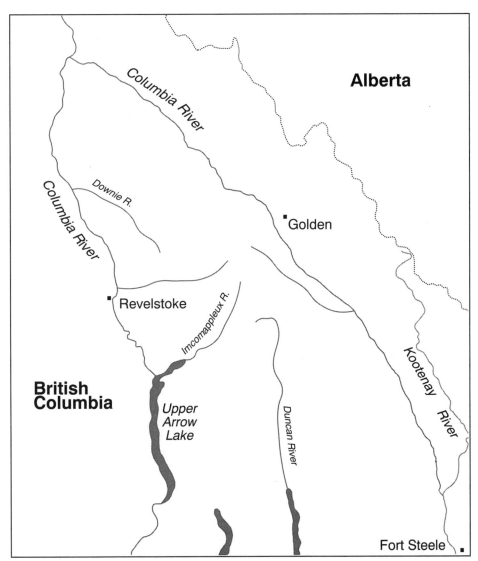

Alberta

Columbia River

Downie R.

Columbia River

Golden

Revelstoke

Imcomappleux R.

British
Columbia

Upper
Arrow
Lake

Duncan River

Kootenay River

Fort Steele

Cartography by Thomas Zajkowski, University of Utah

Columbia River through Big Bend

N

50   0   50   100 Miles
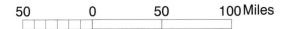

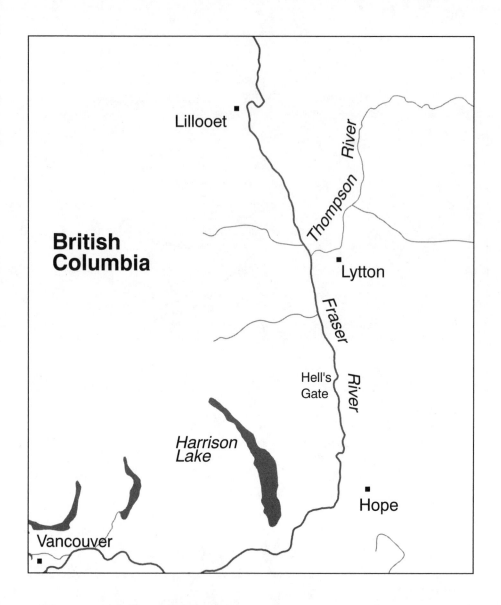

Lillooet

**British
Columbia**

Thompson River

Lytton

Fraser River

Hell's
Gate

*Harrison
Lake*

Hope

Vancouver

Fraser River

N

0   0   30   60 Miles

said all would be drowned. Word of their proposed exploit was broadcast all over western Canada, and reporters from all the newspapers awaited them. When offered a ride on Georgie's big boat, only one had the courage to accept. TV men arrived with their cameras; the roads on both sides of the river were lined with cars, everyone taking photographs.

At Hell's Gate "the water churns and leaps for 1,000 feet as it roars through a giant whirlpool in the Fraser Canyon."[4] At this point the Fraser River is very narrow with high perpendicular cliffs on either side. In his historic voyage down the river in the early 1800s, Simon Fraser quickly decided to portage around these rapids.

But Georgie was not afraid to tackle Hell's Gate in her big boat.[5] She studied the giant whirlpool from above and figured if they got in the center of it the crew might have to ride around in it three or four times before it pitched them out. Her plan was to get as close to the right bank as possible, pour on the power with the eighteen-horse-power motor and let the current carry them through.

She departed at 11:45 A.M. on July 25 prepared for anything. There were no big waves but a lot of whirlpools and boils, for which the Fraser was famous. The water was swift and treacherous. The crew raced through the raging narrows and Georgie swung the boat directly toward the cliff. A great shout went up as those on the shore thought the boat would be smashed against the rock wall. Instead they hit the edge of the whirlpool, were spun around as they shot across it at breakneck speed, and raced on down the river, all in about ten seconds flat. A log in the whirlpool disappeared, then shot straight up into the air. As the party passed around a curve, the log was still going around, disappearing, then catapulting into the air. According to Marjorie Steurt:

> It was a terrifying experience, being in the center of nature's enormous power. We gripped those ropes for our lives. The suspense had built up and built up, until, as we hit the vortex, it was almost overpowering. Our only salvation was the short duration. We yelled and screamed our excitement. There were other nasty rapids below, but Hell's Gate was the climax.[6]

With Georgie on this trip was her Maltese-poodle, Sambo. Reporters took delight in reporting that Sambo could be the most-traveled dog in North America. Georgie told them he had traveled across the United States by jet a number of times and accompanied her on all her boat trips, including the Colorado and Columbia. He had his own life preserver, air mattress, and sleeping bag.

Nahanni River

The last leg of Georgie's northern tour was the Nahanni River in Northwest Territories. She set up camp just above the majestic Virginia Falls, which are more than twice as high as Niagara.[7] The portage necessary to get to the foot of the falls took them along a narrow path through the woods where cranberries, blueberries, and lovely flowers grew in extravagant splendor. The hard path soon turned to soft muskeg that oozed water and clinging mud over their ankles. While staggering through the slush, their shoes were almost sucked off. As the path grew steeper they waded through a stream bed and gullies where the mud was even deeper.

In her journal Marjorie quoted from an article by M. E. Alford: "The Nahanni Valley is a man's country, a seductive region, moody yet romantic. . . . Here, on one short river, there is unparalleled beauty and peace, unrelenting danger, adventure around every bend." Her comment: "How true!"

After lunch on August 1 they were finally ready to depart on the river, using a small triple rig. They passed through lovely canyons and mild rapids before coming to a sharp turn in the river where the whole force of the current pounded against a cliff and poured to the right, forming a cross current of high waves. Later they were caught in a giant whirlpool. Water gurgled over the sides as they were thrashed about, giving them a weird sensation of helplessness. Still, Georgie maneuvered until they pulled through. Then they all bailed like mad.

Below the junction of the Flat River and the Nahanni, the banks closed in and the stream ran between towering rock walls only a few hundred feet apart. Beyond Second Canyon the party reached a wide area known as Headless Valley, so named because three skeletons were once found there, all minus their skulls.

Beyond Headless Valley the party came to First Canyon, the most spectacular of the three. Gray rock walls rise sheer for some fifteen hundred feet. The valley is about fifteen miles long and quite narrow. Below First Canyon the party came to Sulfur Hot Springs and the cabin of Gus Kraus. He had lived on the river for over fifty years and had an Indian wife and an adopted son. They were the river's only inhabitants aside from a prospector named Failey. Georgie's group made camp below the Kraus cabin, had long talks with Gus and his

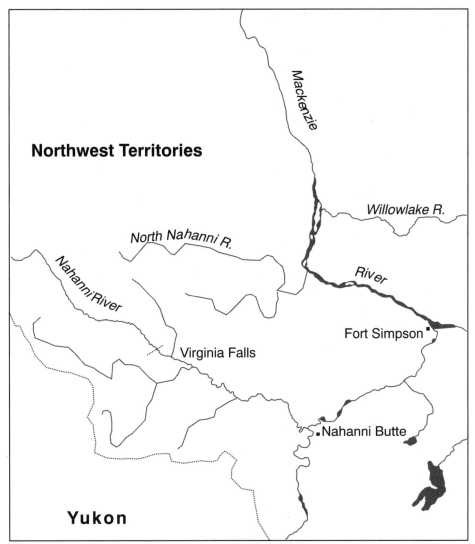

Northwest Territories

Mackenzie

Willowlake R.

North Nahanni R.

Nahanni River

River

Fort Simpson

Virginia Falls

Nahanni Butte

Yukon

Cartography by Thomas Zajkowski, University of Utah

Nahanni River

N

100   0   100   200 Miles

wife, watched them make jerky (and ate some), saw the bushes growing from the roof of his cabin, and bathed in the hot sulphur springs. The water was pleasantly warm, but after people walked around in it for awhile it became liquid mud. They came out dirtier than they went in.

Below the warm springs the country opened up and the river spread out into many different channels. It was a nightmare for Georgie to try to pick the correct one. The daytime was blazing hot and the nights bitterly cold. After forty-five miles of slow water the Nahanni flowed into the Liard, which was so wide Georgie could barely see the opposite bank.

Of the fifteen or sixteen prospectors known to have entered the Nahanni Valley searching for gold, most had disappeared. Some skeletons had been found, others were missing. Mysterious tales about this place had become legend. Floating through low swamp lands, the Liard took the group down to the Mackenzie River and Fort Simpson. They waited three days in the tiny settlement for the plane to take them out. From Fort Simpson they flew to Hay River on Great Slave Lake, then on to Edmonton, Alberta, and their various homes back in the United States.

13 More of Mexico, 1963–1964

$\mathcal{I}$n August 1963 Georgie's wanderlust took her on another trip to the Rio Balsas in Mexico. The party of seven included a man named John (last name unknown), Orville Miller, Ivan Summers, Allan O'Brien, Ellis L. Spackman, Delphine Mohrline, and Georgie. In an article about the trip, Spackman said:

> Georgie is one of the most extra-ordinary women in America. I am sure you have seen her pictures on TV. She has taken more people down more rivers than anyone else. She has been instrumental in working out the technique. And she hasn't lost a client yet.
>
> It is obviously designed for men only, yet the champion is a woman, and not a very big one at that. It isn't fair to us men.[1]

From the journal of Delphine Mohrline Gallagher, we learn more details of that trip.[2] In Mexico City on August 14, it took one whole day to get the rubber boats loaded on the truck from the attic where they were stored and to get Georgie's other baggage off the plane and through customs. At 8 P.M. they were finally on their way for the five-hour truck ride to the town of Mexcala, where they would enter the Balsas River.

By 1 P.M. the following day they had the boats inflated and the baggage securely tied down. They also had on life preservers in anticipation of the rapids; one not far ahead was rumored to be a big one. The party waved *adios* to those on shore and were off.

The Balsas River was even muddier than the Colorado. As the group glided swiftly along, they looked for a suitable lunch stop, since it was already afternoon. When they came to a waterfall with a sandy beach nearby, they pulled over. There they had a "Spackman-O'Brien" lunch, which consisted of peanut butter, cheese, and cracker sandwiches. Then out came the beer to wash it down.

On a previous Mexican river trip, Georgie had taken to drinking beer. To purify the water for drinking, it was necessary to boil it for twenty minutes. Georgie said that after twenty minutes there was not much water left, and, since all the others were drinking beer instead, that was a lot of trouble for just one person. From that trip on her preferred beverage was beer, especially Coors.

Over the Balsas River were vines hanging from trees and thick vegetation. With the sandy beach and refreshing waterfall, Tarzan never had it so good. The party took off again, but within a few hundred yards they spotted a crystal-clear stream rushing down over the rocks from the green hillside. Several voices yelled at once to stop, and luckily Georgie was able to pull in.

The group played in the water and sand like a bunch of kids under a hose in the backyard. Up on the hill they noticed that their antics had attracted the attention of a few natives. "Crazy gringos" was surely the prevailing opinion.

Ivan spoke to two of the natives, who said there were no big rapids, so the group guessed the few riffles already passed were the "big ones" referred to at Mexcala. However, they continued to wear life jackets. They entered Zopilote (Buzzard) Canyon, which had green walls straight down to the river. Jokes were made about the buzzards eating their bones when, suddenly, two of the large birds appeared, winging back and forth in the canyon, screeching and shrieking. The special effect they created on the ride through Zopilote Canyon was most appropriate.

In the late afternoon the party began to look for a place to camp so they would have some of this magnificent canyon to run the next day. They had floated through a few good "hang-on" type rapids, but nothing very challenging. Then, rounding a bend in the river, they suddenly saw a wild stretch of water ahead. There was no place to pull ashore, so into the churning water they went. As the boats lurched and jerked, Georgie yelled instructions to the oarsmen.

Delphine's knuckles were being bruised and rubbed raw, but she could not let go. She saw the bag with Orville's camera in it come loose and grabbed it just in time. The bucket, which was tied on with a four-foot line, flew up in the air in front of Delphine and she tried to get her foot in it to hold it down. Then everything was calm again. It was an exciting few seconds.

O'Brien was following their course on a map and calculated they were near the town of Balsas. They saw a man and a horse on the beach and decided to pull ashore. He confirmed it was the Poblado Balsas.

Ivan and Orville went off to see what they could find in the town. The others accused them of going to look for pretty *señoritas*, but they insisted their only interest was cold *cerveza*. Since everyone provided their own food, they all dipped into their bags and pulled out cans of various sizes and shapes, from which Delphine put together a "Georgie stew." As it cooked, they prepared their beds and warmed their insides with tequila and sangrita.

Orville and Ivan returned, telling them about the religious parade they had witnessed on the main street of the village. The two said people carried statues of saints and the Virgin Mary while chanting to the accompaniment of some instruments played off-key by a group of musicians who'd had a little too much *pulque* (agave liquor). After dinner Delphine tried to provide some entertainment. She sang a Spanish song and danced the Israeli *hora*. When she stumbled over a log, the floor show ended.

In the morning they floated around the bend to a high railroad bridge, where they landed among pigs, chickens, and Half Moon parrots. O'Brien volunteered to stay with the boats while the others went into town. Ivan admired the wide-brimmed Mexican sombreros and tried to find one to fit. Either the Mexicans had small heads or Ivan's was exceptionally large, because he could not find one big enough in any of the stores. Hence his new nickname, "Fathead."

When the group resumed their trip, children ran along the bank trying to keep up with the boats, but the swift current soon left them behind. Downstream they saw a clear stream and pulled ashore. A huge, shiny, green and yellow beetle then caught their eye. John filled the whole lens of his camera with it and said he was going to tell everyone back home that this was the kind of thing they had to fight on the trip. He would say, "I couldn't show you the biggest one we saw because it carried off the boat."

Georgie said, "That's all I need. I have enough trouble getting people, especially girls, to come on my Mexican trips. If I showed pitchers [sic] like that, I would be coming alone."

At camp it poured rain all night. With a down-filled sleeping bag in the tropics of Mexico, the choice was sleeping inside the bag and being cooked alive or sleeping outside and being eaten alive by the mosquitoes. The gringo insect repellant did not work. The bugs for the most part lapped it up. Those Spanish-speaking mosquitoes just did not seem to understand the English labels on the Flit cans.

Orville and Delphine each had a long plastic tube open at both ends, into which their air mattress and sleeping bag were slipped. Orville tucked the bottom end of Delphine's under her feet and told her to keep the head end tucked under also. This did not work at all because she couldn't breathe in that encasement, so she had to leave the head end open. Naturally, the heavens opened up and the rains came, six inches worth, in drops so big and heavy she could feel them hitting her body through the plastic, sleeping bag, clothes, and all. The water ran in at her head end and could not get out at the foot end, so that soon her feet and legs were in a lake of water. This sounds like an uncomfortable state of affairs, but actually it prevented her mosquito bites from itching as much and cooled her off quite nicely.

When the rain stopped, Orville was concerned as to how Delphine was, since it was her first experience at sleeping in the rain. He came over to her bed to see whether she was still there or had been washed away. He then picked her up in the middle to let the water gush out at both ends of the plastic tube.

For some reason, instead of rising with all that rain, the river dropped about three feet, leaving the boats high and dry on the muddy bank. It was a slow and difficult chore for seven people to get them into the water. Georgie told them that from then on each of them should make it a point to look at the boats whenever they awakened during the night.

As the party progressed down the river, rising church towers indicated they were approaching a fair-sized town. The houses might all be made of sticks and brush, but the churches were magnificent. According to the map, they were arriving at Ajuchitlan (A-hú-chit-lon). They pulled ashore along a dirt bank at least ten feet high. John's feet were getting blisters from his sneakers and were sunburned on top. So he and Georgie stayed with the boats while the others trekked into town.

Orville's profession as a teacher of pharmacology led him to an interest in the use of plants and animals as medicine. He was always asking the natives questions regarding this subject. When Georgie's crew told a group of natives Orville was a *brujo* (witch doctor), the natives pointed out a cute little boy of about eight and said he was a brujo also.

Then there was much smiling and conversation and shaking of hands between Orville and the little boy, and it was delightful to watch.

The group traveled on, and when it was almost dark stopped on a rocky beach at a bend in the river. While they were looking around for places to put their sleeping bags, an elderly man hurried down from a nearby hill. Ivan engaged him in conversation and soon learned they were welcome to spend the night at the governor's *casa* on the hill. Georgie would not leave the boats, and John said he would stay with her. The others were undecided until it began to thunder and lightning. When the storm got steadily closer, they grabbed their sleeping gear and followed the man, taking with them a bottle of tequila as a token of appreciation for their host. Georgie said she would visit the governor in the morning.

They all commented how lucky they were to be getting a dry home to sleep in and probably a delicious Mexican meal with dancing señoritas, etc. While walking up the little hill in the dark, they could see the lush landscape and a million fireflies sparkling under the trees. The man stopped at a three-sided building and indicated this was it.

They stared at each other in amazement and said a few things they were glad the man could not understand. The "governor's casa" was a tool shed with one large wooden cot and sacks of copra on a dirt floor, a rack holding picks and shovels, and cement bags piled high. O'Brien tried to choke back a laugh and decided to give his water-proof tent a second chance. A woman, several other men, and children appeared to offer them whatever help they might need. They moved the cot to the back of the shed and brought in two large sand screens. Orville fit the cot best, Spackman and Delphine got the sand screens, and Ivan slept on the ground. The "governor" assured them there were no mosquitoes, so Delphine slept on top of her sleeping bag in complete comfort. For Spackman, the sand screen was a little short. His legs hung over the end, and in the morning all sense of feeling had departed from his feet.

The party was happy to have eaten the food at Ajuchitlan because there was no supper that night. They gave Ivan a bad time about his Spanish and told him he needed a few more lessons, because somehow something must have been lost in the translation. If this man was the governor, they wondered, what was he the governor of? Actually, he was the foreman of a small construction project nearby.

In short order they were all fast asleep, with their host guarding them on a bench out front. When it began to pour, the man came inside and curled up beside the cement sacks. They all thought how very generous he was to give up his bed to strangers. He had offered them all he had. Delphine laughed to herself when she recalled their expectation of that good Mexican dinner and the dancing señoritas, but the nice dry bed she was in was not a dream.

On Sunday, August 18, the party approached a young man in the water with his clothes tied onto his hat using a log to help him along in the swift current. They pulled up beside him to give him a lift, but he did not seem to want to get into the boat. Two words gave the reason why—"*Soy desnudo!*" (I'm naked).

The next day just before noon the group spotted a high transmission line and, shortly thereafter, a newly cut road on the side of the hill. Ivan, Spackman, and Delphine scrambled up to the road and walked a short distance to a native hut, in front of which were six men and several trucks. Ivan learned they were about ten miles from a dam and the men were hauling rocks from this area for its construction. They were told there were no other roads between here and the dam by which to take the boats out, and that three miles farther on the river dropped over a sixty-foot waterfall. They did not quite believe it because they had not heard about anything like a waterfall being part of the river. But this was Mexico, and they could not be positive of anything. At any rate, they were not going to do anything foolish. Georgie said, "We'll send Orville over those falls with the boats—tie all three together in a roll so you will always have a boat underneath. Of course, you might have a little breathing problem—blurpity, blurpity, blurp!"

While in Acapulco several weeks earlier, Spackman had learned of a big dam under construction on the Balsas and had written to the head engineer informing him of their forthcoming trip. A prompt answer was received to the effect that they would be watching for Georgie's group and ready to offer any assistance needed with the boats, and that the group was most welcome to spend the night at their guest house. With letter in hand, Spackman, Georgie, O'Brien, and Ivan rode off in the back of one of the rock-hauling trucks. Georgie put on her jumpsuit even though the weather was much too warm for it. She did not want to shock the Mexicans with her bare legs. Orville had been kidding her about the article a sports writer had written several years earlier in which he commented about her pretty legs, and Orville said she should let the Mexicans see them. Georgie said, "Maybe I ought to cover up my face and leave my legs bare."

While they were gone, Orville gathered seed pods from the datura plants for some of his experiments. For diversion, Delphine started counting her mosquito bites. Three inches up from her ankle bone, she had already counted seventy-five, so she gave up. She estimated that she had 175 on each leg, and they were driving her insane.

Four hours later, Georgie and her companions returned in a station wagon with two trucks behind them. What a reception they had had at the dam, with not only cold beer, but a delicious Mexican lunch. There were bad rapids before the dam, they were told, but not sixty feet high. However, the workers told Georgie if she were to run them "she wouldn't be back in Mexico to eat any more tortillas." They also confirmed that where Georgie had stopped was the last place to get the boats out of the river.

The group sat patiently waiting for the truck driver and some helpers to move them past the dam. They stopped at a flower-filled field to marvel at the terrific rapids on the downstream side of the diversion tunnels. Below they found a sloping, sandy bank alongside the road about fifty feet long, where they were able to carry the boats and baggage back down to the river. About 12:45 P.M., after a good two and a half hours of work, the party was again floating down the river. They had been warned of rapids ahead, so Georgie said they should wear life jackets. But after a few minor rapids the river smoothed out and O'Brien and Spackman dived overboard for a swim. Shortly thereafter they rounded a bend and they heard the roar of rapids ahead. Both swam desperately toward the raft but could not reach it before being swept into the rapid.

The rapids were not difficult for the boats but bad for swimmers. Sharp rocks sticking up made a scary sight. It was a sort of unwritten rule that when Georgie had her life preserver on everyone stayed in the boat. Georgie was provoked about the whole incident, and, while not wanting them to get hurt, she hoped it would teach them a lesson. O'Brien spun around in a whirlpool and yelled for them to throw a rope; they could not get to him, and they lost sight of Spackman altogether.

Spackman had also been caught in a large whirlpool. He reported:

> I tried desperately to break out of it, but in vain. I was spun around ever more rapidly until I was in the very center. Then I felt as though giant hands grasped my feet and pulled me under, life jacket and all.

I thought I would never get to the surface, but finally did, only to be caught in the whirlpool again. Once more I struggled wildly, but was inexorably spun to the vortex and sucked under.[3]

He was finally thrown to the surface where he was able to grab onto a projecting rock and pull himself out. He lay there exhausted and gasping for a while, just thankful to be alive. Those on the raft spotted Spackman clinging to the rock but could not get close enough to pick him up.

O'Brien kept twirling around in his whirlpool, trying to push himself away from the jagged rocks with his feet. Georgie finally maneuvered close enough to throw him a rope, and he was able to get aboard, very tired and scared.

Georgie could not land along the rocky banks, so she just kept going until they reached a sandy beach. O'Brien then put a can of beer and a little food in a bucket and started back for Spackman. They were reunited sooner than expected. Spackman kissed his life jacket, and that told the whole story.

Georgie showed no sympathy. When the two got back to the raft Georgie asked Spackman, "Where the heck have you been?"

"But I almost got drowned," he explained apologetically.

"That's just it," Georgie complained. "There's always some damn fool along who messes things up. I've never lost a customer yet, but if I had to lose one, I guess you'd do."[4]

Off they went to try to find a suitable camping place. They knew they were very close to the mouth of the river, but did not want to arrive there until the next morning. Meanwhile, Spackman could not find his cigarettes. "You thought I was gone, and you already split up my cigarettes and food," he complained. Orville said, "We were just about to split up your money, too." Georgie chimed in, "And your beer."[5]

The rest of the trip was uneventful. They found a nice white sand island for their last camp of the trip. During the happy hour the last of their anti-venom medicine was consumed and the remaining delicacies dumped in the pot for a veritable banquet, a fitting way to wind up the trip.

Family Problems

In a November 3, 1963, letter to Sylvia Tone, Georgie wrote, "Whitey joined AAA [sic] and hasn't had a drink for about 3 months now. It sure seems wonderful, sure hope it keeps up."[6]

Some of the finest adventure films shown on television at that time were of Georgie's trips, "Multiplying [the audience] to almost astronomical figures, in proportion to the few who ordinarily experience such unusual scenes."[7] Georgie had made her debut on *I Search for Adventure* in 1956 and was called back three times. She had also appeared on *Bold Journey*, *To Tell the Truth*, *Queen for a Day*, Art Linkletter's programs, and many others. She showed her films at boat shows, club meetings, and other places as chance provided. Articles about her trips written by passengers numbered in the hundreds.

But on the home front, Georgie and Whitey continued to have their problems. In an undated letter to Sylvia Tone, Georgie wrote:

> Whity [sic] came out about six that nigh[t] but he had fell off the wagon, and it was sad to hear and see. He is just crazy when he drinks. I thanked my lucky stars that I had been able to get the people in so that no one but me would know. It was tough loading the boats on a hill the next morning and of course Whity weak as a cat from the day before, but with my strong back and weak mind I made the grade. . . . Due to Whity I sort of live in a glass house and can't throw many stones.[8]

Grand Canyon on Low Water

On January 21, 1963, a team of steel workers began to close slide-gates of the forty-one-foot-diameter west diversion tunnel at Glen Canyon Dam, shutting the flow of the river to a trickle.[9] With the low flow, very few of the experienced river runners would attempt a run. However, Georgie felt she could make it with her big boat. The rubber pontoons had a shallower draft, floated better, and were more stable in rough water than wooden boats. If one hit a rock, its separate inflated sections would keep it afloat even if a whole section of the bottom were ripped out.

Josef Muench, noted scenic photographer, was one of the passengers on this, the first of fifteen trips he would make with Georgie. With his camera he had stood on every viewpoint along both rims of the Grand Canyon and followed trails into and across the canyon. He had even viewed the rapids and canyon walls from a swaying cable car. Now he would be able to see hidden spots known only to those who traveled on the Colorado River.

Muench had spent a great deal of time among the Navajos, photographing the people and the breathtaking scenery on the reservation.

Georgie looks over her favorite domain, the Colorado River in Grand Canyon. *Photo by Josef Muench, courtesy of Dan Cassidy, Five Quail Books-West.*

Georgie holds on while operating motor. *Photo by Josef Muench, Cline Library, Northern Arizona University, Georgie Clark Collection, #91.13.20.*

He had met Georgie a number of times out on the reservation, most often at the Shine Smith Christmas parties. Muench had recently separated from his wife, and he wanted to get away to somewhere new.[10]

Park Ranger James Bailey was also on the trip between Phantom Ranch and Havasu Canyon. He was assigned to join the party to investigate and photograph that portion of the Inner Canyon which lay within Grand Canyon National Park and which might be affected by the impounded waters of the proposed Bridge Canyon Dam. He was traveling light, as he would have to make the strenuous hike from the mouth of Havasu Canyon upstream to the village of Supai, a distance of ten miles. He noted that Georgie seemed very glad to have him join the trip but disappointed that he had not joined at Lee's Ferry.

On April 9 Horn Creek Rapid was the first and by far the worst rapid of the day. Passenger Fred Darvill got thoroughly soaked. The group stopped just below the rapid for photographs. Darvill wore rain gear until noon, took it off until about 3 P.M., then put it back on until the evening stop. In the afternoon they passed under the old Bass and Hakatai cables. The Bass Cable was made up of four separate cables with a wooden burro car still hanging from the south end. The Hakatai Cable (also constructed by William Wallace Bass) was a single strand with remains of a trolley in the center of it.

One evening the party camped at the mouth of Tapeats Creek, where a bonfire of driftwood warmed them and was the setting for a genial campfire circle, with singing and stories by Josef Muench of his early life in Germany and as a professional photographer. Ranger Bailey added an interpretive talk about the work of a ranger in the National Park Service. Georgie filled in with tales of her runs on wild rivers. Muench was free with advice on how to get the best photographs.

At the mouth of Havasu Creek there was a riffle of fast water that made a landing exceedingly difficult. But Georgie demonstrated her excellent skill in the tricky landing there for the ranger to hike out and others to explore the lower end of this incredibly beautiful canyon.

Following this trip Muench called his estranged wife, Joyce, and told her the story of his river experience. She wrote two articles about the trip for *Arizona Highways*. These and Muench's photographs took up twenty-eight of the forty pages in the April 1965 issue.[11]

14 High Jinks, 1965

The Grand Canyon was Georgie's special place, and she began to spend more and more of her trip time there. In 1965 her schedule called for two Havasu Canyon hikes, one Cataract Canyon run, five trips through the Grand Canyon, one on the Nahanni River in Canada, and one on the Usumacinta along the border of Mexico and Guatemala.[1]

Georgie was a champion of animal rights, even though she didn't spend much active time in the movement. In the spring of 1965 she wrote to California State Senator John G. Schmitz in support of a bill for the protection of poultry and rabbits presented to youngsters for pets at Easter. In a reply dated March 4, 1965, the Senator agreed with her that "many of these children are too young to understand their responsibility toward pets of this type and lack the maturity of control which should be exercised in handling them."[2]

Whitey's Problems

Whitey continued to have severe drinking problems. He would be on the wagon for a while and then try to catch up when he fell off. During his drinking binges he was not always reliable. Georgie tried to be a stabilizing force for Whitey, but that in itself may have contributed to the problem. The rafting company was now Georgie's, and she controlled the purse strings.

Dick McCallum had worked for Georgie since 1957. During that time, besides acting as a boatman, he spent a lot of time with Whitey transporting equipment back and forth. Dick said he got quite attached to Whitey in many ways. He said, "Whitey was kind of a unique guy. He had to be a really unique person to be married to Georgie. Whitey was an alcoholic, so I always ended up . . . taking care of [him]. He was always getting into fights."[3] If a trip was in Idaho, Georgie would fly to an airfield near the point of embarkation, and Dick would go with Whitey in the truck. Because Whitey always stood in Georgie's shadow, it was a difficult situation for him and he would get pretty down on himself.

Desertion

A few years after Dick McCallum went to work for Georgie, Ron Smith and his bride went on a honeymoon trip with her through Cataract Canyon. Smith became enamored with the river, and Georgie soon hired him as a boatman. Smith and McCallum afterwards ran many trips together and soon became fast friends. In 1965 the two formed "Grand Canyon Expeditions" and went into business for themselves.

Georgie was furious at being deserted. To her this was treason. She did not understand this natural evolution in the lives of two ambitious young men. As time passed, Georgie mellowed and again spent time with them when they met at outfitters meetings.

Fun in the Canyon

In 1965 Carol Hintze (known to her friends as "Chintz") made her first trip with Georgie. They saw only one other party on the river, a surveyor and his family from Denver.[4] Sylvia Tone went on a Grand Canyon trip in May.[5] On this same trip were Dick and Marion Smith, Delphine Mohrline Gallagher, Josef Muench, Mae Hansen, and Orville Miller. Dick Smith and Orville were already veteran boatmen for Georgies trips. Muench loved the horseplay and the social life. Delphine had been in Cataract, Glen Canyon, and Mexico with Georgie, but this was her first Grand Canyon run. She wrote, "Certainly this was the greatest of them all—but I recall thinking exactly that after my previous river trips. Am I ever going to get my fill of this kind of vacation?"[6]

There was a great deal of roughhousing on the May trip. In mid-afternoon the party made camp at Nankoweap under a mesquite tree on a nice sandy slope. When the little boats pulled in two hours later, Georgie put a raw egg in Delphine's hand and said, "Get Dick." Only because he was so completely unsuspecting of her was she able to crack it over his head. Later Georgie sent Delphine out on the boat for something. Before she knew what had hit her, Dick threw Delphine overboard and attempted to tear her bathing suit off in the river—he almost succeeded. All the while cameras were grinding away. Delphine remarked, "Let her throw her own raw eggs the next time."

Marion Smith wrote of the party:

> Everyone was more or less of a character in his own right, not the least of which were the Smiths . . . light dilly-dallying was the order of the day. . . .
>
> At Nankoweap the horseplay before dinner got pretty wild. The nurses [passengers on the trip] tackled Dick and sat on him while they shaved him. Every time they nicked him and perhaps when they did not, they made a great to-do about kissing the wound. He remained clean-shaven thereafter.[7]

Orville brought along a 190-proof brew he had made for the trip. Delphine took one small sip and could not talk for minutes afterward. They diluted the alcohol generously with fruit punch and had a party.

As a result of her struggle in the water with Dick, the top of Delphine's swimsuit needed repair. When she had finished sewing it, Georgie attached pieces of plastic fruit from Delphine's hat onto the bra in two appropriate places. Impishly she said she wanted to watch and see who would pick the fruit.

When they came to Kwagunt Rapid, Delphine was riding in the little boats. Often when approaching a rapid in the little boats, which sat lower in the water than Georgie's big boat, it looked as if the river were going over a low dam. One could not see what was ahead until they were right there. As the party went through the rapid broadside, the raft went over a submerged boulder and straight down into the trough on the other side. This was a new hole that took the boatmen by surprise. The crest of the wave curled toward them and the three women in the lead boat with Bob on the oar gasped in unison.

Down into the hole they went and up the other side. The lead boat pancaked on top of the middle one, and they rode through the rapid in that fashion. Delphine was pushed beneath the water with Bob on top of her. She could not yell, but could hear everyone else. One of the women was screaming, "Help," between mouthfuls of water. Delphine was trying to hold her breath and not panic. For a few seconds she thought this might be her last river trip. She opened her eyes to see a fellow named Obie standing up in the middle boat with arms outstretched against the overturned section trying to flip it back into the water. Some camera bag straps were ripped off and several water-proof bags were hanging out over the boat, but they quickly got things in order and went on to meet the others at the Little Colorado River.

As Marion Smith later said, the little boats were more exciting, more dangerous, more quiet, and more friendly with their smaller groups. But those on the big boat got into camp first, ate lunch first, and had more time for exploring.

Georgie's group camped that night at Lava Canyon Rapid near the Copper Blossom (Tanner) Mine in sight of the Desert View Watchtower. That night Georgie gave her signal of one fire, which meant everything was all right. Three fires meant trouble—send down the helicopter!

The following day Georgie began making camp at 75 Mile Canyon. However, one of the little boats was unable to make the landing and they all had to move on. Georgie had something planned for everyone to be together that night. So camp was packed up and tied on the boat once again. They hated to leave, as it was such a lovely, spacious area. They found the little boats at a much smaller beach just above Hance Rapid. A bucket brigade was soon organized to wet down the sand and dust, and it turned out to be an excellent camp after all.

With dinner under their belts, they proceeded to celebrate one passenger's birthday. She received such gifts as flea powder, a handmade tamarisk wreath, a rubber blow-up doll, an original poem, used chewing gum, wet Kleenex, and many more useful items. She also got a swat from each of them as she crawled between all their legs in a line which stretched to the river's edge. She dragged the last man into the river with her.

The next morning Hance Rapid had to be run. This rapid had flipped Mae Hansen out of a small triple rig a few years before, and this time she rode through in her life jacket. They all took a look at it first from the shore. Seeing Mae waiting calmly to give it another try gave Delphine the nerve to ride the little boats again. She rode in the lead boat while the others watched. As they lurched through the foaming water two sections of the boat suddenly buckled and the third was tucked (folded under in the water), washing two men overboard. Both managed to keep their hold on the rope. One was washed back into the boat while the other was grabbed by the seat of his pants and pulled in.

There was so much water in the boat that they tried to land in order to bail. Dick "Ski Foot" Holt (size fifteen shoe) jumped onto the rocky shore with the tie line, but did not get it around a rock quickly enough. He tried to hold the boat himself, which was a sheer impossibility against the powerful current. Dave jumped ashore to help him, but the two of them could not hold it. By then the rope was becoming tangled. Those on the boat were yelling and giving orders at once, which did not help the situation. Dave was pulled back into the water, hanging onto the rope, but Ski Foot had let go and was left stranded on a narrow bar backed by a high cliff.

Dave was soon pulled back into the boat, and they tried to land again as quickly as possible. This time Dave stretched out and hugged a rock on shore while Delphine held onto his feet in the boat, allowing Loraine to secure the rope around a rock. The big boat passed them swiftly with no chance of landing. The second triple rig did not see either Ski Foot or the first group until it was too late. The canyon walls were black and jagged with veins of pink granite running through them. Loraine, who was a mountain climbing member of the Sierra Club, scaled the cliff and went back to rescue the stranded Ski Foot.

Below Hance Rapid the river entered the Granite Gorge with its walls of black Vishnu schist streaked with pink Zoroaster granite, some of the oldest exposed rocks in the world. The boats passed safely over Sockdolager and Grapevine Rapids with stretches of calm water in between. However, the smooth water is never without whirlpools. One cannot imagine the power of a whirlpool until seeing it suck the corner of a boat completely underwater. Georgie always contended that the whirlpools were more deadly than the rapids, especially to a swimmer. She said, "If you have to fall overboard, do it in the rapids."

At Phantom Ranch a crew from the Walt Disney Studios was filming the children's book *Brighty of the Grand Canyon*, the story of a feral burro. During production the burro used as the title character drowned in the river. They retrieved the body, cut off its head, and dragged it along in the river past Georgie's camp site, trying to make it look as if it was swimming, but without success. So Brighty Number Two was called in to finish the film. One can imagine Georgie's fury about such insensitivity and lack of respect for the little burro.

One of the mule train handlers also told Georgie the Park Service was shooting wild burros from airplanes. A ranger at the

Information Center had told them they had a burro problem, that the burros and wild horses did not "belong" here, and that they were "introduced" and had to be eliminated. Animal lover that she was, Georgie was incensed. Sylvia Tone was too. Sylvia wrote, "How about people and damn dams? They, too, have been 'introduced.'"

When Georgie's group got within earshot of Hermit Rapid, she sheared a pin off of the propeller on a piece of driftwood and the motor died. Georgie had run some rapids in the big boat without the use of her eighteen-horsepower motor, but she preferred not to. She called for Orville to hold the bag of tools and hand her what she needed. Every few seconds she would look ahead to see how close they were to the rapid. Nearer and nearer they rode the uncontrolled boat toward the drop-off into those mad waters in a pouring rain. Just on the brink, as though acting out a suspense story, Georgie had the motor repaired, yelled for Orville to hang on, and pulled the cord. The motor started on the first try. They all felt like applauding but were too close to risk letting go of their handholds.

Hermit Rapid really threw them around. Marion was flung forward and slightly injured her leg on the corner of a spare motor. She looked back just as a huge brown wave sprang up behind Georgie and crashed over her. Down Georgie went into the motor well, and the end of the boat appeared to fold over on her. Just as quickly as she went down, the water was gone and she popped up. Discussing this later, Geeorgie told her passengers she ducked on purpose, a practice she always followed in the most violent rapids. Everybody talked about the "good ride through Hermit." Because of its huge, evenly-spaced waves, Hermit is always a favorite of most river runners in the Grand Canyon.

With such high water the group had no place to stop and dry off. Marion said, "I tried doing arm and leg exercises to generate a little heat—they only produced fatigue." After four miserable, wet, and cold hours, Georgie pulled ashore next to a steep hill of slippery rocks and grass at Elves Chasm. There was no "upstream" or "downstream" here. (Meaning that the men go one way and the women go the other to relieve themselves.) "You just turned your back."

With the rain still coming down, Georgie directed Muench to lead the way, and the group struggled up slopes, over boulders, across Royal Arch Creek, then through the catclaw trees to a magnificent, spacious cave. What a welcome relief to get out of the pouring rain! There was enough dry driftwood to start a much-needed fire. They were soon taking off wet clothes and beginning to get the chill out of their bones.

Once everyone warmed up they had lunch. By then one set of small boats had arrived. The people on board had gotten so cold they had to stop and build a warming fire along the way. When the second little boat arrived, it was learned that boatman Dick Smith had a two-inch gash in his scalp. He had been hit by an oar when the boat sandwiched in Hermit Rapid. Two nurses on board had applied a bandanna and a pressure bandage.

Among the passengers were a Japanese pathologist named Wami and Bill, an ophthalmologist. Another passenger, a physician, had left the trip at Phantom Ranch. Luckily, he had left behind some medical supplies, which included sutures. After everyone had been fed and was dry and comfortable, Doctor Bill gave Smith a tranquilizer and prepared to stitch him up. He had able assistants in Wami and the nurses.

He also had quite an audience. Dave wanted to take movies of it all. While the camera was being set up someone bumped the tripod, which fell over and walloped Bill across the knuckles. So Orville doctored Bill up with his purple disinfectant before Bill could continue with his work. Smith's head had been painted heavily with the medicine earlier, so any pictures taken probably would make it appear to have been a bloody mess.

Scissors and tweezers were boiled, the scalp area was shaved, then doused with somebody's private stock of liquor, in which Bill also washed his hands. When offered a shot of bourbon to help him bear the pain, Smith refused it, so Bill drank it himself. Then Bill washed his hands with aerosol shaving cream, rinsed them off with a little more bourbon, and was ready to sew.

A momentary pause in the proceedings was caused by the arrival in the cave of boatman Dick Holt. He had been searching along the cliff for a cave to sleep in when he discovered a perfectly-preserved Anasazi Indian basket. It was small and filled with dirt and rat dung, which Holt refused to dump out. The basket was unusual in that it appeared to be shaped from a woven mat drawn up over a willow ring and secured with sinew.

Smith never made a sound, even though it took twelve stitches to close the wound. His head was doused with Orville's colorful disinfectant, then the bandage was taped on. Smith's wife, Marion, thought she might get sick if she watched the operation, so she went looking for Anasazi pots. When she returned he was resting comfortably.

Chet Bundy met the party at Whitmore Wash. Here they left Georgie's empty food bags and picked up full ones. Among the supplies Bundy brought in for Georgie were enough loaves of homemade bread for two days' lunches. Georgie said of Bundy, "He can take the boats out, lead the trail, and deliver children." That statement revealed the high regard that Georgie held for Chet Bundy, the father of seventeen offspring.

At Diamond Creek the "Royal River Rat" initiations took place. Delphine endured the usual mud baths and broken eggs over her head, plus much more. The men began kissing her, one by one, while she was still blindfolded. At first she thought, "This isn't hard to take!" But for every one she could not identify, a bucket of water was thrown on her. Instead of getting a light initiation, she was getting a double dose.

Georgie then ordered, "Now bend over for the final question. Even though it is very hot or very cold or very windy or pouring down rain on the river, everything is always 'Just the Way You Like It?'"

Delphine knew she must answer. "Yes."

She promptly got a swat on the rear with Georgie's paddle while being dowsed with buckets of cold water.

The blindfold was removed and Georgie handed Delphine the bottle of blackberry cordial. She was suspicious that it would be raw eggs and river water and said she was not thirsty. When they insisted and she took a sip, to her surprise it really was the blackberry liqueur.

Georgie and Josef Muench bet one another that if, while blindfolded, he could not identify the legs of several girls by touching them only from the knee down, he had to wash all the dinner pots. When he said shapely legs such as Charlotte's and Joyce's belonged to *men*, some wondered if he had been nipping at Orville's jug before the contest.

In a letter to friends, Marion Smith wrote:

> I find that I tell more about what we did than what we saw. To describe the scenery is quite beyond me, and almost, I believe, beyond the camera. The distances up above, way ahead, and far behind, are so vast, the great canyon so alive somehow, that its true scale and impact can only be approximated even with motion pictures. One must go there to know it.[8]

Rio Usumacinta

In August Georgie led a trip on the Rio Usumacinta that began in Guatemala and ended in Mexico. The group flew to Mexico City first,

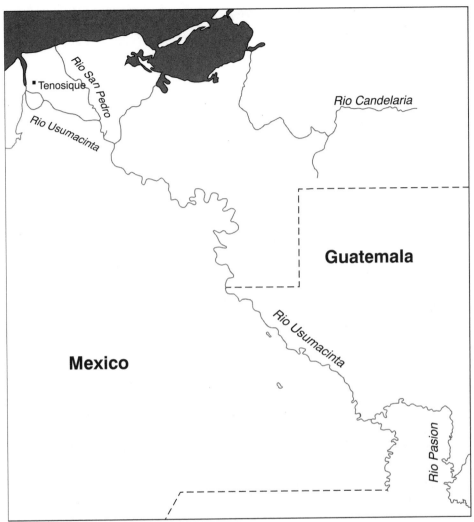

Rio Candelaria

Rio San Pedro

■ Tenosique

Rio Usumacinta

Guatemala

Rio Usumacinta

Mexico

Rio Pasion

Cartography by Thomas Zajkowski, University of Utah

Rio Usumacinta

N

25   0   25   50   75 Miles

then on to Guatemala City. The river journey began in Guatemala on the Rio Pasion, which meanders across the Peten, a relatively flat rain forest on the eastern side of the country.

Georgie and Orville Miller first scouted the river by air.[9] They had been told repeatedly that the Rio Pasion went underground. The pilot said, "You want to see a river go underground?" "Yes," they answered. And sure enough, the river ran into a big pile of rocks and disappeared. It emerged on the far side of a thousand-foot-high ridge. They decided that this outlet would be the starting point of the raft trip, obviously not wanting to try the underground passage. Orville Miller outlined the trip, "We go down the Rio Pasion which eventually joined the Akimbo and a couple of other rivers and became the Usumacinta. This is down in Mayan ruin country."

In the Mayan area of Guatemala the group was on the lookout for the ruins of Seibal which they had read about. This was in the hot, rainy season, and they traveled slowly down the upper reaches of the Usumacinta River, upstream from where it forms a long portion of the boundary between Guatemala and Mexico.

On both sides of the river the green walls of the rain forest were mostly unbroken and nearly impenetrable. Occasionally they would come upon a clearing along the bank where a few thatched huts housed small groups of natives. When one of these places was spotted, the party would slowly come to the shore and wave in a friendly fashion. The equipment and travelers were so strange to the natives that, most often, the women and children would quickly disappear into the jungle. Eventually one or two men might appear, but the group's best Spanish often failed to elicit a response. Most of the people in this area spoke only variations of Mayan dialects, and only occasionally could someone communicate in Spanish.

The question *Donde esta las ruinas?* (Where are the ruins?) was most often futile, so with smiles and waves they would cast off. The dialect spoken in one village was different from that spoken in an area only ten miles away. The party finally came to a larger town and found a young man who spoke fluent Spanish. From him they learned that they had already passed the Seibal ruins. As a result they went back up the river in a long dugout canoe with all nine of them sitting on the muddy bottom, afraid to move for fear of swamping due to its very low freeboard.

The guide finally pulled into the bank at an uninhabited spot which looked much like other places along the river. He led them into the depths of the rain forest, a delightful contrast to the boiling sun on the river. As they entered the jungle, the sky was blotted out by the green canopy overhead and they entered a strange and eerie world. Climbing vines spiraled upward and out of sight. Long rope-like root lines dangled downward to reach the forest floor.

Eventually the group came to a clearing near the top of a hill where Harvard archaeologists who had documented the Seibal ruins had built their headquarters. The buildings were straight rows of plastered houses. The only thing native-looking about them was the thatched roofs. There was a government watchman, or caretaker, at the site.

Beyond these buildings they came to a huge symmetrical pyramid of jungle completely covering a Mayan temple. Trees were growing right up between the stones. In the rotting debris on the ground, sometimes standing, but more often fallen about the base, were huge carved stone stelae, which are a trademark of the ancient Maya. Some of them had been cleaned of their moss coverings by the archaeologists and were amazingly fine in detail. On them was the famous serpent god, Kukulkan, standing out in fascinating detail, entwined with his seven snakes.

Portions of the temple stairs had been uncovered, and near the summit some tombs lay open from the recent raids by anthropologists. Huge banyan trees simultaneously split apart and held together the building stones of this massive structure. At some places there were moss-covered, full-sized carved stone "crocodillees" (as the guide called them). There were also large, intricately carved, wheel-shaped stones called *piadras sacraficios* (sacrificial stones).

Georgie and her friends were all glad they had not missed seeing these ancient ruins. Then they were off again. After an exciting time in the Tenosique rapids, they ended their trip in the town of Tenosique, Mexico.

Santa Rosa Dam and spillway, August 30, 1967, where Georgie's party launched boats on their ill-fated trip down the Rio Santiago. *Courtesy of Robert Baer.*

15 Disaster on a Mexican River, 1966–1967

$\mathcal{I}$n 1966 the Bureau of Reclamation had a bill introduced in Congress that would allow it to construct two hydroelectric dams in the Grand Canyon.[1] The proposed Marble Canyon Dam would be located above the Grand Canyon National Park boundary, and Bridge Canyon Dam would be in the lower part of the gorge near Mile 235. At that time only a fraction of the Grand Canyon was included in the existing Grand Canyon National Park. Bridge Canyon Dam, as proposed, would extend a reservoir thirteen miles into Grand Canyon National Park.

The integrity of the park was threatened according to the Sierra Club, who rather than remain on the defensive mounted a counter-offensive. In April 1966 they sponsored legislation that would enlarge the park to include the entire canyon and would specifically prohibit any dams or diversions between Lee's Ferry, where the canyon begins, and the Grand Wash Cliffs, where it ends.

Other conservationist groups followed suit. Hugh Nash, editor of the *Sierra Club Bulletin*, wrote:

> The Canyon has incalculable value, but dams would destroy much of its biota, turn a living laboratory into a static museum piece, and effectively deny access to anthropologists, archaeologists, biologists, botanists, geologists, and others who still have much to learn from it. And the Grand Canyon has a tremendous educational value for the lay public, which, as nowhere else on earth, can here grasp almost intuitively many of the essentials of geology and geomorphology.

"Unused," the Grand Canyon is already being put to its highest and best use.[2]

"It is anticipated," said the Bureau of Reclamation, "that a minimum flow of at least 1,000 cubic feet per second will be maintained below Marble Canyon Dam through Grand Canyon." In the Colorado River's channel, that would be a miserably inadequate trickle and would preclude most river running, the supreme recreational experience possible there.

Georgie had more or less acquiesced in the building of Glen Canyon Dam. But now her entire livelihood was being threatened. She and other concessioners backed the movement to stop the dams. Georgie wrote to President Lyndon Johnson and got a personal reply from him to the effect that he would do what he could to block the project. Outfitters and many of their passengers wrote letters in opposition to the dams. In July Kenneth Catlin, who had taken a trip with Georgie, wrote a letter to Secretary of the Interior Stewart Udall urging him to take a boat trip through Grand Canyon "as words and pictures are no match for first-hand experience in this case." His letter continues:

> If for some reason it is not possible for you to make the trip I would urge that you personally discuss the situation with someone such as Georgie White, who knows the river well. Georgie has run most of the rivers on this continent and she rates the Grand Canyon trip as the finest and most exciting of all. I feel that the proposed dams would result in a tragic loss of American heritage.[3]

Secretary Udall *did* make the trip and eventually came to agree with the conservationists. Coal-fired generating plants were built at Page, Arizona, and Shiprock, New Mexico, as alternatives to the two proposed dams in Grand Canyon.

A New Crystal Rapid

In December 1966 an unusually heavy rainstorm pounded the highlands of northern Arizona, southwestern Utah, southern Nevada, and south-central California, causing widely scattered floods in all four states. In Arizona the heaviest precipitation was at the North Rim area of the eastern Grand Canyon. From December 3 to December 7, fourteen inches of precipitation were measured at the North Rim entrance station. Debris flows of historic proportion in the Crystal and Chuar drainage basins transported logs, rocks, and mud from the North Rim to the Colorado River. Boulders of up to three feet in diameter were suspended in the flow, and larger ones rolled along the stream bed. The flooding severely damaged modern facilities in Bright Angel Canyon.[4]

The flood in Crystal Creek was the biggest that had occurred there in several centuries. It damaged or obliterated at least three archaeological sites that had been unused and undisturbed since general abandonment by the Anasazi in about A.D. 1150. The debris fan at the mouth of Crystal Creek was enlarged by about two hundred feet. The flood deposited huge boulders in the Colorado River and narrowed the channel, creating a major rapid where there had been only a "miscellaneous" one, in Georgie's vernacular.

Bright Angel Creek began to rise the morning of December 5 and continued in several steps to peak on December 6. Don Dedera of *Arizona Highways* magazine wrote:

> The flood struck the [Phantom] ranch "with the noise of a dozen locomotives," according to ranch manager Dan Doherty. Marooned, the few persons at the ranch began to fear for their lives.
>
> "The big boulders that are in the bottom of the canyon must be all touching one another," said Dan. "The vibration of the flood was transmitted through them, and the ground itself trembled under your feet.
>
> "It wasn't just the size of the flood," Dan recalled, "but the duration of it. It rose up and didn't drop an inch for three days."[5]

Up and down Bright Angel Creek the damage was colossal. Most of the mule corral was washed away, and mules scaled the cliffs for safety. Hundred-year-old cottonwood trees were torn loose and floated down into the river. Phantom Ranch's sewer system and irrigation works were swept away. Two-thirds of the campground below Phantom Ranch eroded into the stream. At the time of the flood, eight miles of new water pipeline, part of a two-million-dollar project for the Phantom Ranch and South Rim resorts, had just been completed and were waiting for government inspection. The flood made a broken, twisted mess of the pipeline and left a legal puzzle: Who is the owner of the wreck? And what can be done?

The pumps at Roaring Springs in Bright Angel Canyon were damaged as water tore through the pump house. The powerhouse half a mile downstream on Pipe Creek was demolished. The flood washed out parts of the trail and bridges along the Kaibab Trail. The Park Service estimated it would take three and a half years and five million dollars to rebuild the pipeline and repair the trail.

Georgie's first Grand Canyon trip of 1967 began Monday, May 4. When she arrived at Crystal Creek she encountered a different rapid, one equal to Lava Falls at its worst. The flood and resultant debris fan had narrowed the width of the river to one-quarter its former size and had doubled the drop and increased the speed of the current dramatically. When the water passed over a particularly large boulder the compression increased, creating a hole-wave combination that seemed twenty feet high. It was to become known to river runners as the "Old Hole" or the "Big Hole" in Crystal.

With her big boat Georgie plowed right down the middle. The raft hit the initial drop with a sickening thud, then plowed over and through a gigantic wave. She then went on through a turmoil of holes and combers, twisting and reeling in the rampaging rapid. In the ensuing years this would become her favorite rapid. On subsequent trips the boulders were still moving, making it a rough new experience each time it was run.

Rio Grande de Santiago Disaster

In late August Georgie led another group down the Rio Grande de Santiago in Mexico. The trip was doomed almost from the start. The group ran into a storm system that hit Mexico with a fifty-year record rainstorm. When the rain let up temporarily, Georgie surveyed the river. She noted, "Wonderful flight over river early this morning. River really high. It will be fast."[6]

Members of the party included physician Robert Baer and his wife, Jean, two nurses, Orville Miller, and a woman pediatrician from Chicago named Lee. They were not aware of it at the time, but other rivers besides the Rio de Santiago fed into Lake Chapala many miles above the dam at Santa Rosa, below which the party would embark. The group was aware of the storm, but when the rain ended they assumed the flooding would soon be over.

At the dam they were greeted by a spectacular sight. The floodgates bypassing the dam were off to one side, with a rock pinnacle in between the dam and the floodgates. From the spillways the water

Aerial view of Santa Rosa Reservoir and spillway on Georgie's 1967 Mexico trip, August 30, 1967. *Courtesy of Robert Baer.*

plunged several hundred feet into the river. Where the water came down off the cliff and hit the river bed it made a gigantic recoil mound of water, like a tidal wave, close to one hundred feet high. Orville said:

> It was spooky, when you could walk up along the side of it on the shore and there was this tremendous big mound of water ten, fifteen times higher than our heads! But the momentum was taking it on down the river and not sideways to where we were.[7]

Jean Baer said when they got down and saw that raging water she wondered whether continuing on was the right thing to do. She mentioned this, but nobody else seemed to be concerned. Georgie just went ahead with the plans, so Jean felt, "Well, she knows what she's doing, and I don't."

They spent the night beside the river and could see that the water had been a lot higher. A third floodgate had been open only a day or two before. The superintendent took them on a tour of the dam and showed them how the floodgates closed. Georgie noted, "Never seen so much water. He isn't sure about letting us go, but Orville convinces him."[8] He said he would lower the water for awhile.

When the flow was cut to perhaps half of what it had been and the big mound of water was considerably lower, they decided they could go down the river. Because it had stopped raining, they supposed the flooding was about over. Also, while they were inflating the rafts they did not notice that the middle raft, which carried the motor, had a slow leak where a patch had come loose. As the party was getting things together, the engineer sent word down that he could give them two hours to get out of there; then he had to open the floodgates once again.

Heavy flooding upstream was working its way down into Lake Chapala. The level of the lake had risen to where it was beginning to inundate the homes of some rich Americans and politicians along the shore. There were gates to control the flow out of Lake Chapala and they were all opened, which then sent a new flood down into Santa Rosa Reservoir. So the group was very rushed and did not notice that the middle boat had gotten a bit soft.

They were finally off, but had gone only a short distance when suddenly a large boulder appeared and they were almost on it. Georgie gunned the motor and cleared the rock, but in so doing the soft middle boat folded halfway under itself. Georgie went under the water with the motor and had to feel her way out. Behind the rock they hit a huge hole. The middle and left-hand rafts went into the hole, which had a big standing wave below it. It turned the left-hand raft upside down on top of the middle one, which had folded in half with the back down beneath the front. Both the motor and the spare were submerged in the muddy water, rendering them both useless for the rest of the trip.

Shortly after they departed, the floodgates had been reopened, so the river was now high in the flood stage, up into the trees along the bank. Georgie's group was almost helpless with only one oar, an upside-down section of raft and the other one folded in two underneath. Finally, just before dark, with Orville plying the one oar and others grabbing tree limbs, they got into an eddy and were able to get to the bank.

They were on a scree slope just below a vertical cliff where some trees grew. The boat was tied to one of them so they could get the nose of the rafts tightly against the shore. At the top of the slope was a semi-flat area. The women, except Georgie, climbed to the flat place at the base of the cliff. Georgie, Orville, and Bob Baer began to untie gear to get things straightened out. The river continued to rise, and every now and then they had to tie the boat higher up the tree. Soon the women began to yell because the water was coming up. Where originally they had been fifteen or twenty feet above water, the river had risen so much it was now threatening the place where they were standing.

They returned to the boats quickly and huddled there, eating from food bags in Orville's section of the boat. The group spent the night on the upside-down boat, frequently untying and retying further up the tree. They really could not sleep, as the six of them were packed like sardines on top of the wrecked boats. If one of them made the slightest move they were either kicking somebody in the face or jabbing them with an elbow.

Next morning the river began to go down. As they continued lowering the line on the tree, they were flabbergasted at winding up about twelve feet below the highest point where they had been tied. When the shore rocks emerged, the group was able to get some bags untied, the boats righted, and the luggage loaded on again. Then they took off down the river. The boat was fine now, except that they had no motor. However, they did have two oars.

Jean Baer remembers that first camp differently. She said:

First catastrophe on Rio Grande de Santiago, August 30, 1967. *Courtesy of Robert Baer.*

Undoing the boats after flip on Rio Grande de Santiago, August 31, 1967. *Courtesy of Robert Baer.*

Georgie and Orville spent a lot of time underneath right here getting the motor out then getting the stuff back on. I mean, that took *hours*. And I remember walking up the bank and finding a dwelling up there and saying to Georgie: "There are some people around here." And she said: "We're okay."

My faith in her judgment went down the drain. What it ended up, ultimately, for me was: I decided my judgment about that whole thing was better. I would not have gone. And once that happened, then I couldn't go back.[9]

The river was fast and rough with a lot of big holes. It was still overflowing its banks. Orville said, "Georgie and I were rowing like mad, constantly, to miss these holes. After a couple of hours I was getting exhausted and I suspect Georgie was, too. But she wouldn't admit it." So they got into another eddy and tied up. Georgie and Orville were up and down all during the night as the river rose and fell. Orville told Georgie, "We're not going to leave here until that river's back down where it belongs." And she agreed that should be their plan, even if they had to sit there for a week. After daylight the water began dropping quite rapidly and it finally ended up a nice, pleasant river. So, off they went.

After an hour or so of pleasant floating in the scenic canyon, they saw a clear stream coming from the side. Since the river was quite muddy they decided to stop and wash up in the clear water. They pulled in on a small sandy bank, and Orville took a tie line and went about thirty feet up the bank to a four-foot-high boulder he could tie to. He started walking back to the raft, untying his life jacket as he went. In a few minutes he turned around and saw that the rock was half under water. The river was coming up that fast! He ran back and untied the rope before it got buried in the river. He said he had a hard time getting the rope rolled up and back onto the raft while trying to hold it, because the current was getting stronger.

About four or five hundred feet below that was a big hole where the river went over a boulder. The water was getting higher and faster, and a big rolling wave at the end of the hole was now probably twenty-five feet below the submerged rock. As the crew rowed away from shore they tried to miss the hole. Unfortunately, as they approached, the boat slid sideways into it. They had been going about fifteen miles per hour until the front end of the boat hit the standing wave. It stopped them completely. The back ends of the raft tucked under, and the front flipped up and over. The boats were still held in the hole, but everyone was dumped into the river.

Orville let go of the oar, grabbed a handle, and wound up hanging on underneath the raft. He thought the fast current under the boat was going to strip his clothes from his body. The current finally tore him loose and he was able to resurface. Apparently he had been holding the raft in place because, as soon as he got free, the boat climbed the wave and went down the river. He managed to reach the hand lines on the bottom of the boat, totally exhausted from being under water for so long and from the swim to catch the raft.

Someone saw Bob Baer at the far edge of the river where he was able to climb out. There were two nurses in the river fifty feet or so ahead of the raft, and some other people were missing.

Orville kept trying to climb up on top of the overturned boat but could not because there was nothing there but slick, wet rubber. Somewhere downstream was the dam at the silver mine. It would mean sure death if they could not make it to shore. He thought, "Well, I'll stay with the raft until I can see we're approaching that dam, then I'll do my damnedest to get to shore!"

Then Georgie showed up. She had reached the edge of the river where she could have climbed out and saved herself. But seeing the raft with Orville clinging to it, she swam after it. She was a strong swimmer and soon caught up with the boat. She came in right behind Orville, who was hanging on to the handles, which were now under the water. Right away she decided to climb up on him and get onto the overturned boat. He said, "Wait a minute, Georgie! Let me get a good breath!" In a few minutes she climbed onto his shoulders and onto the boat. Then she tied a rope across the upside-down rafts, giving them something to hang onto. She then hung onto the rope while Orville grabbed her foot, and in this way he clambered on top of the raft. Once there they were able to think about how to get the other people out of the river. There were two women on the other end of the raft and they were pulled aboard.

About that time they heard a cry from under the boat. "Help! I'm stuck under here!" It was Jean, in the air space underneath the rafts. They told her, "You just calm down and get loose and come on out, and we'll pull you aboard!" Jean Baer later said:

> The boat tipped over on me and I was underneath it and hanging on, bouncing along underneath it. And then I realized that

that dam was downstream and that if we stayed in the river and went over the dam, we'd get killed. So I decided I had to get out from under the boat and I was scared to do it. I was afraid to let go, but I thought I had to. And when the boat would bounce I could see daylight . . . you know, where the boats are hooked together. So I knew which direction to go. I let go and went out and got to the outside of the boat. . . . Eventually we somehow or another got reconnected to the boat and Orville and Georgie were on top of it. And Kay was in the water with me. I don't know exactly how that happened. I think they saw us and we were near it and they threw a rope to us. But anyhow, they pulled her up and then they pulled me up.

Now they were floating down the raging river on the overturned boat without oars or a motor to steer with. They were all on top of the boats except three who were missing. As they floated along they came around a bend and saw a garage-sized rock sitting right in their path. Orville could see that they were going to smack right into it, sideways.

The rock turned out to be a life saver. The boat hit the rock sideways, and the upstream section of the boat, which was upside down, came up on its side so that it was standing on edge. Then, the current began to turn them around the rock and on down the river. While that section of the boat was standing on end, Orville was able to pull it back over onto the middle section in an upright position. The elasticity of the nylon lines, which bound the rafts together, were all that made it possible.

Now they had one raft right-side up and two upside down. Farther on, when they began to drift a bit off the main current, they grabbed at branches of trees in order to slow down and swing in closer to the bank. Finally they came to a place where, by wrapping his feet around the seat on the right-side-up section and his arms around a small tree, Orville was able to stop the boat. It swung into the bank, and Georgie got off with a hand line and tied up.

The group sat there for two hours watching for anybody to come by in life jackets. No one did. Amazingly, those who were together were all uninjured. Some said they were fairly sure they had seen two of the missing people near shore, but they were not certain they had gotten to the bank.

After a while the river dropped and left the rafts draped over some big rocks. They were able to get under them, untie their bags, and get all the sleeping bags and other gear out. They went up the bank about fifty feet above the river where it was safe and made camp. Jean had lost one of her shoes in the river. Fortunately, Georgie had an extra pair along that fit Jean.

From where the party tied up it was about three miles down to the dam near the silver mine. There were continuous rapids the entire way. If they had not managed to stop where they did, it is doubtful they would have made it at all. Orville said, "If we'd gone over that dam, there just is no way that we would survive. I think it'd actually break every bone in your body."

The next morning the river continued to drop. At that point they decided to go back up the river to look for the missing three people. All they took with them was some canned water, one tarp, their money, cameras in waterproof bags, some canned food, and a length of rope about fifty feet long. Sleeping bags, life jackets, and other equipment were left behind with the boats.

Georgie was rather bitter with Orville for having insisted that "we take some women along because we always have men along and it's boring!" She said that of all times, it had to be now. They were literally under-manned, muscle-wise.

It was a fairly easy hike because the flood had scoured the brush and debris off the banks of the river. One of the nurses was dragging behind, and Orville stayed with her while Georgie and the others hurried on ahead.

Soon Georgie saw Bob and Ann (one of the nurses) across the river. The noise of the river had abated enough so that she could shout at them and be heard. Georgie told them to hire an airplane and return to her side of the river where they had seen an airfield during their scouting flight prior to the trip. She thought the group could go on up the river and reach that airfield.

A little later Georgie spotted Kimberly, the last missing person. She, too, was across the river on the same side as Bob and Ann. Only by then, Bob and Ann had climbed so far up the mountainside they could not hear Georgie calling them to come back and get Kimberly.

Kim had been coming down the other shore looking for the main group and had spent the first night alone, without food, and wearing only a bathing suit. She was from New York and had never slept out before. Now Georgie's group was across the river from her. Calling across, she told them she had an injured shoulder. Then the rising river created such an ominous roar they could not hear one another.

At that point Orville, Georgie, and four women were on one side of the river and Kim on the other. The river was so high they could not possibly get across, so Kim had to spend another night alone and hungry. At least now she had comfort in knowing that the others were right across the river from her.

The women passengers tended to stick close to Orville. They clung to him rather than to tough Georgie because he was more sympathetic to them. That night when they were all lying on the tarp together, Jean Baer began to cry. Orville tried to comfort her, but Georgie yelled something like, "Ah! Shut up!" She really could not understand what other women went through sometimes. Georgie was not frightened, nor was Orville once he got out of the river. As for the others, who were not used to these things, it was very different.

Jean Baer said one of the reasons she was so upset for having let herself get into this mess was that she and Bob had little children at home. Their kids were aged ten, eight, and six. Orville's children were older, and the other people had none. Jean felt she and Bob had been remiss in ever allowing themselves to get into a situation like this. She had the feeling Georgie did not see it as seriously as she did and thought at the time, "You've only got yourself to worry about and we don't. We've got responsibilities. Our kids can't have us get killed." Jean figured Georgie's attitude toward it was much more a "fate" kind of a thing. That night Georgie said something to the effect of "What will happen will happen." That made Jean resolve that she would *never* go back with her. "If she wants to get herself killed, she can do it. But that's not for me."

Orville hiked up the canyon another half mile or so where he came to a mass of jumbled cliffs several thousand feet high that came right down to the river's edge. It was apparent they would not be able to get to the airfield that way. They would have to cross the river. They knew they had to get to the girl on the far bank in any case. Jean Baer decided that, given what had happened, she was going to do what she thought was safe. She no longer trusted Georgie. Her first thought was that she would not cross the river, but then she could not face staying by herself.

The next morning Georgie said, "Orville, you go talk to these girls. They told me no way are they going to get in that river again. And we've got to get across." Orville talked to them and told them they all had to get over to Kimberly's side. He said they would be safe because the camera bags and the rope would act like life preservers, telling them they should all stay together and not try it until the river went down. The camera bags, about a foot high and ten inches wide, were watertight and would furnish flotation. Finally the women agreed.

As the river began to recede, Georgie put a stick at the water's edge and watched it go down. When the water level remained stationary for perhaps five or ten minutes Orville said, "Georgie, we can make it now." They got the women, went to the narrowest point, and got them to jump in with "Georgie and [Orville], at the head of the rope, paddling like hell!" The others hung on and helped a little by swimming side stroke. The current carried them about a block down the river, but they made it.

When they reached Kim they found that she had a dislocated shoulder. One of the women, Dr. Lee, was a pediatrician. She and Orville worked on Kim and got her shoulder put back in place. Orville pulled on her arm while the doctor steered it. The nurses helped. Jean Baer had managed to keep some pain medication, which was given to Kim before the procedure.

The group had seen some cornfields a short distance down the river and up on a side hill. They climbed toward the fields and came upon some huts, a pig, a dog, and chickens, but no people. From the cornfield the trail forked, and they decided to try the right fork. Kay soon became exhausted. She was having trouble hiking, so they had to stop often. Also, Kim could scarcely walk because her shoes had shrunk and her feet were blistered. They stopped and camped next to the cornfield overnight—more rocks to sleep on, and bugs of all kinds nearly eating them alive. It began to rain, and Jean cried for the third night in a row. She had had it. Aside from her blistered feet, Kim was doing well.

The next day they saw people on the other fork of the trail, so they backtracked to ask where they were. When Georgie met the group she assumed them to be hunters, as they were armed with rifles. The group was composed of six men and a donkey, and it turned out they had come to hunt bandits that were reported to have been sighted down on the river. This area was part of an *ejido*, a kind of co-op ranch, which was formed when the government took land from a large land owner and divided it amongst the workers. These people were the owners of the cornfields.

They had been told there was a giant (Orville) and a big red bandit (Dr. Lee was wearing a red jumpsuit). But once they saw it was just

Mexican posse that went looking for "los banditos," who were actually Georgie's party hiking out from their wreck on Rio Grande de Santiago, September 3, 1967. *Courtesy of Jean Baer.*

Boat death and grave on the Rio Grande de Santiago. *Courtesy of Robert Baer.*

a bunch of women and that they had no guns, the bandito hunters became quite friendly. They put Kim on the donkey and led the group up the trail.

When they got out of the canyon, they came to a fork in the trail. One of the men said, "Wait here," and they went off down the trail to their ranch. When they returned they had a horse for Kim to ride on. From there they went on to the ejido where they found Bob and Ann waiting.

Bob and Ann had climbed out of the canyon, gone to Guadalajara, chartered a plane, and come back to the ejido, which was as close as they could get to a landing strip. In due time Bob and Ann filled them in on what had happened to them after the upset. Bob said:

> I started in a whirlpool after the boats overturned, and it took me the longest time to pop up. But with these wonderful life jackets I did indeed pop up after about 45 seconds, which I thought was the end of the world. And then I floated downstream and the first thing that I rescued was an oar. I don't know why, but there was an oar. And then one of these river bags came along, and then Ann came along. And so the two of us grabbed onto all this flotsam and we floated for awhile. We were trying to get out before this check dam we had heard about. And we did indeed come out to the shore. It took a long, long time and we camped there on that night.

The pair took inventory of what they had and found that the waterproof container belonged to Lee, the pediatrician. Among the things it contained were her camera, a sleeping bag and air mattress, and a lot of money: three hundred U.S. dollars and a bunch of pesos, along with Lee's checkbook and pen. So they were well off financially. Ann had lost one shoe in the river, but luckily for her there was a pair of shoes in Lee's bag, and they fit her. The bag contained no food but had her first aid kit, which contained a lot of unlabeled bottles. Bob said, "I think I took some aspirin that turned out to be milk of magnesia."

Ann and Bob had been intent on going downstream to where the check dam was. Georgie had to yell across to them, "Stop!" That was when Georgie told them to climb up on their side of the river to a road, and from there get to the airport.

They filled every container they had with river water and started climbing out to find the airport. Some squash and corn growing along the way provided them with something to eat.

Finally, on top of a mountain, they saw a person on the next ridge. Ann had taught Bob that *soccoro* meant "help." And that's what he yelled. The man came down the valley and up to their ridge. He shared his lunch of tamales with them and led them to his village, which was called Cinco Minas (Five Mines). One could not get to this village other than on foot, except once a week by truck. Luckily, the truck arrived within two hours after they reached the village!

They rode to Santa Rosa in the back of the truck in company with some pigs and other people picked up along the way. All of the busses heading to Guadalajara were full, so Ann and Bob rented a limousine to get there. The next day in Guadalajara they rented an airplane and began flying around looking for the main group. They landed at various places, and when they finally landed at Sayulamita, which was serviced only by an air strip, the people said, "The men are gone looking for the banditos."

"What banditos?" they asked.

"Well, there's some blond banditos down by the river and the men think they're going to steal from the fields down there and so they have gone off to hunt them."

Bob said, "We decided we knew those 'banditos.'" Bob and Ann were pretty sure it was their main party because the description of the bandits included a giant, which was Orville, and the red one, which was Lee.

Bob and Ann then chartered two four-seat airplanes, and the newly united party flew back to Guadalajara. Orville remembers:

> The thing that disappointed me once we get back to Guadalajara, you know: we had a great adventure, we're back, alive! Of course Georgie lost all her gear, but that didn't seem to be bothering her in the least. You know she never once complained about losing probably five, ten thousand dollars worth of gear and boats. So, let's celebrate! But these girls didn't want to celebrate. They would just go to bed and stay there, even in the daytime.

Georgie later stated: "Everyone said they were going to get stoned, but due to most of all of the group having 2–step [diarrhea]—went to much needed rest in bed—lot of bites on everyone."[10]

After the others flew home, Georgie, the two nurses, and Orville went to Puerto Vallarta for some rest and relaxation before leaving for home. Orville recalls:

And in Puerto Vallarta, again, they'd get up and eat and go right back to bed. They were just done in! They weren't the least bit interested in celebrating! Including Georgie; she wouldn't go celebrate with me either, although she didn't appear to be done in like these other girls. So I was quite disappointed. I was ready to *really* celebrate. I was alive!

16   Divorce, 1968–1971

$\mathcal{I}$n 1968 Georgie and Orville returned to Mexico and tried the Rio
Grande de Santiago again. They found part of one of the boats
from the 1967 trip on the bank near a village and it still said "Georgie"
on it. Orville said, "So when we showed up with additional boats saying
'Georgie,' there was a lot of excitement. And they had a party for us."

The local people had cut up the boats and used them to patch
knotholes in their canoes and make soles for their shoes. Orville said,
"I thought it was a shame that they cut the boats up. They were perfectly good when we walked off and left them. The boats weren't bad.
They were upside down."[1]

Grand Canyon Friends

In July 1968 Joan DeFato made her first of many trips with Georgie.
She wound up doing a dozen trips with her, about half of them as a
passenger and the others as a helper. On the 1968 trip, Georgie only
took the big boat, and she was the only crew. A man called "Bouncer"
(George Price) was the only person on the boat who had taken the trip
before, so Georgie had twenty-one rookies. She ran the boat all day,
then made the meals with help from passengers to open the cans.
When she got up in the morning, Georgie would gas up the boat,
change the spark plug, go around and jump on all the sections. If they
were not as hard as she wanted, she would pump them up by hand. She
did all this herself; she had just a fantastic amount of energy. Joan said:

> She told me that she would wake up very early, before anyone
> else, and get washed and dressed and just sit there and watch

the sun come up on the rocks. She would meditate. She said she felt she was close to Indians in that way. She would just sit there and plan her day and be at one with the canyon. And then it would be time to go on shore and she would start lighting up the stoves.[2]

After lunch on July 8 they took off down Marble Canyon. Bouncer noted, "Even though I am the only one of the group to have gone through here before, I am just as excited as everyone else."

Brian Dierker also met Georgie in 1968. He later said, "I've never had a bigger influence in my life than Georgie White and Bob Miller. They taught me how to take care of the dudes in the dude business." Bob Miller, who was originally from Wyoming, had a dude ranch in Tucson and in his late fifties decided he wanted to become a boatman. He took a number of trips with Brian and his brother, Dan Dierker. Brian said, "I think I've learned more in regards to my livelihood and my interests in life from Georgie and Bob Miller than anybody." He said Georgie had to be pretty hard to make it in a macho, man's world thing, but she just came on in. He thought it was pretty audacious that somebody would put "Woman of the River" on the side of their boat. "But," he said, "she's been like the center force, as far as my interpretation of what you do for the dudes. Her repeat clientele far surpasses any other percentage of repeat clientele. She had a love affair with her clients. She had an attitude. She had a spirit."[3]

Boatman Al Loewe made a trip with Georgie in June of 1968. During orientation at the start of a trip, he said Georgie would always have a roll of toilet paper and a book of matches. When everybody got off the bus, she would hold that toilet paper up and she would give them her little speech. She would say:

> I know you're all doctors and dentists and everything. Down here we're all river people. We all work together. When we leave a campground, there won't be any of this on the ground. You use it, you burn it. You dig a hole, you do your thing, you burn the paper. And then, probably the next time we come this should be a nice, clean camp.[4]

In 1968 Ken Sleight was president of the Western River Guides Association (WRGA). He contacted Georgie and asked if she would like him to nominate her for membership. In answer, Georgie wrote to him saying that she would be at the November 2 meeting and that he could put her name in for nomination. She wrote, "But I can't attend over one meeting per year."

Sleight said that the WRGA board turned down Georgie's application for membership "because she was a woman and got too much publicity."[5] He said that she was accepted a few years later and that she was a responsible member. She would speak up, state her views, and work for needed change.

In the spring of 1969 or 1970, Igor de Lissovoy and his wife, Lillian, went on a Grand Canyon trip with Georgie on her first run of that season. Igor reported their adventures in the Summer 1970 issue of *The Donnelley Printer*. Igor told of the wonders of Grand Canyon and the great prowess and skill with which Georgie handled her big boat.[6]

In March 1971 Bill Jensen and Jim Falls took their first of many trips with Georgie. They hiked down to the river to join Georgie's party at Phantom Ranch. There was snow and ice along the rim and the wind was howling down through the inner gorge. Jensen said they would sit on the boat and shiver. But Georgie told them, "That's just the way we like it!"[7]

Falls said, "I think what impressed me on my very first trip with Georgie was how she was making us so aware of the environment." "Keep it clean," she said. Falls smoked at that time, and he said you had to carry two containers: one to keep the cigarettes dry, the second to put the cigarette butts in. "If she caught you throwing a cigarette butt—just overboard—into the water, it was a tongue-lashing that you didn't want to hear a second time!"

There was less traffic on the river then. Other outfitters knew Georgie's schedule and knew she liked certain camp sites, so they would pass them by and leave them open for her. That gave her people more time to sight-see. Her trips were twelve days in length at that time.

In the early '70s, it was almost a requirement by Georgie that a passenger should wear a hard hat on their hikes, not just one made of flimsy canvas to keep the sun off. When Georgie conducted the hikes she would say, "Okay, let's go up this pathway. I want to show you something." When they were under overhangs of rock she said, "Somebody above you could loosen a rock and it could come down and hit you on the head!" So they all wore their hard hats.

Some people were afraid of heights. They would frequently say, "Oh, it doesn't bother me." Then they would get up on a high ledge, look down three hundred feet, and freeze. When this happened Georgie would have the boatmen take ropes, go around the people, and anchor the ropes so the person felt safe with something to hang onto.

At some of the big camps people might be spread out or away on short hikes. Georgie had a very loud air horn which she used to awaken the people each morning, or to call them to dinner at night. After years of bitter complaints and sabotage by the boatmen, she switched to blowing on a small brass horn.

Georgie told her passengers, "If you see any snakes, if you see any ring-tail cats, if you see skunks, if you see *anything, you* get out of the way! You're in *their* territory." Jensen remembers:

> At night we'd be sleeping and we'd hear some rustling, 'cause we'd have little candies or nuts in packages sitting out. We'd hear rustling of the paper and somebody would say: "Is that you, Jim? Is that you, Diane?", or whatever. And we'd look and turn a flashlight on real quick and here were the ring-tail cats and they were in there! Gee, they were pretty! They were beautiful! Georgie always said: "If you ever see the ring-tail cats, you are really blessed." I didn't feel like I had to trust Georgie as much as I just wanted to be a part of her life.

With those turquoise blue eyes and that leathery skin, Georgie gave people confidence, right from the beginning. Falls said "she could read the water like most of us could read a 'TV Guide'! She knew exactly where the currents would take her and how to escape serious problems."

Family Problems

Unfortunately, her luck wasn't as good off the river. For Georgie, 1971 was a year of trauma and change. Jane Foster, owner of Marble Canyon Lodge at Marble Canyon, Arizona, said that for several years Georgie maintained a warehouse at Marble Canyon and made it her headquarters for the season. She said Georgie hired a Navajo by the name of Frank Black to work on the equipment with Whitey while she was away on trips. Foster said, "The morning of the day that Georgie would leave on a trip they would start in. And I don't think either of them got sober until the day before she was due back."[8]

Patty Ellwanger, manager of Hatch River Expeditions at Marble Canyon, said that while Georgie was on trips, Whitey would sell some of her boats for money to buy booze. He would often sell one to Ted

Hatch. Ted knew Georgie didn't want to sell her boats, so he would buy them and sell them back to her when she got home.[9]

Georgie's friend Tony (Sylvia Tone) was almost the only one she would confide her troubles to. Excerpts from letters she wrote to Tony, most of them undated, reflect some of her woes:[10]

Whity still on cure. It is the longest he has ever went without a drink in the 42 yrs I have known him. . . . Paul my brother home for a week, health not so good, has blackouts. Mae Hansen going in June, wants heat. . . .

[*On November 4, 1970, Georgie wrote to Tony, saying in part,*] I sure am glad I have Marie myself. I feel at times she needs less work & more of my company while she can enjoy it, I am so busy. *Whity hopeless 1/2 mind—a Real Problem*. . . .

All OK except Whity & he is a mess most of the time, really slipping. . . .

Whity still on wagon. . . .

I am having quite a bit of difficulty with Whity. I hope to convince him to live by himself. He could drink and have no one to yack at him. I would sure miss him, but would have piece [sic] of mind and that is worth a lot. Also I just can't have any friends here (as you know). Slowly I have dropped everyone, but of course I won't drop Marie.

Whity has been in hospital a lot. First an infected arm, then he was operated on last Monday for a ruptured bowel, still in hospital, hopes to get out next week. Marie will take care of getting him and etc. . . . I don't have much hope, but just maybe he will stay from drink for a while. It seems good to see him with clear eyes and a clear brain. It is so rare. *Thanks to you, Medicare is sure a great help*. Rooms at Loma Linda run around *$70 per day*. . . .

Whity's drinking put him so far out I had to put him in a AA hospital for 3 days to dry out. He can't stay here anymore, so I will put him in a trailor [sic] out in small town somewhere. I can't have him at Page anymore so will have peace there. I really feel sorry for him & he is too old to just walk out on. He threatens me when he is drunk & then is like a lamb when dried out. We all have problems but nothing equals the drinking problem.

Orville Miller said, "He [Whitey] was in some of these alcoholic care homes. And he got so violent they kept kicking him out, and so he'd go from one to another. And then he started threatening Georgie's life; he was going to kill her and so forth." Georgie would not say much about this, but she ended up hiding out from Whitey. Orville said she would not let people know where she was, and was using a false name for her address so Whitey would have trouble finding her. He was still husky and strong and could have harmed her any time he wanted to.[11]

On March 3, 1971, Georgie wrote the following letter to her customers from her home in Midway City, California:

Dear River Rat:

I feel terrible telling you this but I am not going to be able to run the river this coming summer.

Personal problems, completely beyond my ability to cope with and do anything else at the same time, have come up and I will just have to be at home most of the time for a few months to take care of them.

Also, as many of you know, my river running has been more or less of a hobby. Naturally it had to pay its way but I have not cared about becoming a big commercial operator. In order to continue as I have been in the past, I do have to have a concession and go along with many new rules and regulations regarding river running thru the canyon. This would naturally require a lot more time, attention to details, and work which I do not wish to take on at this time.

I appreciate your companionship over the past years and I plan to take some trips on a lesser scale next summer. Trips will be more exploratory and less demanding. I do plan to make a Mexico trip this year so if you are planning that trip please let me hear from you.

I love every one of you,
Sincerely,
(Signed) Georgie White

I enclose my check refunding all money received for deposit on a trip and any expenses regarding same.[12]

In addition to her problems with Whitey, who was in and out of institutions, Georgie's brother Paul was in the hospital, and she expected she would have to pay the bill. Also, Marie was not well.

Georgie was not interested in the business end of the operation; she leaned heavily on Marie for that. Georgie would say, "Just give me the numbers and give me the names and leave me alone."[13] Marie kept track of reservations and worried about getting everyone on the bus and headed to the river. It was a perfect partnership.

Jane Foster said Georgie would come into the lodge the last minute before leaving on a trip and call Marie to check on the welfare of her dogs and cats and to see if everything else was all right. Orville Miller said it was amazing what Georgie and Marie could do in the warehouse. "They'd get these 700–pound pontoons up on end and paint them and roll them up and put them on the truck. Just the two women."

In a letter to Sylvia Tone, though, Georgie wrote:

Marie has pains in her chest and shoulders. New deal, I don't know what it is. Paul my brother legs seem to get worse and he is a big man. I probably will have to take care of him complete in time. Marie and I do now, but her savings are running out and since she has doctor bills her husband will have to pay so it sort of will come to me. Please say nothing of this to anyone.[14]

Paul DeRoss died on July 20, 1971, at Harbor General Hospital in Torrance, California, from complications with a perforated gastric ulcer.

Move to Las Vegas and Divorce

Shortly after Paul died, Georgie moved to Las Vegas, Nevada. Her nephew, Paul DeRoss, Jr., said, "I only know that he [Whitey] was in a state institution and they wanted to bill her, so she went to Nevada."[15] Georgie filed for divorce on August 20, 1971. She gave Whitey's address as Riverside County Hospital, Riverside, California.

Georgie wrote Tony:

I accepted concession—Hope Calif don't bother me—Divorce should be O K Last of November—Took my daughter's name back Georgie Clark = Sheriff couldn't locate Whity in Hospital to serve warrant. Said he was discharged—gave old address but they couldn't find him so we have *adv.* paper here in Las Vegas *21* days—then 21 day wait & all is well—For me this really is great as I was afraid Whity would raise a mean stink—I really kept quiet when told this. . . . Glad *1971* is almost over.[16]

When she accepted a concession from the Park Service to continue to run trips in the Grand Canyon, Georgie could no longer throw empty cans in the river. All trash had to be carried out, and there was no more burying human waste in the sand. A portable potty had to be taken along for that purpose. She was also limited as to how many passengers she could take through in a season.

On November 17, 1971, at Las Vegas, Nevada, Georgie obtained her divorce and took back the name Clark. Despite her statements to Sylvia Tone regarding her sadness at the state of Whitey's life, her animosity soon became apparent. In addition to changing to her previous married name of Clark, she blacked out his name on every newspaper or magazine article written about her that was in her scrapbooks.

Memorial to Georgie

In the fall of 1971 a group of seven people headed by John Kelly of Glendale, California, decided to memorialize Georgie while she was still alive. Kelly's letter to River Rats read:

> Bob Pearson and I got to talking this summer; I mentioned that there was a memorial to John D. Lee near Lee's Ferry . . . a lake was named after John Wesley Powell . . . and a plaque was put up near Navajo Bridge for Nevills. Of course the major trouble with these recognitions is that they were all given after the people involved were dead. . . .
>
> Therefore, and inasmuch as Georgie's trips provided an immeasurable amount of pleasure and a large sense of appreciation of the wilderness to a great many people, Pearson and I decided that the least we could do was to put up a plaque for her while she is still very much alive and running rivers.
>
> Bob said that it should be put in Moki Canyon because Georgie's first dog [Sambo 1, who used to go along on all of the Glen Canyon trips wearing his "dog" life preserver] always had a ball in Moki Canyon and that Georgie said if ever there was a paradise on earth for animals, and particularly Sambo, it was Moki Canyon.
>
> So that's the reason for the inscription on the plaque, "Sambo's Paradise." . . .

Six of these great friends who were actually responsible for putting the plaque in place were Chuck and La Costa Sweet, Mary Tinley, Joe Yott, Margaret Rybak and my wife, Marge. We seven got there on a Sears 15' rubber boat and a canoe, all with 3 H.P. motors. . . .

The plaque has been fastened to the sandstone wall in a spot where it is conceivable that the proposed lake elevation of 3700' could eventually cover it. However, we seriously doubt that the lake will go above 3620' for several good reasons. If it appears that the lake *will* rise above 3620' we'll go back and relocate it, although that may require moving a piece of sandstone wall. . . .

I have written Georgie a long letter telling her who, what, why (along with some color enlargements) and also that perhaps many River Rats would be interested in a Georgie operated Lake Powell trip . . . . However, there is a good possibility that she may consider Lake Powell the graveyard of hundreds of needlessly drowned animals and not want any part of such a trip.

If by chance she does go, I'm sure that some of us will want to go with her. If she does not, you are certainly welcome to go next year with the seven of us for one or two weeks.[17]

Keep your sleeping bags dry,

(signed) Kelly

This bronze plaque was placed in Moki Canyon September 6, 1971:

THIS IS AN EXPRESSION OF

AFFECTION AND ESTEEM FOR

GEORGIE WHITE

WOMAN OF THE RIVERS

A VALIANT PIONEER OF THE COLORADO.

A FRIEND OF THE WILDERNESS. AND AN

INSPIRATION TO THE LEGION OF RIVER RATS.

EVERYTHING IS JUST THE WAY WE LIKE IT.

SAMBO'S PARADISE, 1971.

Although she mentioned the plaque to others, Georgie never went to see it. She was never one to look back. To Georgie, Glen Canyon was in the past, its beauty buried forever beneath six hundred feet of icy water.

17 Changing Faces and Changing Rules, 1972–1975

By 1972 a multi-million dollar commercial industry had been built up to accommodate tourists who wished to boat on the wild rivers of the nation. On the Colorado River in the Grand Canyon alone tourism had increased from 70 users in 1955 to 16,432 in 1972.[1] Campsites on the Colorado were usually narrow sand beaches, and in many parts of the canyon they were very limited. The large number of people visiting scenic spots and heavily used beaches posed problems of congestion, disappearing firewood, and disposal of human waste and kitchen refuse. Furthermore, fluctuating clearwater releases from Glen Canyon Dam were eroding these beaches. In order to determine what effect this increase in use was having on the resource and visitors' experiences, the Park Service decided to limit 1973 and subsequent use to the 1972 level.

New Regulations

Georgie was just getting used to being regulated by the National Park Service after having had a free run of the river for so many years when:

> In December 1972, the NPS announced without warning its plan: the number of persons allowed to float the river would be reduced until the total dropped to almost one-half of what the allocation was in 1971 (96,000 passenger days); and there would be a 25 percent cutback of outboard motors on the river in 1974 and each subsequent year until 1977, when all motors would be eliminated. Only oar-powered floats would be allowed.[2]

If implemented, these regulations would put Georgie and several other companies out of business. To fight these harsh restrictions, several outfitters launched a two-pronged attack, using legislative and judicial means.

In May 1973 the outfitters filed suit, asking for an injunction against the NPS actions. They appealed to the Tenth Circuit Court of Appeals in November 1973. When the case was about to be heard, the NPS suddenly indicated there would be no cutbacks in 1974 with respect to motor use and no further cutbacks in passengers, pending further study.

The NPS said it had suspended reduction of passenger allotments to river operators, but kept insisting the phase-out of motorized river boats be accomplished by 1977. The policy brought a wave of opposition.

Siding with the outfitters, Senator Frank E. Moss of Utah testified that "the greatest impact upon the Canyon floor is the constant fluctuation in the Colorado River caused by the varying amount of water permitted to pass through the Glen Canyon Dam." He added, "There exist few facts—if any—to explain what damage is created by river travelers."[3]

Operators like Georgie could make a three-hundred-mile trip through the canyon in ten days. Abolishing motors would mean a thirty to one hundred percent increase in the time required to make the same trip. This meant passengers would be on the water for longer periods of time each day but have less time for side trips, exploration, and appreciation of scenic areas. In addition, the cost of a motor-driven float trip at that time was averaging around $350. With oar-powered rigs, the cost would double or even triple. It would, in effect, restrict floats only to the wealthy.

Nevertheless, in September 1973 the NPS restricted the number of passengers permitted on certain types of watercraft, claiming the action was necessary for safety. Georgie's big boat could now carry only twenty passengers instead of the thirty or more she had been used to taking.

Despite all the opposition by outfitters and members of Congress, the NPS also went ahead and invoked the regulation prohibiting the use of motors in the Grand Canyon. In retaliation, Congress held up funding for the Park Service until the regulation was rescinded. That put an end to the matter.

Death at House Rock Rapid

Mae Hansen and her husband had been on a dozen or more trips with Georgie, and Mae had become her close friend. After her husband died, Mae continued her trips. On one occasion she was washed overboard. When someone asked her afterwards how she felt, she said, "Oh, I must be calm, I must be calm or Georgie will never take me again."[4] Orville Miller said that she did not fight to stay up, to keep her face up and out! He said that she would have drowned if they had not grabbed her by the hair and pulled her out of the river.

At the end of the season, around November, Mae would give a big party for her River Rat friends, a sort of annual reunion. Carol Hintze said, "Half of us camped out in her backyard down in Santa Monica." Bob Pearson said, "Mae was the type of person you would think would be very much at home on a cruise ship or in a more sophisticated setting than, say, on a river trip."[5] But she loved the river trips and adapted herself beautifully.

On July 10, 1973, Georgie led off from Lee's Ferry for another run through the Grand Canyon. Mae was a passenger in one of the triple rigs that followed. She had ridden the little rafts the year before for the very first time and had said then it was so much fun she was certainly going to do it again. The first set of triple rigs entered House Rock Rapid at Mile 17 and was instantly fighting wildly just to remain upright. The rapid, which was normally rather mild, had changed somewhat due to rock movements or other causes. The boatmen said there was a tremendous hole never seen before. When they got through they looked back immediately to watch the second set of rafts and discovered it was already upside down with people hanging onto the outside. Those on the first raft pulled for shore, landed, and hurried as fast as the rocky shores would permit to try to reach the second set of boats and pull them in.

They got the raft to shore in quiet water and two people came out from under the raft where there was about a foot of air space. It was not until some minutes later when they started counting noses that they realized Mae was not among them. It was then they started feeling around under the boats, and found her under one of them.

There was no sign that she had struggled or tried to save herself. The other two people did not even know she was there. Mae was a heavy woman, and nobody will ever know whether she had a heart attack, was struck on the head and could not help herself, or was otherwise restricted by baggage and ropes from moving into an air space. The temperature was 102 degrees outside and 40 degrees in the river. They tried CPR, but it was ineffectual.

Both rafts stopped right there for the night, even though it was early afternoon. Two other charters came by, including Hatch River Expeditions, and both of these big rafts had radios. Despite this, neither of them could make any contact at all with the outside world. They finally said they would go on downriver, trying to make contact as they went, hoping to catch up with Georgie. The next morning the two sets of little rafts took off, leaving the head boatman of the second set with Mae's body. He was there the day of the accident and all the next day, and then sometime on the third day a helicopter came in to make the pick-up. They flew the boatman and the body to Phoenix, where Mae was cremated. Memorial services were held in Santa Monica several days after the trip ended and Georgie was off the river.

Georgie knew about the accident the night it occurred, but there was nothing she could do to help. Apparently she had to go all the way to Phantom Ranch at Mile 87 before she could get through to the outside world. Most of the people on this trip did not know Mae; some had barely met her, some not at all, since it was the first day out.

Although there were several who were shaken up and even frightened, Georgie managed to keep things going as near to normal as possible. The trip still had to go on. It must have been extremely hard for Georgie because Mae was a dear friend, and Georgie did not have many intimate friends.

According to Tom Bradshaw, there was a dispute over what had caused the raft to upset. Some said it was a case of not keeping the pressure in the boat high enough and it shrinking in the cold water, so that when they hit the rapid the limp raft folded up and capsized. A lot of people, including Georgie and Orville, seemed to think Mae had a death wish and really wanted to die in the canyon. They said she had been despondent over the loss of her husband. For Georgie, this may have been a defense, because up to then she had never lost a passenger.

Carol Hintze and Sylvia Tone, who were close friends of Mae's mother, went to stay with and comfort her when they heard about the accident. It was extremely difficult for the mother, as she had outlived both of her children. She said, "Mae went the way she'd like to go, on the River."

Boatmen Talk of Georgie

At an earlier time, Georgie mentioned to Pete Thompson that there were times when her boatmen had difficulty working together in a tight situation. Thompson told her to try using firemen, as they are trained to work together in tight situations. She followed his suggestion, and the firemen proved to be very reliable; they worked well together and soon made up the majority of her boatmen. These firemen loved Georgie and the river, and it was a place where they could let their hair down. They saved most of their vacation time to run trips with her.

Harvey Lee Hall, one of the few boatmen for Georgie who was not a fireman, said:

> I think when fire-fighters started running for Georgie it became a brotherhood and probably that wildness was simply a carry-over from a lot of the hi-jinks that goes on at the fire-house. And guys getting together in any circumstance, but especially fire-fighters; it's just a contest to see who can gross each other out. And I think that's what we were privy to.[6]

The first time Dan Dierker met Georgie was in 1972. He was running a triple rig with Don Neff, who had worked for Georgie back in the '60s. He said Georgie really liked Don. "The first time I met Georgie was up at the Ferry," he says, "We were getting the triple rig ready to go and Georgie already had a boat in the water; was kind of holding court in the evening out there." Dan was going to hop up on her boat and check it out when Don Neff pulled him back and told him, "No, Dan, you aren't jumping up on Georgie's boat unless you're asked." Georgie noticed this and asked them aboard, so he was introduced to her. She had her classic can of Coors beer in hand and they exchanged greetings and talked a bit about Dan's brother, Brian, whom Georgie already knew.

Dan said he was working for Dick McCallum at that time and Dick did a lot of things in the Georgie fashion. He said, "Ours was a rowing triple rig where we had three Green Rivers [seventeen-foot professional neoprene rafts, similar in size to the Navy ten-man, although lighter in weight] side by side. We ran it with two oars. It was an outfitters dream, because you were only paying two boatmen."[7] McCallum's crew was also serving meals out of an inflatable wading pool, Georgie-style. But by that time Georgie was using outboard motors on her triple rigs.

Dan Dierker said it was fun to watch Georgie line up to run Crystal Rapid. He said he and fellow boatmen would stand on shore and tell their passengers, "Okay, now she's going to swing her around there, now she's going to get down in the motor well." They would say this right before Georgie did everything and the people would look at them and say, "Oh, you've seen this before." He said it was always a thrill to watch Georgie ride the water.

Dan never saw Georgie lose her cool. He never saw her screaming-mad angry. "I saw her ticked off, but I never saw her losing her cool or out of control. She was a pretty cool cookie."

When Penny Meo made her first trip with Georgie, she rode on one of the little boats. That first trip was quite an experience for Penny. It was different from anything she had ever done in her life. She said, "It was the first time I'd actually gone on a vacation without Mom and Dad or anybody else." Penny did not have much contact with Georgie her first trip except at the beginning and at camps and lunch stops. But she fell in love with the river and kept coming back.

Penny used her vacation time every year to go down the river with Georgie and soon began going twice each summer. She said:

> I will say this for Georgie, she's helped me come out of a shell that I had been in for years. I used to be the type of person that would go off in a corner and cry when somebody strange or new would talk to me. And with running the river and working the Sports and Boat Show with her I learned to be able to talk to people better. You know, they didn't scare me off. So I owe her a lot in that respect.[8]

When Jeff Webber graduated from high school, his parents gave him a river trip as a graduation gift. When they arrived at Lee's Ferry he met Georgie. Jeff really fell in love with running the river. When the trip was over and they were de-rigging at Temple Bar, he said to Georgie, "You don't have to pay me anything. I just want to learn how to do this, because I've never experienced anything quite like this before. This is the most thrilling thing I've ever done."

Georgie sat back and looked at him with those piercing blue eyes that could look right through you. Then she said, "Meet me at Lee's Ferry next May." And she walked away.

So the next May, even though he had not been in contact with Georgie for months, Jeff packed up his car and drove the several hundred miles to Lee's Ferry. When he arrived, not a soul was around.

After sitting there for about three hours he began to think, "I can't believe I drove eight hours for nothing." Other boaters had come in and began rigging their boats. But no Georgie. He thought, "She probably forgot all about me."

Then late in the day Georgie's truck pulled in. Jeff was sitting on the hood of his car and as the truck went by Georgie stuck her head out of the side window and said, "Jeff. Are you ready to go to work?"

Georgie had remembered. Jeff said, "I think that one thing she really liked was that I was there *ahead* of her." Georgie put him to work tying boats together, getting the gear separated, and other preparations for the trip. He worked that way for about four summers.[9]

Ludwig "Lud" Fromme and his wife, Kathryn, took their first trip with Georgie in 1972. Lud was thrilled with the experience and quickly found out how she got her boatmen, who were mainly Los Angeles City firemen. He told Georgie he was seriously interested in becoming a boatman for her.

The next year she needed a replacement and called Lud, asking if he could get a first aid card, get CPR certified, and be there in time. He later said, "No way was I going to turn that down. I made it, never to have regrets." The bottom line was that he ran mainly two trips a year from 1973 to 1989, when he retired as her senior boatman. Lud wrote:

> I learned a lot from her about the river—having started from scratch. She had a good handle on gradually getting her boatman to "think" a little like her—which helped a lot in critical situations—because the boatman in charge would ask himself—what would Georgie do—and it usually worked out for the best.[10]

In a letter to the author, Lud recalled several things that stood out in his mind about Georgie. For instance, if a boatman would goof off or make an obvious mistake in judgment, she would avoid talking to him. If she was avoiding a specific boatman, it meant that he was on "her list." If the error was serious enough, he would not be invited back. This happened once when a boatman was careless in tying up the thrill boat on which he was assigned. He tied the boat to a large rock on an island and went off hiking. The tie needed to be high enough that rising water would not dislodge the line. The water rose while they were away, and the boat broke loose and floated away.

Ron McIntyre's boat flips in Crystal—the man at bottom is Lud Fromme.
Photo by Don Scutchfield, courtesy of Lud Fromme, by permission of Kathleen Scutchfield.

Georgie White with her big boat at Lee's Ferry in the mid-seventies.
Courtesy of Mildred Hooper.

Lud wrote, "We were downstream at a lunch camp when we saw the boat coming. Georgie thought they were playing a joke by laying low so as not to be seen, but it soon became apparent that the boat was empty." Fortunately the boat was stopped before it got too far. Another outfitter "delivered" the passengers and embarrassed crew to Georgie's camp. She never said "boo" to the boatman responsible, and he never worked as a boatman again.

One thing Michael Denoyer remembered about Georgie was that she always had a smile on her face. He said, "I don't know if she was just naturally happy or if it was the Coors beer that made her happy. Anyway, she always had that big smile on her face."[11]

In 1973 Denoyer was working for Whitewater River Expeditions. The manager of the company, Paul Thevenin, and Denoyer had driven to Lee's Ferry to rig their boats. When they pulled in at the ramp, Georgie's rigs were spread out all over the place; Georgie and her crew were nowhere to be found.

Denoyer asked Paul, "How are we going to get our boats in?"

"Just go on down there and untie one of Georgie's boats and move it up or down stream a bit, so we can slide our boats in. She won't mind that."

So Denoyer went down and untied one of her boats and moved it downriver a short distance. After he tied up the bow line he looked up and saw Georgie coming down the ramp with a big smile on her face.

All of a sudden the smile disappeared and she said, "Young man. What are you doing moving my boat?" He told her he just moved it down a little bit, just enough so they could have room to push their boats in. The next thing Denoyer knew she put both hands on his shoulders and shoved him back, and said, "You don't touch my boats. Don't you go messing around with my boats."

He said, "I'm sorry. We just needed enough room to get our boats in the water."

About that time she shoved him again and said, "I don't want you touching my boat." She shoved him pretty hard—and would not let up. Then she took a swing at him and hit him on the shoulder. He later said, "It wasn't going to kill me, but I sure could feel it." Then she took another swing and hit him again. Denoyer was backing up all this time and trying to figure out how to get out of the situation gracefully. He was not about to punch a woman out, thinking, "She would probably kick my butt anyway." Then she said, "You don't think I'll hit you between the legs, do you?"

Denoyer was not about to find out. He looked behind her, saw about a dozen Los Angeles firemen, and did not want to mess with any of them. He pushed her away, walked past the firemen, and headed toward his own truck. When he got there Thevenin was rolling up the windows and locking the doors. He didn't want any part of it.

Denoyer said:

Anyway, that was my introduction to Georgie. We used to laugh about it in later years. She was just a very kind lady. I had all the respect in the world for her. She had lots of input from a lot of folks. She was the one who started commercial river running in a big way as far as I know. With all her shows and parties and movies—and after the shows she'd get more people signed up for the following year. She really got the word of Grand Canyon river running around. She was quite an inspiration.

Georgie believed in entertaining her passengers, and her boatmen fell into the spirit of it. Libby "Foxy" Weimer reported one stunt the boatmen pulled off from time to time:

After Blackberry and supper, we hear lots of noise and commotion in Jeff's camp. . . . Coming into camp is this creature led by animal trainer Jeff. Jeff's hat is a bailing bucket, his whip a rope attached to a stick. The space-blanketed creature is none other than "Jomo," the elephant whose trunk is fashioned from an inflation hose for the boats. After a few insipid tricks we wonder what was so hilarious in Jeff's camp. Jeff asks for a volunteer—"Foxy Lady." What now? Jeff asks me to lie down on the sand in front of Jomo and again the elephant performs perfunctory tricks such as putting his foot on my chest ever so gently. Then Jomo is requested to step over the lady, carefully, oh, so carefully. Jomo steps over me halfway— Wham—squirts about a quart of water on me as if he's peeing. Brought down the house! Inside "Jomo" were Skutch and Charlie, both boatmen.[12]

Shenanigans like this were part of the attraction that brought Georgie's passengers and boatmen back again and again.

18 Georgie's Effect on Passengers, 1976–1979

$\mathscr{P}$ark Ranger Tom Workman first met Georgie in May of 1976 when she was sixty-five years old. Her light brown hair was stiff and tangled from long contact with river silt, and her dark, tanned skin hung in loose folds around her knees and elbows. Her face was seamed like the rocks of the canyon she loved. But the muscles underneath that skin were tough as rope, and those turquoise eyes flashed with authority.

Workman was the first National Park Service ranger to be assigned to the Lee's Ferry ramp area. He said when he first met Georgie he thought, "Is this woman nuts?" Then, as he learned more of her history, he realized what an incredible person she was. He enjoyed being stationed there because he got to talk to her so often. From the beginning he and Georgie became fast friends. They shared the same birthday and exchanged cards or telephone calls on that day.[1]

Tom told of an incident that occurred during the motor-oar controversy, while the Park Service was still trying to phase out motors. Georgie had been edgy and worried about it. A private trip was waiting to use the ramp to launch, but Georgie was rigging her boats and taking up the entire area. She told them, "I've got my stuff here, and when I'm done you can bring your gear in and rig your boats." This did not sit well with them, and they complained to Workman.

Tom went over to her and said, "Georgie, you've got to be a little cooperative and work things out here on the launch ramp." That started an argument, which really took Tom by surprise because they had never argued. Tom could see her frustration as she kept referring to "these rowing people." He realized she was taking out her frustration on them over the whole situation. Finally he said to her, "Listen. You're an outfitter and if you don't come in line, you won't leave me any alternative but to either mark it down or give you a citation."

At that she retorted, "Oh, you can go ahead and do that." And then she railed about "You Park Service . . . this and that." Then Georgie broke one of her own rules. She started to cry. Tom started crying too. Everybody in the ramp area was watching this confrontation, and Tom did not want to talk any longer after he began crying, so he just walked away.

The next day they apologized to each other, hugged, kissed, and made up. Then, with everybody looking on, Georgie grabbed Tom by his long hair, yanked him over backwards, and jumped on top of him. They both began laughing uproariously as they rolled around in the dirt. Afterward, she let the paddlers launch their boats.

Tom Prange was one of Georgie's fireman-boatmen. He remembers the influence Georgie's philosophies had on him and other people. One of these was her expression "Just the way we like it." She tended to take life as it came, and that was difficult for a lot of people. She stressed that. He also remembered her saying, "You can feel sorry for anybody you want to that's hurt or has bad luck, but don't ever feel sorry for yourself."[2]

In recalling other things about Georgie, Prange said, "Her back massage would take about two pounds of skin off your back! And I had my hair brushed by her several times and that was like losing your scalp!"

Prange told of an Asian woman they had one trip. He said she was a true Oriental and had a very reserved look—the quiet type. She could give foot massages by walking on your back. He said, "And I mean, she just left 'Brownie' [Don Brown] and I useless a couple of times, you know, just by this massage."

Prange said they hiked up a canyon one time, and he found some rocks that were exactly the same size as eggs. He took a carton up there and filled it with a dozen of those "eggs." Then he put them in with Georgie's supply and made sure they got into her egg ration for the next day. She was sure that the Asian woman had done this because of her stoic look and "no one else would have the patience." She explained it to Prange several times how it had to be this woman. Then she talked one of the men into going down to the woman's sleeping bag to slip those rocks in after dark, and he almost got killed by this "stoic" lady.

Tom Bradshaw said on his early trips with Georgie she would talk at the drop of a hat. He said:

> You could just ask her, "What do you know of . . . what is this place down here?" And she would take you on a great story that you'd just be enthralled with and you would hope that the boat didn't move too quickly because you felt that the story was going to be much longer, and it usually was, than the flow of the river would allow you to remain there while she was telling the story. I missed that in the later years. But I did have the benefit of it.[3]

On her second trip, Bradshaw's daughter, Kelly, rode on the single boat on which a boatman named Don "Scutch" Scutchfield was the leader. During the night no one woke up to tend the boat, and in the morning they found the S-rig high and dry due to the falling river. Scutch got up and was fumbling around while everybody else was just beginning to stir. He suddenly heard or saw Georgie's boat coming from a distance. He started screaming, "Mother's coming! Please help me! Everybody, please help me! Please! Mother's coming!" He ran through camp to get everybody out of their sleeping bags. Soon a group of people was out by the boats and he was going, "One, two, three, heave! One, two, three, heave!" They got the boat in the water just in the nick of time, so she never saw it. Georgie waved as she went by and he waved back. Afterward Scutch walked around saying, "Oh, thank you! Thank you, everybody, so much!" She definitely had everybody under control, even when she was not there.

Rosalyn "Roz" Jirge went on her first river trip with Georgie in 1977. She had seen Georgie on the television program *Bold Venture* when she was a teenager and was fascinated by Georgie. She could not believe that anybody would do what Georgie did, especially a woman. Roz was never brought up to go camping or get dirty, so she shoved the whole idea of going down the river to the back of her mind. Almost twenty years later, she and her husband went to a camping program given by *Sunset Magazine* in Menlo Park, California. There she learned Georgie was still running rivers.

Roz thought, "Oh, my goodness, Georgie White is still alive. And she's still doing this thing. She must be ancient by now." Roz was told about a party Georgie was giving in Berkeley in January, and she talked her husband into attending with her. She was fascinated by the movies of previous years' trips, but her husband, Jagdish, took one look at those films and decided it was not for him. A few years later, in 1977, she told him, "I really want to go." He told her, "If you want to go, you go alone."

During the trip Roz asked if she could help Georgie at the San Francisco Boat Show the following year. Georgie said, "Sure." From then on they were bosom buddies.

One day while they were waiting for the small boat, Georgie decided to hold the initiation for the first-timers, all very apprehensive as to what was going to happen to them. In speaking of the initiation the night before, Penny had warned Roz not to speak unless spoken to, but she would not tell her anything else. Georgie just laughed wickedly.

The first-timers were blindfolded, then led around an obstacle course. Afterward, Georgie went down the line of inductees and asked questions about the rapids and campsites. Roz answered her first two questions correctly, then goofed on the third and easiest one of all. The result was bailing buckets full of water in her face, enough to practically drown her. One time she giggled quietly (she thought) at someone's incorrect answer and really got it. After agreeing that everything was "just the way we like it," they were swatted on the rump, allowed to stand up, their blindfolds removed, and then given a good, healthy swig of blackberry liqueur. Roz said, "It was really fun— I haven't laughed so much in years."

Open Dam and Great Rides

Michele Strutin, a writer for *New West* magazine traveling with Georgie in 1978, reported that while approaching President Harding Rapid Georgie had fixed the river with an iron gaze, ready to cramp the boat on to the left, swing around to the right, and hit the middle of the rapid, avoiding the treacherous rock in the center. Somehow the boat went too far towards the bank, the left pontoon slid high up on the rock, and passengers and boatmen were suddenly staring down into the laps of the people sitting in the middle. Then the undertow grabbed the right pontoon, sucked it under, and rolled the whole doughnut 180 degrees.

Some of the gear was gone, still tied on but somewhere below the churning water's surface—and three people vanished with it. Soon the heads of a boatman and two passengers broke the surface. They scrambled to get back on the boat before it would crash into the opposite cliffs. Passengers in the middle pontoon reached over the side,

Initiation into Royal River Rats. *Courtesy of L. C. B. McCullough.*

pulling their comrades out of the water as Georgie angled hard into the current. Georgie said it was the first time a pontoon had turned in ten years.[4]

Prior to the start of the trip, two park rangers had informed Georgie they would have good water part of the way. There was a V.I.P. in the canyon, and extra releases would be made from the dam to assure him a good ride. Georgie told her group, "Hey, you know, there's a man from Washington—Mr. Whalen [William J. Whalen, Park Service director]—going down with the Park Service this trip. They're going to open the dam for him and we'll get some big water."[5] She explained that Whalen was going down the Colorado to get first-hand experience to help answer the motor-versus-oars controversy. The Park Service would open the dam floodgates when Whalen was downriver in order to illustrate that the river ran fast enough to obviate the need for motors. As a result, Georgie's party had great rides through Unkar, Hance, and Hermit Rapids on about twenty thousand cfs of water.

Strutin, who had been riding with Georgie, transferred to one of the triple rigs. At Crystal Rapid the boat was pulled quietly, ominously, by the current. It rolled into the first hole, then the second, and finally the third—the "hole with no bottom." The boat plunged and then climbed high up the wall of water and danced almost upright. For a second the rafts stood poised on end, and then they flipped, riding out Crystal upside down. Some people were thrown out into the river; the rest clung to ropes underwater or became trapped between the boat and the slapping water. The boatmen were on top first, pulling people from under the boat. It took three hours to untie and right the boats, then retie them and attach the soaked gear.[6]

Family Trip for Jirge

In July 1978 Roz Jirge made a second Grand Canyon trip with Georgie. This time she was accompanied by her nine-year-old daughter, Asha; her brother-in-law, Ralph Weisner; and nieces Leslee, age fourteen, and Hayley Weisner, age twelve.

Since the Park Service allowed only forty people per trip, Georgie divided her passengers up with forty on her side and forty with the firemen. She ran the lead boat herself. Behind the big boat ran two sets of triple rigs and a single S-rig. The two trips were required to camp separately.

Georgie fixing Asha Jirge's hair in a Navajo bun. Georgie loved young children and took them on her big boat for their safety and to shield them from the sometimes bawdy activities of those on her other boats. *Courtesy of Rosalyn Jirge.*

Camp in Marble Canyon, July 1976. *Courtesy of Dan Jewell.*

The boats were packed with food, extra motors, portable toilets, and cases of Coors beer. It took a while to sort out the passengers, but generally the older people and families headed for the big boat. The fearless types went for the smaller "thrill" boats.

The second day on the river was relatively calm. Hayley wrote in her journal, "We went to Redwall Cavern. It doesn't look that big at all from far away: it looks like a little hole in the wall. But from close up it looks like the biggest thing in the world." She added later, "A man named Major Powell thought that he could fit 50,000 people in. But I don't."[7]

On Roz's family trip, Hermit Rapid's waves were huge. It proved to be the best ride of day three. Leslee, Asha, and Hayley were enjoying all of the big rapids. Roz was concerned that her little daughter, especially, would be fearful of the high, rough, waves, but Asha fooled her—she laughed all the way.

A couple of days later the water had dropped to less than five thousand cfs. Georgie pulled up to a beach at about 10:30 A.M. to wait for the water to come up before running Bedrock Rapid. Roz said their stay on the beach turned out to be great fun.

Hayley said, "We went to about Mile 125 and we stopped to wait for the water to come up. While we waited this guy named Scott taught Asha and me how to make drip mud castles. It wasn't easy at first, but after a while we got pretty good, if I do say so myself."

They pulled up to camp on Lake Mead, and Roz could hardly believe her eyes. Gone was the lovely soft sand and the beautiful slim peninsula that had jutted out into the lake the previous year. The entire area was covered with rocks. Georgie pointed out sleeping areas on both sides of the boat. Arms loaded with a camera bag, canteen, and the plastic bag holding their rain suits, Roz shinnied off the raft. Then, as she stepped over a mooring line to follow her brother-in-law, she tripped and took a dreadful, twisting fall, letting out an involuntary scream. Horrendous waves of pain went up her right ankle. The ankle began swelling immediately and the pain was excruciating. She tried to laugh and joke about it, but inside she was almost dying of embarrassment and shame. How could she have been so careless? To make it safely through the rapids and then trip coming out of the boat!

On Tuesday, July 18, Roz heard Georgie's alarm clock go off at 3:30 A.M., then fell back to sleep for a while. She awoke later to the sound of pots clanking in the kitchen area. When the hot water was ready, Georgie fixed some coffee laced with blackberry cordial and brought it to where Roz was sleeping. When asked if it was not too early for that type of liquid, Georgie laughingly said it was necessary because "she was out of cream and sugar."

At the end of her journal Leslee wrote, "If I can raise the money, I'm going again next year, too!" Asha wrote, "We hugged everybody and kissed everybody (almost). I didn't want to go . . . . This has been my favorite vacation in a long time. I want to do it again someday."[8]

Passengers frequently composed songs about Georgie and their trips. The Jirges' family trip produced the "Royal River Rats' Salute to Georgie." It was sung to the tune of "She'll Be Comin' 'round the Mountain when She Comes." It began:

> She'll be comin' down the rapids with her Coors!
> She'll be comin' down the rapids with her Coors!
> She'll be comin' down the rapids
> She'll be comin' down the rapids
> She'll be comin' down the rapids with her Coors!

The song continues for fourteen verses, each line repeating as above:

> She'll be ridin' a silver raft when she comes!
> She'll be wearin' a leopard-skin swim suit when she comes!
> She'll be yellin' at the boatmen when she comes!
> She'll be drinkin' blackberry cordial when she comes!
> There'll be 87 drunks when she comes!
> She'll be eatin' canned tomatoes when she comes!
> She'll serve hard-boiled eggs at 10 when she comes!
> She'll yell "slide down in your seat" when she comes!
> She'll be yellin' "watch your feet" when she comes!
> She'll be runnin' on one spark plug when she comes!
> She'll be grinnin' at the rapids when she comes!
> She'll be blastin' on that air horn when she comes!
> And her name is Georgie Clark when she comes!

Georgie blowing her horn to call in the troops, Bridge Canyon camp. *Courtesy of Rosalyn Jirge.*

19 Georgie Breaks an Arm, 1980–1982

$\mathcal{I}$n 1980 Tom Vail was a passenger on one of Georgie's small triple rigs. The raft required three boatmen, but when they launched from Lee's Ferry, there were only two. One of the boatmen had not shown up. After they pushed off, Chuck Kane, the trip leader, asked Tom if he wanted to row. Tom later said, "He probably asked me because I'd brought the most beer, so I must be the most qualified. I said, 'Sure, that sounds like fun.'" So Tom rowed a triple rig on that trip.

Halfway through the canyon Kane's group double-camped with Georgie. Chuck took Tom over to introduce him to Georgie, and that was his first meeting with her. Georgie had a way of testing people when she met them:

> We ended up standing right next to each other . . . she put her arm up on my shoulder and she says, "Oh, you're Tom. I hear you're doing a pretty good job." And with that, she swung around and kneed me in the groin. Not hard enough to put me to my knees, but enough that I felt it. And, I'd heard enough stories about Georgie at this point that I knew what she was doing. . . . "How's this kid going to react?" So my reaction to it . . . I put my arm around her, and I said, "Okay, Georgie, you and me, up into the bushes, right now!" Of course, my biggest fear in the world was that she'd go with me.[1]

Tom went on to become a steady boatman for Georgie.

Roz Jirge continued to make annual trips with Georgie. On an August 1980 trip they made a stop for "egg break" at about Mile 30 and met up with the firemen's group. On Georgie's boat egg break, a brunch of sorts, was just that—hard boiled eggs and salt. Here, Roz learned how the other boats fared. She noted, "Egg break is a feast on the little boat. There were corn tortillas, eggs (of course), bacon bits, salami, chilies, olives, mushrooms, smoked oysters—the list seemed to go on and on." In later years Georgie took her cue from the jealous complaints of the passengers on the big boat. She brought many of the goodies suggested by the firemen, although she drew the line at smoked oysters.

In 1980 Brian Rasmussen also took a trip with Georgie. He was twenty years old and had spent the summer working at Marble Canyon Lodge. Before going back to school at Northern Arizona University in Flagstaff, he purposely quit his job at Marble Canyon Lodge two weeks before school started in order to try to get in a river trip. He had been on two trips before and was hoping to get his foot in the door with one of the outfitters. He hung around the Lee's Ferry launch ramp looking for a possibility to go down the river.

During his two years of employment at Marble Canyon Lodge, Rasmussen had come to know Georgie, and she just happened to be rigging out a trip while he had that window of time to do one. He asked her and she said she could use an extra hand. He ended up swamping (being a helper) on one of her motor rigs, the "Swinging Single."

The one event that really stood out in Rasmussen's mind in the time he spent around Georgie occurred early in the trip, on the second or third night. The usual routine before dinner had been that a few bottles of blackberry cordial be passed around. There was also hot water for tea or coffee. It was cocktail hour and would get to be a big, festive occasion, with everyone socializing and visiting.

On this night near the Little Colorado River, with the sun going down and the colors intense on the cliffs, Rasmussen was talking to Georgie. She put her arm onto his shoulder and asked how everything was going. She also told him even though this was a fun and festive occasion, and everyone was partying, "you still have to remember where you're at. You're in the Grand Canyon." With that she spun him around to look at the upper cliffs, which were still lit by the setting sun. It was a very spectacular scene, one that he never forgot. While the others were busy partying, Georgie made sure that he appreciated being in the Grand Canyon.[2]

Georgie Sidelined as Pilot

By June of 1981 Roz Jirge had advanced from paying passenger to kitchen helper for Georgie. On arrival at Lee's Ferry she found the boats mostly tied. She said, "There was poor Georgie, with 'one wing clipped,' trying to direct all of the new people." Georgie had broken her left wrist on the previous trip in a freak accident. (As she bent over to adjust a sandal, Georgie's boat had lurched; she flung her arm out for balance and bumped it against the ice chest.)

Prior to her leaving Las Vegas for Lee's Ferry, the doctor had put a heavy cast on Georgie's arm to make sure she would not try using it. She did not like that one bit. The news of Georgie's broken arm traveled fast. Up and down the river, all during the trip, boatmen from other companies stopped to ask how she was doing. Their concern, deep love, and respect for Georgie really touched Roz.

Bill Huff would run the big boat all the way on this trip. It would not be easy, as the water was extremely low—only three to eight thousand cfs. Still, he did a good job running the big boat with Georgie directing him all the way through hand signals. Roz felt sad seeing her sitting there, unable to run her boat. Roz even had to help her tie her shoes, tie her life preserver, and rope her in. Roz said she did not take any photos of her because "it's just not the Georgie we know and love."[3]

Georgie would try to teach her crew the "sign posts" along the river. She asked Roz to pick out Nankoweap and bet her an "Irish Mist" in Las Vegas if she missed it. Roz thought she meant the Indian ruins, not Nankoweap Canyon; needless to say, she lost. She also did not realize Georgie wanted her to pick out the canyon of the Little Colorado River, and she lost again. Roz noted, "The face full of water thrown by Huff has probably burned the location of Nankoweap Canyon in my mind forever."[4]

Georgie allowed the group only a short stay at the Little Colorado, where the water was clear and incredibly blue. Some of the passengers swam in the blue water, while others went to see Ben Beamer's cabin. They could not remain long, however, as Georgie was anxious to get to a particular camp near the sacred Hopi Salt Mines. At the time Roz was unaware that it was illegal for Georgie to camp there. In later years, Ranger Tom Workman made a direct but gentle request to Georgie asking her not to use it. She was fortunate not to have been given a citation for breaking that very important rule.

When they reached camp at the Overhang, a quarter mile below Deer Creek Falls, most of the passengers would not put their beds down inside the cave, in spite of the threatening weather. They were afraid of the bats residing in the crevices.

A canyon wren had made its home above the cave and was singing its glorious, trilling melody. A ring-tailed cat had a den to one side of the cliff. Georgie left food out for it. During the night the beautiful creature scampered right behind their beds and ate the goodies. A skunk also wafted by, cute and stinky. One of them must have sniffed at Roz while she was sleeping; in the morning she discovered little critter prints in the sand right next to her head.[5]

Georgie and Roz got dinner going and waited for Pat Tierney's triple rig. The small boat finally pulled in and they learned that Karen Morse had been seriously injured in Specter Rapid. Karen was one of the rare women Georgie would consider using as a boatman. An oar had hit a rock and slammed into her face. Several teeth were broken and three of them were driven into her jaw almost up to her nose. Her husband, Bob, was almost beside himself with grief. Karen was with Don "Brownie" Brown's group. Boatman Al Stocks (a paramedic) managed to suture her mouth and administer morphine for the pain. They had stopped at Dubendorff Rapid to await a helicopter.

Georgie was upset about this, she said, because of the difficulty of signaling a plane in order to get a helicopter down. She said it would have been wiser to bring Karen to the comfort and safety of the big boat where she could be taken to the helicopter pad below Lava Falls. She was also afraid the chopper would not get there any earlier than if they had gone to Lava, one day farther downstream.

As it happened, though, some park rangers were at Dubendorff when Brownie and Tierney got there. The rangers rowed down to Deer Creek Falls, climbed above the falls, and radioed for help in the more open area of Surprise Valley. In Roz's opinion Georgie's worry was not that it would take as long to get Karen air-lifted from Dubendorff as from Lava Falls; Georgie did not want an accident charged to her company's record and didn't want to pay for the expensive medical evacuation.

Brownie's group pulled in at Lava Falls after running all the way from Dubendorff without any stops, not even Deer Creek Falls. They were running a separate trip, with no support from a second boat, and they wanted to run Lava Falls at the same time as Georgie in case of an accident. From Brown's group they learned the good news that a helicopter had picked up Karen at 7:30 that morning. All of them, and especially Bob, were very relieved that she was now safely in a hospital at the South Rim of the canyon.

After Brownie's perfect Lava run, the big boat continued down the river. Bob went on the small boat to the helicopter pad, where he got a chopper out to join Karen. On the right bank below the Pumpkin Bowl, at an unusually-shaped and colored hot spring at Mile 212 where they had stopped for a pleasant soak in the warm mineral water, the party spotted two wild burros. These animals had somehow managed to escape the round-up by the group "Friends of Animals," as well as the guns of the park rangers. Georgie was ecstatic. She loved those animals. She hoped that one was a male and the other a female and that they would manage to start another herd.

Only three boatmen were allowed to drive the big boat through the main rapids at the time Georgie had her broken arm. These men were Bill Huff, Bob Setterberg, and Chuck Mills. Others were allowed to take over in the slower waters of the lower canyon and Lake Mead. Other than that, Georgie never let anybody run her big boat.[6]

Later that same year (August 1981) Roz Jirge made a second trip on the river, this time as a regular passenger. She opted to ride on one of the smaller boats piloted by Harvey Lee Hall, with Orville and Tom Prange manning the oars. She had some old fears (named Crystal and Lava) she needed to face. At Lee's Ferry the passengers sorted themselves out as to who would ride on which boat. Georgie's boat was being run by Bob Setterberg, as Georgie still had to avoid using her left arm. She was out of the cast, but she had to wear a splint when working. Her boat pulled out first as usual.[7]

Because Roz was getting psyched up for the next day's big rapids, she only managed a fitful sleep. She kept dreaming about Crystal and the "Eater" and "Big Red." Having ridden through the holes and waves in the relative safety of Georgie's boat, she knew just how gigantic Crystal's holes really were.

When it was time for them to make the run, Roz noticed how quiet everyone had become. Crystal was serious business. She prayed Harvey would keep right to avoid the biggest hole. Unfortunately, there were some huge boulders on the right side. Boats as big as Western River Expedition's J-rigs had been wrapped on them and ended up staying there all night long. Roz did not want to camp in the middle of Crystal Rapid.

Georgie with boatman Bob Setterberg, one of only three men allowed to operate Georgie's big boat. *Courtesy of Rosalyn Jirge.*

The thrill boat in Granite Falls Rapid, 1980: motorman Don Brown is being thrown forward; Orville Miller and Tom Prange are at the oars. *Courtesy Rosalyn Jirge.*

The thrill boat at Emery Falls, August 2, 1982. *Courtesy of Ludwig Fromme.*

Everyone made final checks on their life preservers, then they pushed out for the run of Crystal. Roz was near panic. But the ride turned out to be wonderful. Harvey purposely took the boat into the big hole, but he placed it so perfectly it went up and over exactly the way it should. The wave went over the passengers, and suddenly there was a yell. A man had been knocked out of the boat. His wife panicked when she saw her husband in the water. She stood up, let go of the ropes, and began trying to crawl into the outside boat to help him. Roz could see he was already clambering back on, or at least hanging on to the side ropes, so she grabbed the woman and yelled over the roaring water for her to hang on—he was okay. It would not have done any good if she were to be tossed out of the boat along with her husband. All of this took place in the middle of the half-mile-long rapid, and it was over in a matter of seconds. Roz found herself enjoying the rough ride in the little boat more than she had expected to. Her fears vanished and she felt free at last.

After the usual dinner of tomato soup, ham and lima beans, Roz moved her gear close to the kitchen. The "survivors" party was a beaut, with "Stupid" (straight grain alcohol mixed with Koolaid) flowing like mad. That potent stuff tasted like Koolaid but made people do some weird things. One man's wife had got a huge, wet kiss from one of the boatmen. She appeared shocked at the time. Roz suggested she tell him not to kiss her, if she was offended. Apparently she was not. She took off with the man, who came back smiling. The next time they saw her she had taken a walk with another boatman. He came back with the same smile. Then it was a third one's turn. Three boatmen in a row and she was not through yet. She left with the first one again, and later, at about 11 P.M. when the party broke up, her husband could not find her. He was humiliated, but managed to keep his cool.

At the end of the trip Roz declared it to be one of the greatest trips she had taken. She said, "Being on the little boat all the way made it a totally new experience. I enjoy the big boat, but the little one gives you more of a feeling of being a part of the river, rather than just being on it."[8]

20 The Year of the Big Water, 1983

Lake Powell began to form behind Glen Canyon Dam on March 13, 1963. The lake reached "full pool" at the 3,700-foot spillway level on June 22, 1980.[1] Then, heavy precipitation in the Rocky Mountains in the winter of 1982–1983 and rapid snow melt in the spring of 1983 caught the Bureau of Reclamation completely off guard. Therefore, they did not draw down the water level in Lake Powell far enough to take care of the heavy runoff. During June water was surging into the reservoir at the rate of 111,480 cfs, and releases from the dam reached 92,000 cfs, the highest amount of water ever released from Glen Canyon Dam.[2]

In mid-June, as the reservoir neared the spillway level, Reclamation Bureau employees installed four-by-eight-foot sheets of three-quarter-inch plywood bolted to a framework atop the spillway. The water level rose, but miraculously the plywood managed to hold back several feet of Lake Powell. Boaters on the Grand Canyon run were in for high water not experienced since pre-dam days.

When releases from Glen Canyon Dam reached sixty-one thousand cfs the dam began to shake. The concrete linings were being ripped out of the spillway tunnels, and the weir flow shook the dam so badly they could only use one spillway. On Wednesday, June 29, Reclamation officials reported the water level at the dam at 3,706.75 feet, an increase of a quarter of a foot from Tuesday's maximum level. They also reported they were releasing 92,000 cfs from the east spillway of the dam.

Tom Gamble, chief of Colorado River Storage Project power operations, said a "rumbling" noise reported to be heard near the east spillway by engineers descending into the dam had ceased since the releases were increased from 70,000 to 92,000 cfs.[3]

Beginning June 25, 1983, the Grand Canyon National Park superintendent ordered passengers on both commercial and private river trips to walk around Crystal Rapid, allowing only boatmen and swampers to run through it. The closure was due to several incidents at the rapids, one of which resulted in the death of William Russel Wert, 63, of Carbondale, Colorado.

According to the park newspaper, *Visitor Information*, this closure was due to the extreme hazard of Crystal Rapid. Four motor rigs and numerous oar boats had flipped in that huge rapid, and ninety people had been washed into the water. In addition to the one fatality, there had been fifteen injuries.[4] The closure remained in effect from June 25 to July 21.

Georgie did not comply with the order as far as her big boat was concerned. Joan De Fato, who was a passenger with Georgie during that time, said she thought Georgie had permission from rangers to do so because her big boat had never upset and she didn't have enough power to get that huge rig into the eddy below Crystal to pick up passengers. Georgie kept right on going down the middle with all her passengers on board. Closure of the rest of the Colorado River was considered unnecessary. Many other rapids on the river had been virtually washed out because of the high water levels.

In his 1983 *Guide to the Grand Canyon*, boatman Larry Stevens tossed in a plus rating to indicate that Crystal Rapid gets more severe when the river moves faster than 35,000 cfs. On a toughness scale of one to ten, Crystal is rated at or near ten at all water levels, with a ten-plus at high water.

Six People Overboard

Georgie embarked on a trip through the Grand Canyon in mid-June on this high water. The river was moving fast and with incredible power. Below Phantom Ranch she did not realize how fast they were going until they were having "egg break" on the boat above Crystal Rapid and reached the rapid far sooner than expected.

Daryl Bates was one of Georgie's boatman on the big boat that day, and he was seated on the rear of the right side pontoon. Bates said there were also two kids, one about twelve and the other fourteen, on that side.

Bates said that when they arrived at Crystal, Georgie plowed right down the middle as usual. As they hit the big hole they encountered "a huge wave, bigger than you were used to seeing in Crystal." He braced himself, and instead of washing across as a wave usually did, it covered them completely. Then the back-flow came at them. Bates recalls, "All of a sudden I sunk down and my feet went straight up over my head. I was braced to go one way and all of a sudden I was pushed the other way. I was pitched upside down and couldn't hold on."[5]

A ranger who was on shore said Georgie went into the hole and the boat stood on end. Her big boat was thirty-seven feet long and twenty-seven feet wide, but it went into the hole and up the wave and just stopped there. There was water above her and water below, and the boat just shook. It went back down, went up again, and then back down. The second time it went down the right-hand section of boat tucked under. That was when Daryl and five passengers went off, along with all the luggage on that side, including Georgie's personal bag and camera bag. The third time the raft went up, it went over the explosion wave.

When the right pontoon dropped down, the wave washed over the group. Then it washed back into them like a tidal wave. As he went down into the water, Daryl said, "I actually thought I wasn't going to come up. I thought I was gone."

He remembers it as being like when an ocean wave hits you unexpectedly and "you're down under and going all over the place." He was getting ready to take a gulp of water when he looked up or came up and opened his eyes and could see light. At that, he popped out and got a breath of air. Then he was pulled back down again, but was not down quite as long before he popped up again. After going up and down several times, "I was kind of terrified because I wasn't expecting it."

Daryl said he was pointing his feet downriver, drifting with the current until he got into calmer water. He did not know how long it took—maybe a minute. Then he heard someone, he thought it was Georgie, yell, "Get the kid!" At that point he did not have any idea where anyone else was, and he looked over on the right towards the shore and saw one of the boys in the water. The boy was thirty or forty feet away. Daryl tried to swim toward him but the current was so fast he could not get there before being swept past the boy.

Georgie pulled the boat up behind Daryl, and he was able to get back on. As soon as she picked him up she started heading for shore.

That's when he found out others had been washed off the boat too, and that the others had made it to shore.

As soon as Georgie landed and tied up, Daryl started climbing back over the steep terrain to get to those who had made it to shore earlier. Because Georgie was using only a twenty-five-horsepower motor, she did not have enough power to bring the boat into the eddy at the foot of Crystal. It took Daryl about forty-five minutes to get back to where the two boys were. By the time he got there, park rangers who had been up on the bluff overlooking the rapid watching the trouble had already arrived with their kayaks and a small raft and were trying to calm the two terrified boys. It was not far via the river to where Georgie was tied up. The rangers ferried them all down, and they got back on her boat.

Georgie proceeded down to a beach near the "Ross Wheeler," an iron boat abandoned by the Russell-Tadge party in 1915, a place they normally stopped at for a break. Several bags had been ripped off the boat when the people went off in Crystal. Georgie complained that they were not tied on well enough. (When boatmen loaded the bags in the morning they would lay them out in position along the raft. Those were old Navy bags that had D-rings in the back. The boatmen would run a nylon line through the D-rings and tie the ends to a rope on top of the boat with a double half-hitch.)

When Georgie accused the boatmen of not tying the bags on securely, Daryl said to her, "Look, Georgie. The bags were tied on. The line is still there that the bags were tied on with." The force of that monstrous wave had ripped off the patches that held the D-rings to the bags, and the D-rings were still there with the line running through them!

Georgie, of course, would never admit to being wrong. If anyone was washed off the boat they were not holding on, and if bags were lost they were not lashed on properly. She was later quoted as having said about this incident, "Well, they sure don't make passengers like they used to."[6]

Upset in Crystal Rapid

While they were stopped at the "Ross Wheeler" waiting for the other boats to come through, somebody came by and told Georgie's group that Chuck Mills, who was running one of Georgie's S-rigs, had flipped his boat in Crystal and was tied up below it. At that point there was nothing Georgie could do but wait, since Chuck's group was too far upriver. They learned that none of Chuck's passengers were hurt, so after awhile they continued on downriver.

Leading the other half of Georgie's trip, Chuck Mills had left Lee's Ferry a day after she did. He operated a single large raft with fifteen or sixteen passengers. Running with him, Ray Gorospe was the motorman on a triple rig.

Chuck Mills said that on the second day the small boat began to have motor problems. When they got into shore that night just below the Little Colorado River, they worked on the motors. They tinkered around with them again the next morning, getting a later start than they would have preferred.[7] Before they left camp in the morning a note from the Park Service, dropped down from a helicopter, said, "We are releasing up to 80,000 tonight, so camp high, be safe."[8]

They had camped that night just above Lava Canyon Rapid at a place Georgie called "Copper Blossom" (the Tanner Mine). Gorospe had already gone through a couple of spare fifteen-horsepower motors, so they took Chuck's twenty-five-horsepower spare from the single boat and put it on the triple rig.

They pulled in at Crystal about 3 or 4:00 in the afternoon, and went up on the bluff to take a look. Chuck said, "It was a lot different. There was just one big hole almost the width of the river, maybe three quarters of the way across. Me and Ray talked it over and we stayed and camped there that night."

They headed into the rapid about 8 A.M. the next morning. Ray Gorospe went first in the triple rig so that if he had any trouble, Chuck could come through and try to help out. He lined up the triple rig and turned it so they would have the long axis of the boat going through first.

They took off down along the right shore, headed pretty much to where they wanted to go. Gorospe said, "As soon as we got in there I realized that we were dealing with something that we had never dealt with before. The force of the water was so strong it was pushing us right towards the hole." The strong hydraulics sucked the boat into the hole. Gorospe yelled, "Hang on. We're hittin' it." They went completely under water.

When they came out, one boat was tucked underneath the others and three or four people were in the water. Fortunately, the middle boat, which carried the motor, was still upright. So Gorospe was able to get around Big Red, a huge rock below, and over to shore before they got to Tuna Creek Rapid, less than half a mile below. He told everybody, "Hang on, Chuck will be here, and we'll get our bags out of the water and we'll be fine."

Then it was Chuck Mills's turn. He remembers:

> I'm going at a little bit of an angle, trying to get it over to the right side where there was a better channel, and we got into the main part of the rapid. I was trying to get over to the right and we hit a wave there and it wound up flipping the boat. . . .
>
> As soon as I realized what had happened I noticed or felt I had a rope wrapped around my ankles. I struggled a bit, then popped up and got a couple of breaths of air. Then it pulled me back down. I reached around for my knife to cut that rope loose, when all of a sudden it just loosened up and my foot came out. Anyway, I was able to get out from under the boat and I started to get on top of the boat, which is now the bottom of the boat, and I realized that I'd messed up my leg.[9]

Mills was able to climb up on the boat where he saw that everybody was in the water. He got everybody up on the boat, except two of the men who had made it to shore.

Gorospe said he was sitting there looking up the river to see Chuck come through, and when he saw him, something did not look right. As they drew closer, he could see why. Instead of silver, he was seeing black—the bottom of the boat. As they went by only Chuck and a few people were on top; all the rest of the passengers were in the water. Ray decided all they could do was get their boat straightened up, get back on the river, and try to pick them up.

While they were working on their boat, another boat came through, made it okay, and parked on the left. The next few outfits that came through were all upside down. So there were people everywhere, floating along in the water along with equipment and gear boxes.

It took Ray and his crew half an hour or more to get their boat turned around, get it rightside up and lashed together with everything tied back down, and get back on the water. When they got into the current, they saw several people floating in the water but were unable to reach them. These were people from the other concessions. Ray said he tried to throw ropes to them, but even with the motor and the oars the current was too strong. As they drifted down, they saw the Park Service come in with helicopters and drop men down into the water, pulling people out. They finally caught up with Chuck at around Mile

The thrill boat in the "Big Hole" in Crystal Rapid moments before capsizing and leaving four-teen people in the river. *Photo by Don Scutchfield, courtesy of Rosalyn Jirge, by permission of Kathleen Scutchfield.*

111, where his raft had drifted into an eddy, and they were able to get a bow line around a rock and tie up. Other boaters had picked up Chuck's missing passengers and brought them to rejoin him.

More boats stopped to check up on them, and they radioed out to the Park Service for help. Fortunately Chuck's party had landed near a flat spot where a helicopter could land. By noon or one o'clock they were on their way out of the canyon. Chuck Mills said, "We could have turned the boat over with everybody's help, but I couldn't walk and nobody else could run the boat. So I made a decision to cancel the trip."

All the passengers flew out, including those on the triple rig. Chuck Mills also had to be evacuated because his knee was injured very badly and he could not walk on it. Ray told the helicopter pilots, "Georgie's downstream. If you see her tell her we've got problems and tell her what happened to us. Tell her we've got three guys coming down in one triple rig."

When Gorospe and his two boatmen finally caught up with Georgie, he told her what had happened and where they had left her other boat. He said, "Typical Georgie; she never got real excited about anything. She just looked at me and said—she used to call me Half-Breed—'Okay, Breed. It sounds like you did the best you could do.'" And that was it.

Georgie's Lost River Bag

Georgie's personal bag had been washed off her raft in Crystal Rapid. The story of its recovery is related by Mark Austin and Gill Ediger, who were boating with a private trip that launched about the same general time as Georgie. Austin said his group spent a lot of time hiking, but eventually they got down to Lake Mead. Along the way they picked up tons of river booty, placing it up on the shore in obvious places so people could find it on their next trip. They could have only hauled a fraction of it out on their own small boats. Austin said:

> So we got down to the Lake and I saw this black bag floating. And so I pulled up to it, you know. That was one of many. And, anyway, this one particular one I reached over and grabbed it. We had to row to it a little ways. And I reached in and grabbed it and I started digging through it. It didn't take me long before I figured out I'd found Georgie White's personal river bag.[10]

What first tipped them off was the leopard-skin print clothing in the top of the bag. Austin had heard many stories about Georgie, but he had only met her briefly a couple of times. He continued:

> We're digging through this river bag and there was her lucky horseshoe. And I'd heard rumors that she had this lucky horseshoe. It was not a horseshoe. This was like a mule shoe. This was a small horseshoe, or mule shoe. And she claimed it was from "Lucky," the famous burro of the Grand Canyon. And whether that's true or not, who knows. But, at any rate, she told me that when I returned the river bag to her.

Gill Ediger, who was in that same group, kept a log of the trip. According to his log the party spotted the bag while being towed across Lake Mead. He tells it this way:

> We saw a river bag floating along the way, and I whistled at the tow boat. He made a circle and we snatched it out of the water. Turned out to be none other than Georgie White's (only all her ID's said Georgie Clark). We dug through all her gear and laughed a bit at what we found: very few clothes (one change), a purse, a billfold w/pictures from 1938, etc, an address book, a check book for Georgie's Royal River Rats w/the last entry on 20 June (only 4 days earlier), a big stack of business cards for same, a funny little horseshoe, a bag of minimal cosmetics, and an aircraft frequency radio (required by NPS on all commercial boats) worth at least $1,000, which we proceeded to drop in the river and lose.[11]

Austin said the "horseshoe" was wrapped in leopard skin cloth, and inside the bag they also found four hundred dollars in cash. Everything was totally waterlogged. Finally they "dug out a driver's license and there was old Georgie smiling away."

After they got off the river they stopped in Las Vegas, where Austin tried to call Georgie. He telephoned Georgie's sister, Marie, but she had not heard anything about all of the problems on the river. His call to her was the first she knew that anything was wrong. When he told Marie that he had found Georgie's river bag in Lake Mead, she became extremely worried. She asked, "Is Georgie all right?"

Austin could see that she was just getting more concerned. He said, "Well, I'm sure she's all right." While they camped near Serpentine Rapid, several boatmen had stopped by to talk to them and by then everybody knew what had happened. Austin explained to Marie that Georgie was fine and would be in touch with her soon. It took him quite a while to calm her down.

Marie said he could just drop the bag by, but Austin explained that he would really like to return the river bag to Georgie in person. After some time and several calls, he finally set up a time and returned the bag to Georgie at the Showboat Hotel. The first thing she said to him was, "Is my horseshoe in there?"

"Yeah," he told her.

She asked, "And everything else?"

"Yeah."

And then she said, "Well, we don't really need to talk about this. You want a Coors?" That was *it*! That was her total response.

When Austin tried to continue the conversation with her about it by asking what happened, she said, "Well, you know I've never had one problem. . . ." And she just went on and on as if nothing had ever happened. She just did not want to deal with it. But then, about two weeks later he got a nice letter from her, thanking him for returning her belongings.

21 Tragedy at Lava Falls, 1984–1987

*B*y 1984 Georgie, now at age seventy-three, had made some concessions to age. She seldom led hikes in the side canyons but remained with her boats, and she avoided most of the nighttime partying enjoyed by the boatmen and passengers. Soon after supper, while others sipped the traditional blackberry brandy and coffee, Georgie would slip away to her raft to unroll her pad and sleeping bag. By 8:30 P.M. she would be asleep. But her love of the rapids was as strong as ever.

In August 1984 Ray and Norine "Nori" Abrams embarked with Georgie for a trip through the Grand Canyon. This was Ray's sixth trip with Georgie and Nori's second. Ray was almost like a boatman—he enjoyed helping in every way he could. They were a fun couple, both heavy set, but Nori more so.

On the night of August 24 the party camped at Fern Glen Canyon. The next morning they had "egg break" at about 10 A.M. Some of the passengers went on a hike, but Ray and Nori stayed with the boats.[1]

The trip had gone well up to that point. Their crew was very safety conscious. They made sure everyone wore their life jackets and told them to hang onto the safety lines through the rapids. Georgie always took precautions with passengers who she thought might have difficulty. This included having them switch to a seat on the center pontoon rather than ride on the outside sections of the raft. For added safety she would have the boatmen lash them to their spot with a so-called sling Georgie had devised many years before. The sling was made of rope tied in such a way as to hold the passenger in place in case he or she lost their hand grip on the rope. At the same time, it could be quickly released if necessary. Lud Fromme said, "Georgie, myself, and Jose Couce, the other boatman, practically insisted that Nori switch to the inside section and allow us to put her in a sling."[2]

However, she adamantly refused to move from her favorite outside seat. Abrams said neither he nor his wife wanted to take the risk of her being tied to and possibly trapped under the boat in the event of a flip in Lava Falls.

The two smaller triple rigs left camp first, followed by Georgie's big G-rig. The seating order of passengers on the left pontoon was as follows: Don Scott, Ray Abrams, Nori Abrams, Craig Bosson, Cathy Couce, and Jose Couce. Fromme was positioned on the rear of the right-hand pontoon.

As Georgie approached the head of the rapid, her passengers were instructed to hold onto the safety lines with both hands and not to wave to the folks on shore. The boatmen had double-lashed all the river bags to the boat and double-checked everyone's life jacket.

As usual, Georgie did not stop to scout the rapid but plowed right down the middle. As they entered the first drop, Georgie turned off the motor and crouched down in the motor well holding onto a safety line. The raft plunged directly into the "ledge hole," with the bow of the boat facing down river, not sideways as was practiced by the smaller triple rigs. As the boat hit the hole, it was momentarily stopped, and swung so that the bow was facing the left bank. At this point the pontoon on the left side was tucked under and a wave swept over it, washing four or five people into the river.

Fromme said he was not aware of the trouble on the other side until he heard someone screaming for help. He scrambled over as quickly as possible, still not knowing that Nori Abrams was overboard. He soon became aware that a young teenager who had been sitting about amidships was overboard and screaming for help. Fromme got to him and pulled him back on board. Fromme said, "If he had not panicked, he would have realized that all he had to do was to hang onto the ropes alongside the raft until he could pull himself back on, or be helped. But with his screaming, I had to go there first." Fromme then became aware that three people, including Jose Couce, were trying to help Nori get back onto the boat.

Ray Abrams said he was under water approximately twenty to thirty seconds. After surfacing, he got hold of a safety line on the pontoon with his left hand, grabbed his wife with his right arm and supported her with his right leg under her body while yelling, "Hang on, hang on." His wife was conscious and gasping for breath as they continued down through the rapid for another thirty or forty seconds towards a black cliff on the left side. In the meantime Couce and two other passengers were trying their very best, without success, to get Nori back on board. The major problem was her weight. Ray Abrams helped his wife stay next to the boat, but she was still gasping for air as they entered the next rapid, Lower Lava.[3]

As they approached the cliff, Nori was sucked away from Ray into a whirlpool. Ray said, "We were both sucked under. I lost hold of the boat and my wife, and when I came back up she was gone." Sometime during this process, Ray's left shoulder was severely wrenched. But, with great difficulty and help from another passenger, he was able to get back on the boat. Georgie had gotten the motor going again, according to her regular Lava procedure, and had full control of the boat.

In a few minutes Nori was spotted floating face up about sixty or seventy yards away toward the center of the river. Georgie was trying to get back as close to her as possible, but the big boat would not turn easily. Still, Georgie was soon able to maneuver into the area close to Nori. When the boat got within about thirty feet of her, Couce and Fromme dove in and got to her. With Georgie's help the two soon brought her alongside the raft. It was impossible to get her onto the boat, so they held onto both her and the boat. Fromme said, "I kept talking to her, trying to get her to help herself, thereby helping us in our efforts. Needless to say, I was not aware all this time that she was already gone."

Georgie picked the first sand beach she could find, and finally got Nori on shore. Several passengers took Abrams off the boat and over to one side as CPR was begun by Couce, nurses Nancy Dawson and Gwen Heaton, and Bill Estes, a doctor of internal medicine in his third year of residency. Abrams was restrained at first from going closer and then decided to stay where he was, occasionally consoled by Gwen Heaton, while the four took turns working on Nori.

Abrams recalled that during a break from working on his wife, Couce and Estes examined his arm and wrapped it in a sling, as he believed he had dislocated his shoulder while hanging onto the raft or being pulled aboard.

The foursome worked on Nori for more than half an hour, but they knew very shortly that it was all over.

Nori's body was wrapped in an orange tarp and carried by several passengers to Georgie's boat, where it was tied down to a pad on the bow. Then everyone reboarded and continued downriver to the helicopter pad at Mile 183.

Upon arrival at the helicopter pad, one person got out the ground-to-air radio while other passengers made the letters SOS on the beach with life jackets. Abrams stated that he saw five or six planes fly over and that at least four attempts were made to radio out. He was not sure Georgie knew how to operate the radio, as Couce eventually took it from her saying, "Come on Georgie, let me have the radio— you push the button this way."

Abrams said Georgie suggested he fly out to Las Vegas with the passengers when the helicopters came in as prearranged. She told him the helicopters coming in from Las Vegas would not be able to take Nori out because the body would have to stay in Arizona until an investigation could be completed. She said, "You would have to wait for the ship to come in from the South Rim. What good would it do for you to be on the South Rim, when everyone else would be going to Vegas. You'll have more support there." This seemed reasonable to Ray, and he agreed to fly out. At Las Vegas he called his friend Howard Cornbleth, who picked him up and took him to Sunrise Hospital, where he was found to have a separated shoulder. The other passengers were taken to the Showboat Hotel where they would remain overnight.[4]

Then Madison Aviation flew in on a scheduled flight to pick up passengers departing the trip. At this time the pilot was notified of the incident and called Grand Canyon National Park to report the accident. Rangers Kim Crumbo and Brien Culhane were dispatched to the scene. Upon arrival they found only the boat crew, as the passengers had already flown to Las Vegas. The victim's body was flown to Tuweep by helicopter with Culhane attending. From there it was transported to Grand Canyon National Park Airport by airplane and turned over to Coconino County's Deputy Russell.

Thus Georgie's claim to have never lost a passenger was shattered. Yet Georgie would not admit this. Like in the death of Mae Hansen twelve years earlier, Georgie tried to convince herself that this death was somehow self-imposed. In some ways she blamed herself, if only in small part, for Nori Abrams's death. She told Roz Jirge she almost refused to take Nori on the trip when she saw her hobble painfully off the bus at Lees Ferry. She said she very nearly told her to get back on the bus and return to Las Vegas; that she was not in good enough physical condition to make the trip. Nori and Ray Abrams were Georgie's friends, however, and she did not want to disappoint them. She also blamed herself for not insisting Nori move to the inside raft before entering Lava Falls. She said Nori was an adult, however, and had to take some responsibility for her own death.

Paul Miller's Adventures

Orville Miller's son, Paul, went on several of Georgie's river runs with his dad. On one such trip in the mid-1980s, they had a near tragedy in Tuna Creek Rapid less than a half mile below Crystal. The water level was unusually high at that time and there was a large boulder on the left side just upstream from the rapid. This boulder was normally high and dry up on the bank. On this trip the water was over its base and going around both sides.

Harvey Lee Hall was the motorman on the triple rig. The oarsmen were Orville Miller and Bob McElroy. Everything to the left of the rock was shallow water pouring viciously over a jumble of boulders, but one could not really see that from their location. To McElroy, it looked like either way would have been good. There ensued a brief argument, with Orville yelling, "Don't go to the left of that rock!" They finally decided to go to the right, but by then it was too late.

According to Hall the boat came out of Crystal Rapid full of water, hard to maneuver, and with a dead engine. He saw the big rock sticking up and kept trying to start the engine. By the time it fired, the boats were still so full of water they could not make much headway. Bob and Orville were rowing to the right as hard as they could, and they slammed into the rock dead center.[5]

Those in the middle boat, including Hall, were in bad shape because they were trapped between the raft and the rock, pinned there by the full hydraulic force of the river. Hall tried without success to reach the knife at his belt, thinking that if he punctured a cell in the raft it might relieve the pressure. All he could do was wiggle his fingers.

Fortunately, the boats freed themselves after about forty-five seconds when the raft in the main current pulled them loose. Had this not happened someone could have been killed. As it was, one woman, Donna Sahli, had very serious injuries. She was floating unconscious in the river when the crew pulled her out. Three people were also left stranded on the rock.

Luckily, another boating party, Grand Canyon Dories, had stopped for lunch just below Crystal Rapid; they witnessed the entire incident. They quickly assessed the situation and came to the rescue, shouting instructions to those stranded on the rock as they passed by, telling them to jump in so they could pick them up. The other crew dropped them off where the damaged boat had landed, then radioed for a helicopter to pick up the injured.

When they first hit the rock, Orville was hit by a big wave and washed into the river. The same wave forced Paul and the others in that section down into the bottom of the raft. They were able to hold on and were not washed out immediately, but they were under about four feet of water, holding their breath. Paul said:

> So finally, I couldn't hold my breath anymore and I realized I had better get up to the surface and take a breath. So I scrambled to the surface, got a quick breath, and realized that what I was standing on was another person, not the raft. And I just got really mad at myself that, like: "You S.O.B.! You're not going to get a breath of air at someone else's expense!" So I reached down and grabbed this woman; she was all tangled up in the ropes and stuff at the bottom and had been under water for a fair amount of time like I had. And so I just one-handed her to the surface. I just got her head up as fast as I could. And she got a breath then. But by doing that I'd let go of the raft. And so, just at the same moment, the raft shifted a little and the water came tearing into the boat again full force, and we swung further out into the current. And it blasted me right out of the boat.[6]

Paul ended up going through Tuna Creek Rapid in his life jacket. He kept waiting for his head to pop up. Sometimes he would get up into the froth, but he could not catch a breath until he washed out at the foot of the rapid.

As soon as he could, Paul looked around and spotted his father ahead of him in the river. Orville was exhausted, but soon the boats came floating through and picked him up. Paul and another young man made it to shore while the wrecked boat passed. By going to shore, Paul and the other man missed the raft, so they had to jump back into the river and swim on downstream. Paul said, "One of the main reasons we had gotten out of the river there was because, downriver, there was this big curling wave . . . and we did not want to wash into that thing."

The rafts had gone downstream a mile or more. The two jumped back in, and they could not avoid the wave and hole that were pretty much taking up the entire channel. Paul, knowing he would have to hold his breath for awhile, hyperventilated a bit before he went in. He was sucked under and counted to twenty before he popped back up on the other side.

The pair eventually caught up with the rafts where they had eddied out against a rock wall and were treating some of the injured. Donna Sahli, who had suffered the head injury, also had a broken arm. After putting a splint on her arm and applying first aid to the injured, there was nothing to do but head down the river. Although a person held her when they went through rapids, the twisting and jolting of the raft made Donna cry out in pain. Donna's face and head were so distorted that her friends did not recognize her. Two of the crew, Penny Meo and Ron Hancock, saw to it that Donna did not fall asleep during the night. Due to the shock she was suffering, this could have been extremely dangerous. The next day they motored the short distance down to Bass Camp, an area large enough for the helicopters to land and airlift the injured to the hospital on the South Rim.

On another trip Paul remembers a flash flood at Elves Chasm. He said that on many of the hikes he had seen the results of flash floods—uprooted trees, jumbled piles of boulders, and washed out bushes—but never before witnessed an actual flood. To reach Elves Chasm it is necessary to hike up a narrow, steep box canyon. It took twenty to thirty minutes of rather difficult climbing to get to the waterfalls. There was no possible escape up the sides in the narrowest part if a flood came.

On this trip, while Georgie's party was swimming and playing in the falls at Elves Chasm, a thunderstorm came rolling in and a cloudburst started pouring rain on them. They decided they had better get out of there.

No sooner were they out than a monstrous flood came roaring down in a wall of water, ten or twelve feet high, rolling boulders the size of Volkswagens, and roaring like a freight train.

Paul said some people had not quite made it out of the canyon when this happened, and they had to do a quick scramble up the sides. They were lucky to be at the mouth of the canyon where the sides were climbable. He said it was a spectacular thing to see.

After they returned to the rafts they suddenly heard a loud hissing noise directly above them. About a thousand feet up was a sheer cliff, the rim of the inner gorge of the canyon. A waterfall, about the size of Yosemite Falls in spring, suddenly burst through a notch in the rim. There was nothing there one second, and all of a sudden this waterfall came pouring down. The water was a brilliant pinkish-red, caused by the color of the sandstone and soil it was eroding. Paul said:

> I'd never seen a red waterfall before like that. It was spectacular. I loved being down in the Canyon when it was raining like that. You just never knew what you were going to see. Sometimes, you know, three to five layers of waterfalls stacking up the different canyon walls. I think that's always the best time to be in the Canyon.

Marty Hunsaker Arrives on the Scene

In Las Vegas Georgie hired a man by the name of Martin Hunsaker to transport equipment from her warehouse to Lee's Ferry and back. In 1984 he told his sister, Lee McCurry, "I'm hauling stuff for this crazy woman, who keeps trying to get me to go on the river with her! She's plumb crazy!" He told Lee, "I don't know. I'm not going!"[7] In spite of this, he decided that he would make one trip with Georgie in 1985.

Lee McCurry met Georgie's trips at Pierce Ferry several times in 1985, and on the last trip of that year her brother, Marty, asked her to make some macaroni salad and pick up some Kentucky Fried Chicken so they would not have to cook that night. Lee and Marty spent the night on Scorpion Island with the group. The next day, when they were ready to return to Las Vegas, Georgie decided, "Lee's brought all of this food for us so I didn't have to cook, so I'm going to ride back with her."

After Marty made his first trip on the river with Georgie, he was hooked. He kept going back and soon became a boatman for her. Georgie then had to hire another trucker to haul her equipment to and from the river.

Death of Georgie's Sister, Marie

For many years Marie had been Georgie's most trusted aide, taking care of the details that Georgie did not care for. Though thin in stature, she also helped Georgie do physical tasks in the warehouse. Marie would also care for Georgie's pets while she was away on trips. But for the past few years Marie had been suffering from the increased effects of Alzheimer's Disease. Orville Miller said of Marie:

She was a fine person. And, again, she developed Alzheimer's, which was unfortunate. And this is an insight into Georgie's character: Marie began totally fouling things up: reservations-wise and records-wise. She was losing checks. She lost a couple of my checks that I paid for trips. And she'd do it with others. People didn't know whether they were on the trips or not. And for several years Georgie was losing a lot of business. Now, never were any of these checks *cashed*! I don't know what became of them: two of mine were lost. They weren't cashed; they just disappeared. Marie wasn't cheating anybody—maybe throwing them out in the garbage or something, because they never appeared in my bank statement.[8]

For several years, this had been cutting into Georgie's business. As an example, passengers were required to sign a release to the effect that they acknowledged some dangers existed in river travel and they exempted the outfitter from liability in this regard. But Marie would bring the wrong set of releases to the hotel. Passengers would be asked to sign a release again when many of them had done this three or four times already! Marie deteriorated to the point where the things she used to do with precision were now getting fouled up on a regular basis.

Georgie knew what the problem was, as did her close associates. At times they would talk to Georgie about this and suggest that she get someone to take Marie's place. But Georgie would tell them that when she was a young girl Marie practically raised her, that Marie, being older, was like a mother to her and took care of her. And she was *not* going to tell Marie she could no longer do this job. She did not want to hurt Marie's feelings. She said, "I don't care what it costs me! I'm not going to tell Marie she can't do this. Until *she* recognizes it herself, I'm going to let her keep doing it, no matter what it costs me!"

Apparently Marie finally realized that she was no longer handling things properly and told Georgie she should get somebody else. That was when Georgie hired Lee McCurry to help look after Marie.[9] McCurry said:

So in '86 she had me start taking care of Marie because she didn't even know who *Georgie* was at that time. And, we'd go to breakfast and Marie would say: "What is *your* name, Honey?" Georgie'd say: "It's Georgie." She'd say: "Well, I ought to remember that. That's my dead sister's name." So, see, the

Alzheimer's had gone that far, you know. Then she passed away in '87 and, in the meantime, I was answering telephones for Georgie, because we had her [Marie] in the day care center. And then, from then on, she kept me on as a secretary.

On July 4, 1987, Marie died, leaving Georgie the only surviving member of her family. Word of Marie's death reached Georgie at Pierce Ferry. She took Roz Jirge aside to tell her the sad news. "When I looked at Georgie I could see tears standing in her eyes. She just would not let them fall down her cheeks. I hugged her and told her it was all right to cry this time, but she could not, or would not. Then I told her, 'It's okay. I'll cry for both of us.' And I did." Georgie began to blame herself for Marie's illness, insisting that she had worked her sister too hard in the warehouse and in the office. No amount of reassurance from her friends could change her mind. She never stopped missing Marie and she would speak of her frequently.

Better Food

Roz Jirge said that in about 1984 or 1985 the Park Service told Georgie she would have to serve salads. She would bring lettuce and that was it, except for a few fresh tomatoes, because she loved those so much. Roz said to her, "Georgie, a salad is more than just lettuce." So Roz started bringing other vegetables from her husband's garden, including English cucumbers, plus a few other things that she would purchase. This became a whole production. Finally, when Georgie heard people raving about the salads, she said, "You don't have to bring all those extras, anymore. I'll do it." From then on Georgie started bringing croutons, "gazabo" (Georgie pronunciation of garbanzo) beans, and other salad ingredients. Jirge said that

> In about 1987 or 1988, she [Georgie] started bringing steaks and hamburgers and chicken. About three meals would include fresh meat. And then eventually, she switched it over until, I think the last year, almost all of the meals were barbecued. Her old way was just fast and easy and it may not have been gourmet; in fact, if you talked to a lot of people, it was downright awful. But it was okay. It was simple, nutritious, and it took no effort.[10]

Georgie liked to keep everything simple and efficient but was forced to change her menu because people, as she said, had changed a lot. Jirge noticed this at the boat shows when people did not ask how exciting the trip was or how beautiful the canyon but "What is the food like?"

When Georgie made the change she still did not serve the food on fine china. Jirge said, "You haven't lived until you've tried to figure out how to eat a steak without a knife and fork. What Georgie did was use tortillas. We used tortillas for everything. In fact, you could eat the plate."[11]

Georgie's use of the English language was colorful, to say the least. She mispronounced names, places, things. "Gazabo beans" was probably the most comical. However, she also called Shinumo Canyon "Shamingo." Hakatai shale, one of the many sedimentary rock formations in Grand Canyon, became "Hatakai." Crew person Penny Meo was Penny "Moe," and Georgie's sister suffered from "Old Timer's Disease."

Another Woman of the River

Teresa Yates first met Georgie in 1985. At that time she was married to John Weisheit. Teresa worked only four trips for Georgie, two in 1985 and two in 1986. Teresa, like Georgie, developed a deep and abiding love for the river and the canyon.[12] Beginning in 1980 John and Teresa had made a few trips with rented gear in Desolation and Gray canyons on the Green River and also on the San Juan. Then they chipped in with family and friends to buy some used ten-man rafts for vacationing. These rafts needed patching, but John and Teresa did not know how to go about it. Teresa explained:

> So we went to the library and looked under "white water rafting" and there was no information on how to fix up these boats. But in looking for some information we found Georgie's book: *Thirty Years of River Running*. And we started flipping through it and we saw a picture of her sitting on a 10-man military surplus raft. So we figured if there's anybody who knows how to fix these, it's her![13]

They took the book home and wrote Georgie a letter telling her they were private rafters, that they had just purchased some ten-man rafts, knew nothing about them, but would like to fix them up. They asked questions such as: How do we repair them? What materials are needed? And where can we get the materials?

Georgie answered immediately, saying, "Here is what they are made of . . . . Here is what you do . . . . Here is where you get the materials . . . . And good luck with your fixing of these rafts."

Meanwhile Teresa and John read her book. They wrote back and said: "Thank you very much for all your information. Really enjoyed your book. Seems like a very interesting life." They thought that would be the end of it, but Georgie wrote back to them and said, "I've got two spaces available this summer. Would you guys like to swamp for me on a trip?" And so of course they said "Yes."

They had not been down the Grand Canyon yet—were just working up to that, figuring they had better get some experience elsewhere before they tried to row the Grand. Teresa said it was really neat to go down with Georgie and see it first before they committed themselves to a trip down there by themselves. That was in 1985. John went in May and they both went in August and in September.

Then something turned Georgie off. She stopped inviting them to work on her trips, so they had to do their boating with other outfitters. It would seem Teresa and John were accused of soliciting Georgie's passengers for private trips down the Colorado River. Both vehemently denied this, but Georgie chose not to believe them. In fact, they were planning a trip down the Salt River near Phoenix, Arizona, and two of Georgie's passengers asked to accompany them.

Teresa came back into Georgie's life at a later time, after her divorce from John, when she was driving motor rigs through Grand Canyon as Georgie, her heroine, was doing.

22 Another Tragedy, 1988–1989

*I*n 1988 Karen Smith went on her first Royal River Rats trip, although not on Georgie's boat. She was one of fourteen passengers on an S-rig on which Marty Hunsaker was the boatman and trip leader. They got into a some trouble at Crystal Rapid. The current caught them, as Karen later said:

> We were going to the right of Crystal and the current caught the boat and Marty was at the helm and he was holding the boat motor so *hard* that he broke the handle off of the motor trying to get us out of there. We went into the hole and it seemed like we were under water forever! But, you know, I don't know how long. But then, all of a sudden it spit us out, spun us around, and we smashed into the wall![1]

One of the passengers fell out and three people were injured. With the motor out of commission, they floated along until they came into a little eddy and waited there. There were two doctors on board, one of them a head-and-neck surgeon and one a general practitioner. They took care of the injured people. A Hatch River Expeditions party picked up the girl who had fallen overboard and brought her back to Marty's boat.

Passengers were always told to hang on with both hands while going through any and all rapids. One of those injured was a man who ignored this and was trying to take photographs in Crystal. He gashed his leg rather badly. No one had broken bones, however, and the injuries were not serious.

In 1989 Marty Hunsaker did not fare as well. Tanya Wilcox, a swamper on Marty's boat, said that on the third day of their trip they approached Crystal Rapid and pulled to shore on the right side above the rapid so that they could scout it. Boatmen Chuck Kane and Al Korber were on another S-rig traveling with them. Georgie had gone through the rapid about an hour earlier and would wait to have lunch with them at the "Ross Wheeler," which Georgie called "Iron Boat Camp."

Korber scouted the rapid with Marty and his group. After looking it over, Marty said, "Okay. Let's do it." So Marty, Tanya, boatman Paul Semerjian, and their thirteen passengers returned to the boat and began their run. Korber was to come through last. He and his passengers watched from a nearby bluff as Marty began his run; Chuck Kane remained with the boats.

On his approach into the tongue, Marty was a little to the left in the current when his motor conked out. He was cranking like crazy to get it started again when the current swept the boat into the left side of the rapid, just where he did not want to go.

Kjeld Harris was a passenger on Marty's boat. He remembers:

> As we went into Crystal Marty decided to go to the left side against the sheer wall instead of on the right side of the boulder, the more or less safe way around Crystal. We high-sided on the left side, got pushed up on the rock wall, high sided by a rock, by a big wave near a rock, came back down and flattened out upright, and then got hit again by a wave coming from right to left. Got pushed up the wall and flipped us over.[2]

Tanya said Marty never intended to go left, but meant to make the safe run along the right side and got pulled left by the current when the motor died.[3]

Harris was a scuba diver, and he remembered his scuba training. He followed the direction of his bubbles and was able to push off from the canyon wall where the current had him pinned against a rock. He came up under the raft while it was still going through the rapid. He began looking for an air pocket but could not find one, so he pulled himself along the raft, getting beat up against the rocks, and finally came up on the upriver side of the raft gasping for air. He grabbed hold of the side of the raft and, with great effort, pulled himself up onto it.

Harris said that a small woman named Joyce Sloninger was pinned in the space between the main part of the raft and the metal compartment where the food storage was kept. She was screaming very loudly. He managed to pull her out and onto the bottom of the boat. Just after he freed her, the raft slammed hard against a rock in the middle of the rapid. Had she still been in there she probably would have been killed.

As the boat started to come out of the rapid, working on instinct and adrenaline, Harris began to drag people out of the water. He pulled boatman Paul Semerjian out, and Paul then helped Harris get other people onto the overturned boat. Tanya held onto ropes on the side of the boat and was hanging onto the back of Marty's life jacket so that he was able to look around a bit easier. Tanya wrote:

> When I came up . . . I was only about five feet from the upside down raft. I swam to the raft grabbing onto a rope. There was a male passenger who had already climbed on the top of the upside down raft. I was in the water hanging onto the raft. Marty came up right by me—he reached up for the raft and most of his hand was gone. When Marty was motoring he had a rope with a loop to keep him steady. He was unable to free his hand before we went over. I grabbed the back of Marty's life vest. Marty and I saw one of our passengers in the main current not trying to get out. Marty was yelling at me to get a head count and let him go. I let Marty go and was pulled onto the raft.[4]

Marty was able to get close enough to the woman for her to hear him, and she began reacting to get out of the river. Marty was swept downstream.[5]

Georgie discouraged passengers from diving off a boat to save someone in the water—it just put more people in peril. They never planned on upsetting, but for passengers the first choice was to get to the boat and the second choice was to get to the bank. According to Chuck Kane, "Once a boatman has passengers in the water, they are like your kids. You have a moral obligation to go out and find every one of them and see that you get them to shore."[6] However, a boatman is severely limited as to what he can do while swimming in a rapid with a life jacket on. Marty's sister, Lee, said, "He knew better than to do that. But his concern was for her. He didn't care about himself. And this is the way Marty was—he was always worried about the other guy. And he felt like he was responsible for them."[7]

Kjeld Harris said:

I saw Marty Hunsaker go by me in the water and I said to him, "Marty. Are you all right?" He looked at me and gave me the OK sign and said to me, "Get a head count." At that point we started counting people and we accounted for everybody except Marty who kept floating by us in the river.[8]

The people were on the bottom of the raft and Marty went by them in the swift current just below the rapid. At that point Harris thought about jumping in and grabbing Marty because he looked tired. But he figured that Marty had been doing this for a long time and knew what he was doing.

Fortunately, the boat drifted into an eddy on the right side below Crystal Rapid. Al Korber's party had watched them run and flip. His group came down immediately, picked up three passengers trapped on the far side of the river, and brought them across to where the crippled boat had landed. They started looking around for Kim, the woman Marty had left the raft to aid. She eventually showed up a little farther downstream.

Everyone was now accounted for except Marty. They were relieved because they felt he was experienced and could take care of himself. The down side was that he was in ill health and no longer young. Marty was afflicted with diabetes, which left him with the eventual probability of having one of his legs amputated.

They needed to get downriver, so Chuck Kane took temporary charge of salvaging the boat until they could meet up with Marty. They disconnected the motor frame, dropped it down and out, flipped it over, and put it inside the upside down boat. The craft was not very seaworthy, but all they wanted to do was get downstream to where they would have a lot of manpower to flip it over and rig it correctly. In that way they managed to motor down to where Georgie was camped. Kane, a veteran boatman for Georgie, did a masterful job of manning the crippled boat with its mangled frame and with a motor that had only one forward gear and no reverse.

Tanya Wilcox said, "Just myself and the other boatman and Chuck Kane were on the crippled boat and we put the rest of the passengers on Al's boat. Al was able to get them all back down to Georgie—we were all able to get back to Georgie."

While the two crews were re-rigging the damaged raft, two boats from Hatch River Expeditions came by and stopped to check on them. Boatman Curtis "Whale" Hansen stated:

Me and Steve Hatch got there about an hour after it happened. We made the normal run and got down to the bottom where those eddies are, and there was Marty's boat, upside down . . . they had all the people and they were pulling gear out from underneath of it and everything. So I stopped and talked to her [Tanya Wilcox] and she told me that Marty and another passenger had gone on down and could we go find them. So I went about a hundred, two hundred yards downstream and found the passenger and she was on the shore and I picked her up and I was able to motor back up to where they were and drop her off. So in the meantime I sent Stevie down to look for Marty.[9]

Steve Hatch, Ted's son, was running the other boat alone as the only crew member. He had about a dozen passengers on his boat, four or five of them children aged twelve to fourteen. Steve saw that Whale was tied up next to the overturned boat, so he ferried over to see if he could be of some help. Steve said:

Whale yelled over and said: "Stevie, go down, look for Marty, he's going to be down there a ways, he went after some people!" I couldn't put that together myself. I didn't know what another swimmer could do to help anybody out! At least in the water. So I thought: "Okay. Well, I'll go down and look for Marty!"[10]

Finally somebody said, "Look. There's a gear bag in the river." It was about fifty to one hundred yards ahead. Steve said, "Okay. Well, we'll grab that gear bag, but keep your eyes open for Marty." As they got closer Steve noticed that the object never turned. It never switched angles, but always stayed upright in the water. He kept watching it between glances off to the shore to look for Marty.

So we got closer and closer. I couldn't tell what it was. It *looked* like a gear bag, but it was floating way too high. Got closer and closer and I went: "That's a life jacket!" I thought: "Okay. Well, we'll pick up this life jacket." Kept getting closer and I thought: "Why is that life jacket sticking so far out of the water?" Because we came up closer and closer and went: "Something is wrong! This life jacket's sitting just like it should be with a person in it, but it's too high out of the water."[11]

Upon realizing that it was Marty, Steve instructed his passengers to move to the left side of the boat. He came up to Marty on the right side, shut off the motor, ran up front alone, grabbed him, and started pulling him aboard. As Steve went to grab him he looked down into the water and saw that Marty was submerged almost to his eyebrows. His face was completely under water. Steve recalled:

> So I knew Marty didn't have much of a chance at that point, because I knew he wasn't conscious. So I grabbed him and tried to pull him in. I'm just floating all alone out there with no crew and I couldn't pull Marty in! I pulled and pulled and pulled! Couldn't get him in! So I yelled for some help across to the others. Well, I said: "Somebody come and help me! You kids, turn away! I don't want you to look this way! Turn away and somebody make those kids turn away. I don't want you to watch this!"[12]

At that point Dr. Frank M. Weinhold, a radiologist, came over and helped Steve pull Marty in. Steve then checked the boat to make sure his passengers were safe and that they were not going to crash into any rocks.

They unfastened Marty's life jacket, unbuttoned his shirt, and together checked for body core temperature, all the vitals. Steve noted, "He was cold as a beer out of the river. And he had no signs of life." Dr. Weinhold did everything *he* could, looked him over without starting CPR, and said, "There's nothing you can do for this man. He is gone. And he has been gone for awhile." It had been an hour and a half or more since the upset in Crystal Rapid. There was no way Marty could have survived that long in those frigid waters. Hypothermia would have killed him if nothing else. Weinhold noted no external signs of trauma.[13]

At that point Steve said he was almost emotionless. He covered the body with his raincoat and motored over to shore. About five to ten minutes later, Whale arrived and pulled up next to Steve's boat. Brad Hudson, the swamper, was with him, and they sensed that something was wrong.

Steve said he had not shed a tear at that point, but he was very close. He said, "Brad, come over here and run my boat." When Brad came on board, Steve said to him, "Brad, don't look up front, but Marty is dead. Marty is gone. He's left us!" Then Steve jumped over to the other boat and told Whale, "Whale, Marty's gone! He's on my boat!"

After conferring about the matter, Whale said, "Georgie is down at Upper Bass Camp. I'll go down and talk to her. You stay upstream until I wave you in." Whale remarked:

> So I pulled in there and told her that Marty was dead and why I was all upset and everything: my voice cracked and everything. She just looked me right in the eye and she says: "Well, he was a smoker!" And, you know, she didn't even hardly bat an eye.[14]

Marty had been more than just a boatman to Georgie. He accompanied her to meetings with the Park Service and was involved with helping run her business, so Whale had expected more of a reaction than that.

When Whale waved Steve in, he pulled to shore and Brad came down and tied up the boat. Then Georgie's crew members, Herb Heitmeyer and Janet Macky, came over and helped move the body on shore to a shady spot where they covered it with wet burlap to keep cool. Later, assisted by one of the passengers, a doctor, they shrouded the body in a tarp and life jackets and placed it in the water. The floating body was attached to shore with several tethering ropes.

Roz Jirge was on the trip and, although she saw the Hatch boats pull in, was busy setting up lunch. Later, as the meeting went on, she joined them and learned of Marty's death. She gave Heitmeyer her tarp to wrap Marty's body in. She said: "As long as I live, I shall never forget the sight of Marty, wrapped in that blue tarp, floating in the water. I decided to take a cue from Georgie and keep busy caring for our passengers. It helped distract me from the tragedy."

Kjeld Harris said that when the overturned boat, accompanied by Al Korber's boat, arrived at Georgie's camp, they began asking where Marty was, and when they could not see him it dawned on them that Marty was in the tarp. Harris said, "We just about flipped. All hell broke loose. Everybody started crying. Everybody sat around talking about it a lot that night." It was an emotional time for everyone involved, especially those who knew Marty well. Tanya told the author:

> It was a great shock to me, because I'm a truck driver and Marty was also a truck driver. He is the one who introduced me to Georgie, and I started running the rapids with Georgie through him—with Georgie before Marty started running. It was quite tragic. I know his daughter and his sister, Lee, real

well. I took it quite hard when I hit the beach and found out that Marty didn't make it.[15]

Radio contact was made with a commercial airliner that night, and Park Service investigators Mark Law and Tom Workman arrived by helicopter the next morning. With ample room and plenty of help, Georgie's crew had worked most of the night de-rigging the boat and flipping it back over.

Georgie called her passengers together and gave them a little talk about how they should not let this affect their trip, that life must go on. In spite of this, according to Park Service records, a total of eight people flew out the next morning by helicopter.

Kjeld Harris said, "Me and my girl friend at the time decided to keep going down the river and completed the trip. That's when I got involved with Georgie's Royal River Rats. She asked me to come back to be a swamper for her—do swamper work and then boatman work."

Georgie, in keeping with her nature, was philosophical about losing Marty. In discussing the accident with ranger Tom Workman, she basically said that "Marty died in the canyon, and that was a nice place to die, if you've got to die, and it was real short."

Georgie met with Marty's family prior to his funeral. She did not attend the service. Instead, in typical Georgie fashion, she went to work in the warehouse, preparing for her next trip one week later.

23 *Birthday Party, 1990*

$\mathcal{G}$eorgie's loves, the things that kept her coming back to the Canyon, were the rapids, the river, and the river community.

Carol "Fritz" Fritzsinger was a young boatwoman working for Dick McCallum of Expeditions, Inc., in 1990. Fritz said she thought Georgie just acknowledged her as another woman running the river. Once she was leading a trip that was preparing to launch at Lee's Ferry at the same time Georgie was there. Georgie came over to her and said, "Now, you tell your boys that they need to get out of my way. I've got a big boat and, you know, I need lots of room on the river." Fritz recalls, "And it just tickled me, that she just recognized me as another woman on the river and that she related to me as 'a woman and her boys,' the way she was." For awhile after that, the men she worked with were nicknamed "Fritz's boys."

Fritz and Annie Anderson were talking with Georgie one day and asked if she would do a trip with just guides sometime, so that they could float the river with her—just have a little trip where they could get to know her personally. Georgie thought that was a great idea.

Afterward Fritz decided she had better follow up on it, so she wrote Georgie a letter, and Georgie immediately replied. Fritz thought it was great that Georgie was still warm to the idea. She said they still had to work out the details. Later Fritz wrote again and got back an immediate answer to the effect that she was still interested and trying to figure out when she could do the trip.

So Fritz wrote to her a third time. Georgie wrote back saying, "You know, I need to be twins. I'm just too busy; I'm doing first aid, and Marty's gone now, my sister's gone." She wrote a long letter about how she had to patch the black bags and fix the boats and get everything ready for the season and that she would not be able to do it. Fritz remarked, "I was just really amazed that she would take the time to write back to me and I'll always treasure those letters I have."[1]

Dan Dierker said he also spoke to Georgie about the proposed training trip for river guides. He said, "The one thing I regret is that we never got to get the boatmen training trip together. It never came together where we could do a training trip of forty boatmen with her to drive us down. I would have loved to have done that."[2]

On the days when Georgie was getting ready to launch a trip at Lee's Ferry, she would eat her meals at nearby Marble Canyon Lodge and make it her headquarters. For the last few years she ran trips every two weeks, so she spent some time with Jane Foster, owner and operator of the lodge. Over the years they became close friends.[3]

In the mid-'80s, in addition to wearing clothes made of leopard-spotted cloth, Georgie began to fly a flag made of the same material. It was a little wedge-shaped pennant attached to a tamarisk branch mounted on the back of her raft. The staff at Marble Canyon Lodge obtained some of the same material and made a tablecloth for her. This special tablecloth was always used for Georgie's meals when she and her boatmen ate there. Jane Foster recalled:

> Georgie first used cotton bandannas flown on the back of the big boat on an old fishing pole, before going to her leopard-skin pennant. People snatched those for souvenirs and some years we'd have a terrible time. I would try to have a supply of several dozen of those here for her, because she'd take them out on her boats. And then either people took them for souvenirs or some way they'd disappear all the time. So we had to have replacements for them.[4]

As mentioned earlier, Teresa Yates had once been spurned by Georgie. Teresa found work with other outfitters and became adept at running motorized rigs, as well as rowing single rafts. In 1989, after Teresa and John Weisheit were divorced, Georgie warmed up to her again. Being divorced herself, Georgie perhaps felt some compassion for another divorcee. At any rate she recognized that here was another woman doing just as she had done and doing it well. Instead of feeling threatened, Georgie now went out of her way to be friendly with Teresa. A strong bond developed between the two women, to the

Georgie in riffle below Vasey's Paradise. *Courtesy of Rosalyn Jirge.*

Georgie still helps de-rig the heavy rafts, 1985. *Courtesy of Ludwig Fromme.*

point where Georgie would accidentally call Teresa "Sommona," her dead daughter's name.[5]

Teresa said Georgie was an inspiration to her from the beginning of their acquaintance because of Teresa's desire to learn to motor. After going down with Georgie, Teresa realized that motors were definitely something that she could at least set a goal to do, and this was something that Georgie encouraged.

Teresa said, "She had a lot of attitudes and thoughts and opinions that were definitely what I agreed with." With Georgie there was always a positive side to any situation—things could always be worse. And even though it may, at one time or another, seem a very negative situation, you could always glean from it and learn from it. You might be faced with a situation that was not exactly what you wanted at the time, but if you continued on with certain goals you might look back on that negative time as positive. On every river trip you learned something. You learned from your experiences as best you could and moved on to the next one, with the idea that you were going to learn more.

Garrett Schniewind was one of many young boatmen who admired Georgie. He recalled:

> For us, you'd see Georgie coming down cause you couldn't miss her boat. The triple rig was the largest thing ever on the river. And so, you'd see her coming from back up-river and it was always something that our customers kind of enjoyed seeing. Some of them even would say that they hoped they'd get to see her as she came by on the river. They had heard about her before, and they wanted to have a chance to see her.[6]

People thought it was special to see Georgie because at age eighty she was still down in the Grand Canyon, doing what she wanted to do and doing it her way. On a river trip, besides the excitement and beauty of the canyon, people have time to reflect on their own lives. People like Georgie, who were out there living on their own terms, really gave others something to think about. To see someone living with such honesty was something to behold.

Pat Stadt, one of Georgie's kitchen helpers, said that Orville Miller, Georgie's old boating friend, had a birthday party for Georgie at his home in Sacramento in October of 1990, a month ahead of the actual date. Pat said a number of Georgie's old boatmen showed up and it was fun to "just kick back and listen to their stories. She was quite a lady."[7]

Georgie was still the chief cook in May 1990. *Courtesy of Bob Atherton.*

The Big Party

Patty Ellwanger, manager of Hatch River Expeditions at Marble Canyon, said that during a first aid class in April of 1990 she realized Georgie would be eighty years old in November. She got the idea to give a birthday party for Georgie and mentioned it to Ted Hatch. He told her to go ahead. When she asked how much money she could spend, his response was, "Whatever it takes." Patty spoke to the river guides and they were enthused about the project.

As the summer went on the momentum grew for throwing a big barn party at the Hatch warehouse near Cliff Dwellers Lodge. As the time grew closer they realized that it was going to be a gala affair.

Steve Hatch said that his dad, Ted, always had a great concern for Georgie and her welfare. One reason he cared so much was that she was his tie to the old days. Steve said:

> My dad isn't in the old days anymore. When my grandfather, Bus, died in '67, to my dad the old days were dying. That was two years before I was born. And Georgie was my dad's tie to his childhood—to when *he* was down here as a young man running boats and doing them as fine as anybody could. Back in the old days. And times have changed and skills have changed and now he's in the office and one of his boys is down here.[8]

Patty said they all got involved in arranging a menu and catering food. As plans progressed, they added a band for dancing—then fireworks. Members of the Grand Canyon River Guides Association helped organize the program and do the decorations. Dan Dierker and his friend Brad made a huge artificial cake of papier-mache shaped like a triple rig. They convinced Dan's brother, Brian, to jump out of the cake dressed in a big red cape like Superman. Their sister, Andrea, sewed the cape. They devised a trap door and got balloons.[9]

This notice appeared in *Grand Canyon River Guide News*:

> Georgie's 80th at Hatchland—You're Invited
> Ted Hatch, Patty and Billy [Ellwanger], and the folks at Hatchland are throwing an 80th Birthday Party for Georgie White, who just about started it all. The party is November 10, 1990 at Cliff Dwellers. The object is to bring together as much of Grand Canyon river running history as possible. Put it on your calendar, and don't miss the GCRG Fall meeting

either. Same time, same place. Chili, courtesy of the Hatch folks, is on the menu, bring your own beer.

Ted Hatch wound up paying for several kegs of beer despite the above notice. Patty ordered a real birthday cake that was placed inside the one made of papier-mache.

Tom Vail said he spoke to Georgie sometime before the party. She told him she might not even go, as nobody was going to attend her birthday party, it being way out in the middle of nowhere. How wrong she was! Vail knew there were going to be a lot of people there, but even he didn't realize how many would show up. He estimated that it was probably the biggest gathering of river people ever. Roz Jirge and other friends convinced Georgie she should show up.

Patty Ellwanger said the party started with a clean-up crew and a decoration committee, which started the day before. The next day, November 10, Georgie arrived about 2:30 in the afternoon. Orville Miller recalls that a group of Georgie's crew—including the women who were kitchen helpers such as Joan De Fato, Karen Smith, Phyllis Wilkin, and Roz Jirge—pretty much filled Marble Canyon Lodge, having made reservations well ahead of time. Joe Muench was there, along with Bill Jensen and Jim Falls. Several of Georgie's firemen-boatmen came in from Los Angeles, including Don Brown, Tom Prange, Bruce Blackwell, Ray Gorospe, Chuck Mills, and Don Scutchfield with his wife, Kathleen. Orville estimated there were thirty of essentially "her" river people. Jane Foster and four or five waitresses and cooks from Marble Canyon Lodge came to the party. Fifty or sixty RVs showed up, due to the lack of hotel space. Guests came from all over the country. Bart Henderson flew in from Alaska, Bob Whitney from New York, Bob Pearson from Maine, and Dave Shore and Don Briggs from San Francisco, just for this party. Patty Ellwanger said that five hundred people signed the guest book, and she did not think everybody there signed it.

To kick off the party, Ted Hatch gave a short speech. He said, in effect, that it was time they got away from waiting until somebody died to put a plaque for them on a rock somewhere in the canyon; rather they should honor them while they were still alive. Everybody agreed that this was a most appropriate sentiment.

The decorating crew had placed eighty big candles around the papier-mache birthday cake. Someone took an acetylene torch and lit them. Brian Dierker was in a barrel down inside the cake. They had rigged up and practiced an act where he came out of the cake and grabbed onto a trapeze. They had even devised a pulley system from the rafters by which they lifted him up. Dierker came out of the cake bare-chested, wearing leopard skin leotards and the black and red cape made by his sister. Dierker said:

> The thing that impressed me to the end of it is how Ted Hatch is one of those guys who could throw a party for a gal like that, drop six grand, in the right place. And then he included all the boatmen, and everybody got together and said well—and this was a great honor to me—they said well, who'd jump out of the cake. You know, you always think of somebody jumping out of the cake. And everybody said, well, Brian, cause everybody knew she had an affection for me and I've always had an undauntable affection for her.[10]

Nathan Avery, one of Ted Hatch's employees, was in on the conspiracy. He owned an old Cadillac with bull horns on the hood, and he had cut off the top to make it into a convertible. He backed the Caddy into the warehouse and sat waiting. Dierker popped out of the cake in his Superman outfit, grabbed hold of the waiting trapeze and flew up to the warehouse ceiling. Then he was lowered down next to Georgie, swept her up in his arms, and carried her, cackling as only Georgie could, to the back seat of the waiting Cadillac. Avery drove them off into the night. They had a silver bowl full of ice and Coors beer in the car.

Ted Hatch hired professionals to set off commercial fireworks, as big and beautiful as any you would see on the fourth of July. The purpose of getting Georgie out of the warehouse was to let her view the fireworks from a nearby cliff, away from the huge crowd. Lew Steiger reported:

> It was a clear night sky and the stars were shining and you could see way out there. Way, way out there. Clear past the Milky Way. And the fireworks were huge, the biggest. They kept going too, one after another: bright showers of color that lit up the cliffs on either side. You could've seen the spectacle from miles away . . . from the Echo Cliffs and the Paria Plateau, the Kaibab Monocline, Saddle Mountains, the road-cut up to Page, the Navajo Bridge.[11]

When they returned to Hatchland after watching the fireworks, Georgie was wearing Brian's cape. Tom Vail walked over to her and said, "Georgie, the last time I saw that cape, Brian had it on." She got a big grin on her face and said, "Yep, but I got it now."

Ted had hired a good band, and after the fireworks they began playing. Ted danced the first one with Georgie. Patty Ellwanger remarked, "One of my favorite scenes was watching Ted and Georgie dance. Georgie is a wonderful dancer. I was impressed. She could really do the Two-Step." The party continued on all night and into the next day. The band quit playing about 4:30 in the morning.

Don Briggs, a guide and filmmaker from San Francisco, was working on a film about the history of river running on the Colorado. He was quite certain this party was going to be an event that needed documenting. So he raised the money from some of the outfitters and the Grand Canyon Natural History Association to film Georgie's party. Georgie was a big part of that history, so this fit right into his project. Briggs said, "I wouldn't doubt that that's the most people that had ever been in Marble Canyon at one time. I can't imagine any other event that would equal it."[12]

In addition to filming the highlights of the party, Briggs visited with as many people as he could and asked them to tell him their favorite "Georgie Story." Most of his video was asking a person that single question and recording their response. Some were first-hand experiences and some were rumors that had grown out of proportion through many tellings. One story going around was that Georgie's big boat had flipped in Crystal Rapid during the flood of 1983, when, in fact, that never happened.

According to Briggs, after the fireworks were over, Georgie returned to the party and opened her birthday gifts. One was a case of a special brand of blackberry liqueur that Georgie especially liked. She was excited about that. Then, they had a *real* birthday cake. This huge cake also had candles on it. Georgie blew out the candles, then she started dancing with Ted Hatch, all the while wearing Brian Dierker's red cape.

"I think Ted Hatch was just like a little kid," Briggs said. "He was having *such* a good time. Of course, I guess he's always that way. You know. Ted's just like that. He sort of never grew up. Thank God! He was so—he is so wonderful!"

Roy Webb, Green River historian and guide, was also there. He wrote:

There was dancing, back slapping, hugging, kissing. Kids were running around through the crowd, old friends and new were seeing each other for the first time in years, or at least acted like they were. People were having their pictures taken, formally and informally; the cameras ranged from big, commercial video jobs to battered and scratched Instamatics.[13]

Webb said the people were drawn by two common denominators. "It was, first, to honor one of their own, one who had more than beat the odds and stayed on the river longer than almost anyone else there." She had, after all, been at it for forty-six years. "And second, looming over there about two or three miles away, barely visible in the fading autumn light, there was the Canyon. *The* Canyon. The Grand Canyon, also known as the Grand, the Crick, the Big Ditch. The one and only, penultimate, ne plus ultra Grand Canyon." It was the common denominator in that whole, diverse crowd. "Georgie's birthday provided the excuse, as if any of these people ever needed an excuse to get together and party."

Webb further mused that "it might have started out as Georgie's birthday party, but it soon took on a life of its own." Says Dan Dierker, "The boatmen are kind of rowdy and they had differences of opinion, but you couldn't buy a fight that night." After enough of that good draft beer, Webb began reflecting on all the river running history gathered together right in that one warehouse: "must have been literally centuries of experience."

Webb said he "went outside, into the clear, cold November night, and there, looming in the near distance like a half-forgotten thought, was the gash of Marble Canyon." Knowing that Badger and Soap Creek and House Rock Rapid were not very far away, he wondered how they would look in that same moonlight.

River guide Lew Steiger reported the party for *Grand Canyon River Guides, The News*. He quoted Georgie as saying she could run across the ocean in her big boat. "'I'm positive it'd go right across if you could keep in gas.' She nods earnestly and laughs. 'It'd take some people to hold on, though. They'd have to be able to hang on. And they'd have to have the heart for it.'" Steiger wrote:

> Georgie was on a roll that weekend. "I think its good different things still occur," she said at one point. "Because people are so well spoiled today. In the old days nobody ran the river, only a couple of adventurers that you never hardly saw. It was

rough, and it was tough. There was no way out and no other boats or helicopters or anything like that. On our boat we were dependent on one another and right there, whether it's rocks or punctures or anything, that's what you got and how you're going to get out. It's up to you to get through . . . .

"The Canyon's good for people," Georgie says. "They got to learn, you know, it isn't everything just to earn so much money all the time and to keep wanting to climb the ladder up no matter who they step on. In the Canyon, it's the person themself that counts. So if you're the president or the ditch-digger, I don't care. And nobody else does either. Not while you're out here. After all's said and done, it's mainly how you got along and this type of thing. With each other." . . .

"Georgie fell in love with the place and saw its potential," Dan Dierker growled. "I don't think she originally just looked at it as a commercial venture. I think she's always felt the more people you take down there the better mankind is. Because it's a place that enriches humanity at large. You know, as long as you don't get them all down there at the same time of course. . . . But essentially we're honoring this lady because we're all kind of her progeny. And hey, she's still down there isn't she? She still thinks it's the best place in the world. And if you ask me, she's right." . . .

"Home," Bart [Henderson] said the next day just before he left, "All those people, they were coming home."[14]

Georgie received many cards and letters for her birthday reminding her of special things that had happened on her trips. These were placed in a special album. Following are a few excerpts:

Evelyn Venstrom Preston wrote: "The water—the first day one would not drink it, the next day one would let it settle before drinking it, and after that one would just go ahead and get a drink."

John "Homesteader" Lonk wrote:

Being a city kid I was sitting on the front of the boat and the first rapid had a hole that looked like it was the center of the planet. All I could think of was "What in the hell was I doing out here." Since I was at the front of the boat I was also a lander. We came to a spot where Georgie wanted to land, off jumped Frank Rich and myself to hold the boat to the shore. A back eddy caught the boat and violently swung the boat tearing the rope out of my hands and dragging Frank Rich into the water and under the boat. Frank popped up and was hauled aboard. Georgie tried to land again but the current was too strong and she went downstream. Meanwhile I was running over the shore boulders to where Georgie could get close enough to the shore for me to jump on. Later Georgie was in front of me, eyeball to eyeball and said "Were you trying to homestead?"

Kim Steiner remembered:

We then came up on Dubendorff Rapid, and, with the water being somewhat low that day, our motor mount got caught up on the rock now known as "Georgie's Little Bastard". The passengers abruptly stopped talking and were quiet as we hovered in the middle of the rapid, the rock keeping us from going anywhere. We all looked from one to the other, and back at Georgie, wondering whether we should be concerned or not (all of the passengers, except the crew, were novices at white-water rafting). We looked at Georgie, and Georgie looked back at us, from each passenger to the next, holding our questioning gazes. Her face was expressionless, those steel-blue eyes calmly and capably watching us, letting us know there was nothing to be afraid of, no reason to panic. The entire hang-up probably lasted a total of twenty seconds (but to hear us passengers talking about it later that evening back at camp, we were caught for "at least 5 minutes!"). What really impressed me the most about Georgie was her ability to have such a calming influence on us. A wave came and washed us over the rock, freeing us.

Lud Fromme wrote:

I think that many of the boatmen will agree with me on the following. If she liked you and was pleased with your work and efforts etc. you could depend on being "pushed around" and some playful punches or boxed around the ears etc. from Georgie. This was a sign of satisfaction with your work and her way of saying "you're OK with me." Beware if she ignored you and did not talk to you. For sure that boatman did something wrong—and he very probably knew what it was. In some cases it also meant that he would not be asked back for the

Georgie dancing with Ted Hatch at her eightieth birthday party. *Courtesy of Susette Weisheit.*

Victim of Georgie's "kangaroo" court. *Courtesy of Ludwig Fromme.*

next year. And, of course, we all know about the kangaroo courts. Despite all the complaining and arguing—it was probably an "honor" to be at the rough end of her fun time. I guess we wouldn't have it any other way.

From Charlotte Anderson:

On our 1970 trip Georgie had the big boat and two sets of little boats. Carol Hintze and Charlotte (Chintze and Char) were on one of the little sets run by Al [Loewe] and Orville [Miller]. Orville was quite a prankster and we had a lot of fun. One evening near the end of the trip, Georgie took us aside and said she would really like to "get" Orville. She told us she had been trying to find some "friends" who would attempt to "pants" Orville at the end of the trip. We told her we'd think about it. Orville was always doing something to someone! The last day Georgie made it clear that any shenanigans had to wait until the boats were broken down and stored and all the work was done. Well, we waited and then lured Orville down to the waters edge and about six of us pounced on him in the shallow water. He fought valiantly, but was no match for the vindictive females. Al stood by, about six feet away, shouting, "I'll help you, Orville! I'll help you!" Within a few minutes we had Orville's pants in hand, and then, feeling sorry for him, I offered him the Top of my bathing suit! He put it on and then put his shirt around his waist and came out roaring for Georgie. He knew she had instigated it. Now Georgie introduces us as "the ones who pantsed Orville!"

From Chintze: "A friend painted a yellow strip down the back of her rain suit because she was chicken. At the end of the trip she was changing it to purple for Royal River Rat."

Yes, Georgie sure enjoyed her birthday party, and a whole lot of others did, too.

24 Final Run, 1991

$\mathcal{B}$y the 1990s it is estimated that two and a half million people annually are boating on the wild rivers of America with commercial outfitters, spending over $250 million in the process. Two Eastern rivers, the Natahala in North Carolina and the Ocoee in Tennessee, account for five hundred thousand rafting passengers each year. This and the growing number of private trips form a big slice of adventure tourism today.[1]

In the Grand Canyon, where trips are limited by the NPS, gross sales by licensed outfitters amounted to $21.8 million, compared to $86.3 million for land-based concessions.[2] "These days it's not unusual for 10,000 river-rafting, mountain-biking visitors from all over the U.S. to congregate in Moab [Utah] on a weekend."[3] Georgie had made a significant contribution to this new and exciting type of travel.

In 1991 the Park Service invoked a new regulation prohibiting boatmen and crew members from drinking alcoholic beverages of any kind while transporting passengers on the river. They also decreed that consumption of alcohol upon establishment of a camp must be moderated to the extent that "boatmen could satisfactorily perform their camp duties and provide proper direction and service to the clients in camp."

According to Mark Law, River Subdistrict ranger, this was "a reaction to the fact that there were a lot of people down there that thought their role as a boatman was to sit in the boat and drink beer all day." He said what they were finding was that this was *not* exactly what many of the passengers expected or wanted to experience when

Georgie with Dave Toeppen at Outdoor Show in Chicago, January 1991. *Courtesy of Bob Atherton.*

they were down in the canyon. The Park Service took a lot of heat for putting in this regulation, but many of the operators themselves were for it.[4]

This new regulation did not sit well with Georgie. She was both owner and boatman, and she was used to starting the day with a beer and then drinking some throughout the day. She did switch to non-alcoholic beverages during the daytime, but they were not to her liking. As the season wore on she began to lose weight.

Dan Cassidy and his wife, Diane, went on a trip with Georgie in late May and early June. Dan had been on a number of dory trips through the canyon in earlier years; he knew the river pretty well, this being his twelfth trip.

Dan said the trip consisted mainly of long days on the river, getting up at a quarter to five or five at the latest, having hot water to make tea, hot chocolate, or coffee, plus a box of cereal, and that was breakfast. In his log of the trip, Dan noted that there were "different types of people, smokers & drinkers. Not the dory types at all." He told the author, "You'd usually get on the river somewhat hungry. It seemed like she always had about thirty-five boxes of cereal for forty-three people." They were packed and on the river by seven, or shortly thereafter. If one missed getting a box of cereal and did not like the leftovers served at egg break, they had to wait until two in the afternoon to get something to eat.[5]

Dan said they didn't stop to see much of anything, and when they did stop, like for egg break or lunch, Georgie always managed to land at a place where nobody could go anywhere. They would go by some of the most marvelous side canyons and stop at a dead-end rock pile for lunch. This was because "she didn't want anybody to spread out—she didn't want anybody to get lost or bit by snakes. She was always talking about snakes. You were not allowed to go up in the bushes."

On the six-day trip, the only place the party really stopped was the Little Colorado River for thirty minutes, and at Deer Creek for two or three hours. They went by Havasu without even slowing down. Dan said, "Havasu Creek isn't a place I need to stop anyhow—I've hiked there and stopped there so many times on dory trips, but I thought there were a lot of people that would have liked to have seen it."

Another thing that annoyed Cassidy was that passengers had to sit in one position with backs against the middle tube, so they could only get one view of the canyon. And Georgie would not let them take their cameras out because she did not want to be responsible for getting them wet.

When Dan tried to ask questions of Georgie, she refused to answer, saying she did not do interviews. Perhaps she sensed some of his resentments. He said, however, that he was glad to have gone on a trip with Georgie.

Losing Weight

When Georgie realized she was losing weight, she attributed it to not drinking regular beer on the river, and she became more subdued. Roz Jirge said Georgie had *lived* on beer; it was one of the main parts of her diet, along with avocados and tomatoes. "During the day I never saw her drink more than she could handle. However, after Marty's death, she seemed to become more withdrawn and the beer-drinking at night would often make her very intoxicated, more than I was used to seeing."[6]

Teresa Yates remembers meeting Georgie at Pierce Ferry and being so glad to see her. She said:

My boat was coasting in to the shoreline, I pulled my motor because it's shallow there, and I coasted in and parked the boat and I was already running up front, because she was already walking very briskly from her de-rig area over to see me. So we were just excited to see each other. And I ran off my boat and just picked her up and realized how light she had gotten! And started swinging her around and she says: "Put me down! Put me down!"[7]

Georgie told her, "You're not supposed to *do* that! I'm trying to look like I'm *fatter* than I am!" And she said, "I'm losing weight because I can't drink Coors!" And she added, "You're picking me up like a feather! You're showing everybody I'm not *there* anymore!" Georgie told her, "I'm wearing floppy clothes to look bigger than I am so they don't know how thin I am." Teresa said that was the first clue that something was wrong with Georgie's health.

Ted Freeman said, "I remember the first trip I was on—it was just a non-stop running commentary all day on the big boat. She had something to tell you about every rock all the way down the river." But in 1991, the second trip he took with Georgie, she was very quiet. "She wouldn't talk much. Maybe she knew then she was pretty sick."[8]

Karen Smith was along for the last trip of the season. She said the water was low and when they went through Crystal it was a completely different ride. She said Georgie would normally hit the wall on the left side and the left side of the raft would stand on end, but this time the current pulled them over to the right and they missed the wall. The raft got hung up on the rock pile next to Big Red. It was Karen's first time being stuck on a boat in the middle of a rapid. Water was rushing by and some of the passengers started to get excited. The boatmen, Jim Coburn and Ron Hancock, along with helpers Karen and Phyllis Wilken, talked to the passengers to get them calmed down.

Georgie yelled orders to the crew. A couple of the passengers were still excited and nervous, so Phyllis and Karen tried to calm them by singing songs and telling jokes. Hancock was busy taking pictures, so Coburn, in between talking to the passengers and reassuring them that everything was okay, went back and talked to Georgie to find out what she wanted them to do. Coburn had people on the left side of the raft move over to the right front. He put more and more people up there until they sat three in a lap, winding up with about twenty-two passengers and four boatmen in that location. They alternately rocked back and forth and jumped up and down for forty-five minutes. Eventually they rocked their way off the rocks and went on.

Karen said the incident made it "a *fabulous* trip! It was very exciting for me, because I'd never done that before." She said that between Coburn and Georgie and Hancock it was done with such finesse—they knew what they were doing. "That is what made it so great!"[9]

Natalie Jensen and Marnie Bellows worked as waitresses at Marble Canyon Lodge and frequently served Georgie when she was preparing for trips. One day Natalie told Georgie she would like to go on a trip with her, maybe work her way, and she would like to go together with her friend Marnie. Marnie was the one who prepared Georgie's plates at meal time. She would put little grapes around on the plate and arrange the fruits and vegetables to look like a sand painting. Sometimes Georgie would say, "I just don't want to eat it! It's too beautiful!" And then she would giggle.

To them it was a dream come true when Georgie offered them a trip free of charge except for the cost of the helicopter out at the end of the trip. They wound up on that last trip of the season with Georgie.

Of the trip Bellows said:

> You look back there and she'd be getting whipped back and forth and she'd just be laughing her butt off, like it was the first time she'd ever done it. It was just like: getting thrown all over the place back there—She did love it. And you could see that, every minute down there how much she enjoyed and how much she enjoyed other people enjoying it. And that was really a big part for her, that she turned people on to the Grand Canyon experience. And it was in her own way—it wasn't like some of the trips where you get catered to left and right. It was a little bit of the rough and tumble side of the Canyon. It was a little bit of getting away from your everyday life and getting a little sand in your eyes and a little grit in your teeth![10]

Marnie and Natalie were amazed when Georgie would call the ravens in so she could feed them; and she would tell them stories about her young life. Some of them were strictly stories, such as telling them how she had been in the circus as a young adult. She claimed to have worked with the circus where they had a raven who could imitate sounds, and she told them how it could even do a rattlesnake.

Of the incident in the Rock Garden at Crystal Rapid, Bellows said, "I've never been so scared in my life!" Natalie Jensen remembers:

I looked up when it all happened. We stopped and the first thing I looked back at Georgie and Georgie was up looking at passengers heads . . . making sure everybody was there. That was the first concern for Georgie. Then afterward it was, like: "Boatmen, boatmen, okay, let's get a plan and let's talk to these people and let's decide what we're gonna do." Exactly that. I mean, it was very . . . really calculated. She just was like: "Okay, let's just . . . we gotta get out of this situation." That's the thing.

"Sometimes you take what you get," was Georgie's comment afterward. "It's pot luck out here."

Bellows said that on the evenings Georgie felt like telling stories she would "just kinda light up. You could see the aura around her! She was just like this little angel or something!" They were fascinated by her tales of the old days, of finding a body in Cataract Canyon—she told of being on the Groucho Marx show and how she upstaged Groucho when telling of that incident; telling of trips to Mexico and Alaska, and of swimming the river with Harry Aleson.

Georgie also made some remarks that sounded profound to Bellows and Jensen. They remember her speaking about aging and how so many people, as they get older, just want to sit at home and watch television. She could not stand to watch TV because every time she turned it on there was a woman crying and she could not stand to see those women crying. She did not believe in crying. She told them, "Don't sit home and wait for death to come. You go out and enjoy. Live today for what it is."

In the fall of 1991, after the boating season ended, Georgie began getting ready for the 1992 season. Her brochures were sent out with dates and prices for the trips, and reservations were taken, but Georgie's health continued to decline. She had an aversion to doctors; although she loved them as friends, *going* to a doctor for medical reasons, that was a different story. Yet, in mid-December, she said to her secretary, Lee McCurry, "You know something's wrong. I just feel bloated." Then finally on a Sunday she said, "I think tomorrow you'd better take me to a doctor."[11]

She could not get an overnight appointment to see a doctor, so Lee took her to a hospital emergency room. Georgie must have had

Georgie laughing in motor well as she takes on Crystal Rapid. *Courtesy of Dan Hunting.*

a premonition of what was wrong because she turned over her power of attorney to Lee before going to the hospital. After three hours of tests, the doctors told her something was very wrong and she would need to remain in the hospital. Two days later Georgie called Lee and said, "You gotta come down. I want to talk to you." Lee said Georgie told her, "I can tell you right now, the answer's no." Lee said she knew right then it was cancer. Georgie was hospitalized for one week and then insisted on going home. The doctors told her they needed to do an exploratory operation, as they did not know where the cancer was located. Georgie told them, "It doesn't matter where it's at. It's cancer." To that the doctors told her they might be able to save her life—add five or more years to it. To which Georgie replied, "And live in pure hell—what you're gonna do to me with chemotherapy!" She added, "All you're gonna do is put me through five years of hell and pad your pockets! *I want outta here!*" So Lee took her home.

As she was told she had only a very short time left, Georgie asked Lee's son, Robert, to take all of her animals to the veterinarian and have them put to sleep. She did not feel any of them would be happy with anyone else. Later, as her life continued longer than she had expected, she missed their companionship.

Later Lee took her to a different doctor, a gynecologist. Lee said he was very kind. Georgie was a fatalist, and she came to an understanding with the doctor, who became her physician for the remainder of her life, that the writing was on the wall as far as Georgie was concerned. The only thing she wanted him to do was try to keep her as free from pain as possible, and that is precisely what he did, nothing more.

She was able to finish out her days on her own terms. Once a week the doctor would drain the fluids collecting in her abdomen. Lee said it was extremely hard to see a person who was old enough to be her mother, and who had been able to do more than she could, go "pfft" and become just the opposite. Georgie got to the point where Lee had to help her dress and undress. She lost so much weight she was almost like a skeleton, just the bones with skin hanging on her. It was obvious that Georgie's river running days were over.

25 Memorials for a Legend, 1992

G eorgie sold her business to Bill George, owner of Western River Expeditions in Salt Lake City, Utah. Lee McCurry said, "She thought the world and all of Ted Hatch and of Bill George. But she had said, back in '86, 'If I was ever to sell to anybody, it would be Bill George, because I know he's got the money to buy me out.'"[1] Georgie sent the following letter to her clients:

Dear River Rats:
    After a lifetime of adventures and 47 years of leading white water expeditions on the Colorado River in Grand Canyon, I have turned my valued "river rats" over to Western River Expeditions, a company which has operated trips in the Grand Canyon and other areas for the past 35 years.
    This decision has not been easy, for as I stated in the epilogue of my book "Georgie Clark—Thirty Years of River Running": "And so I am off down the Grand Canyon again doing what I love best, for I am Georgie Clark, Woman of the River, and if I have my way, I shall repeat these trips through the biggest rapids in the world, over and over and over again . . . Forever!"
    Unfortunately, life is at best precarious and uncertain, and I am compelled by cancer to part company with the river and thousands of people I have come to know and love through our countless shared experiences.
    My office manager, Lee McCurry, for this year will continue to coordinate trips and receive your payments, although

the trips actually will be operated by Western River Expeditions.

I chose Western to purchase my company and operate my trips because I know they provide a quality experience with some of the very best guides, equipment and Dutch-·Oven meals in the business.

For this year, your confirmation information, including trip rates, terms for final payment, cancellation policy, meeting place, time and transportation, will remain unchanged. The only difference is your final payment will have to be made by check as Western does not accept credit cards.

Please know that although I will be unable to be with you physically on your trip, I will always be there in spirit. Enjoy your trip. For you, as it has been hundreds of times for me, running the Grand Canyon of the Colorado is truly the adventure of a lifetime.

Cordially,

Georgie Clark

Georgie then cut herself off from everyone but Lee McCurry and her two children. She would not take any telephone calls, although she enjoyed hearing messages on the answering machine. She did write letters to some of her oldest and dearest friends, including Bob Atherton, who was on her 1955 Grand Canyon trip, and L. C. B. "Mac" McCullough, who used to visit her at the San Francisco Boat Show each year. However, as the days stretched into months, Georgie changed her mind. She began to telephone some friends and agreed to say her farewells in person.

In April of 1992 Bob Pearson flew out from Maine and spent several days in Las Vegas. He was able to get together with Georgie and Lee for lunch one day. He had not seen Georgie for about a year and he noted that "in her mental attitude, in her mind, she was as sharp as ever. But physically—her illness had really taken quite a toll on her."

They went to eat at J.J.'s, a favorite haunt of Georgie's out on the Boulder Highway. Just before they returned from the cafe, Bob was talking to Georgie in Lee's van and he noticed a collapsible wheelchair in it. At a later time, while talking to Lee, he mentioned the wheelchair. Lee told him there were times when Georgie was in an area where she felt nobody knew her, and she would allow herself to be pushed in this wheelchair, but if she had the remotest idea there was anybody around who knew her, she absolutely refused to use it.[2]

Return to the River

In April Tom Prange and Don Brown, two of Georgie's boatmen from the Los Angeles Fire Department, decided to visit Georgie. Prange said:

> We were sitting there in her favorite restaurant . . . it was "J.J.'s", or anyway, the coffee shop. And she didn't look good at all. She had her jacket on and I didn't realize how light she was until I went to help her get up after we had finished eating. She was nothing but bones at that time. But in seeing her, her face was real drawn and everything at lunch, so I could tell . . . she'd lost a lot of weight and wasn't in very good health. And I thought, "Wouldn't it be great to take her to Marble Canyon?" And not knowing, you know, where we could get a motorhome or anything. I mean I didn't worry about it. But I asked her.
>
> I also knew that the key to the whole thing was Lee, because it seemed to me—the information that I had—that Lee was pretty much controlling what she did and how she did it and all that. So anyway I brought it up at lunch with Lee sitting right there, and I had the encouragement from Lee.[3]

As soon as Tom mentioned the idea, Lee began to figure which days would be the best for Georgie to go. Her fluid was drained on Mondays, and on Tuesdays she was sick from that. So, "Wednesday, Thursday, and Friday would be good days." With that they decided they could do it, and made a tentative date. It did not look as if Georgie had much time left.

Three weeks later, they picked Georgie up on a Wednesday morning and headed for Marble Canyon, Arizona, in Brown's motor home. Before leaving, Georgie called only two people to meet her there, Teresa Yates and Ranger Tom Workman.

Teresa said when she found out Georgie was sick, she started sending her cards—lots of cards and pictures of her and her puppy. She did not receive anything back from Georgie for quite a while, but she just kept sending the cards and pictures. While on river trips Teresa also sent cards from Phantom Ranch. She said, "I finally received a phone call from her. The answering machine came on and she started talking. And I just ran for the machine, because I was out-side at the time she called!" They talked on the phone, and that broke the silence. Georgie wrote Teresa a short letter, and from then on their answering machines started talking to each other. Georgie called and told Teresa she was going to Lee's Ferry, wanted to see her, and gave her the dates. Teresa called back and said she would be there.

Don Brown could not speak clearly, as he had had throat surgery, and Georgie could not understand him. Therefore, on the trip, Brown drove and Tom sat back with Georgie. They fixed a place for her on a fold-down couch next to a big picture window, right behind the dri-ver's seat, and they propped her up with pillows so she could see out. Tom sat next to her all the way to Marble Canyon and chatted with her when she was awake. Georgie recalled many odd things—told them quite a few stories that they had not heard her tell before. But even then she could only stay awake for about fifteen or twenty min-utes at a time. She would talk and then go to sleep.

At Marble Canyon Georgie had her favorite room. Brown and Prange had a room just around the corner so they could check in on her. They brought her wheelchair along, and she allowed them to use it to bring her over to the cafe. According to Teresa, those at dinner with Georgie that first night, besides Brown and Prange, were Al and Marilyn Korber and Teresa.

The next day they took her down to Lee's Ferry to visit Tom Workman. Workman said he was prepared to see a woman who was feeble in both voice and body. He was amazed to see that, although she was extremely frail in body, the inflections of her voice had not changed. Her voice and spirit were as strong as ever. Workman said he wondered how you would talk to a person who was dying. They talked of old times. Then Georgie brought up the subject of death herself. She said to him, "I'm dying and my doctors say there's nothing they can do, and that's it. I wish I could stay longer but I don't have a choice." She talked as if she were going on another adventure—and that was the way it ended.

Georgie wanted to be left alone at the launch area. Tom Prange said:

> And I had no idea. I mean, I didn't know whether she'd wheel herself into the River or what! I had considered that could happen. But we went up to the launch ramp area and parked the motorhome so that she was facing—you know—looking

down at the water. And I think we left her there for a couple hours. She just wanted to be there by herself. She didn't want to get out, so we didn't wheel her around or anything, but had her to where she could look down at the water and the boats putting in.[4]

Later they took her up to the old Lonely Dell Ranch of Mormon John Doyle Lee, for whom the area was named. Once again they left her where she could look out the window. She wanted to be alone, so Brown and Prange walked around through the fields and orchards, talking about old times on the river.

That same day they took her for a short visit to the Hatch warehouse, where Patty Ellwanger was holding a first aid seminar. Patty said, "Everybody noticed those piercing blue eyes. And as frail as she was and as tired and as sick as she was, those blue eyes were always the most sincere, dominating thing in her personality."[5]

During the afternoon Georgie was in her room with the door open so people could come and go to visit with her. Jane Foster said they brought out the leopard-spotted tablecloth for dinner that night and set up her place.

Teresa along with Al and Marilyn Korber drove up from Phoenix to meet Georgie on Wednesday and have dinner with her. Georgie asked Teresa to come back for breakfast the next morning, so she camped out at the Badger Overlook Road and returned to Marble Canyon Lodge in the morning. Teresa left for home about 11 A.M. She said, "I didn't go down to the Ferry with her. I asked her if she wanted me to go with her and she didn't express that, so I just thought she might want to do it alone. So I left it at that."[6]

On April 28 Orville Miller, Joan De Fato, and Roz and Jagdish Jirge met Georgie at J.J.'s Restaurant. They were the last of her river friends to see her alive. Georgie made no attempt to walk to the table; Lee brought her in the wheelchair. She was so emaciated she appeared to be all eyes and mouth and thick blonde hair. She was still unwilling to be seen with gray hair; just prior to visiting Marble Canyon, Georgie asked Lee to dye her hair. Her voice was as strong as ever and she was very accepting of her fate. The visit was short, not more than thirty minutes. She had almost no strength left. Jagdish helped her into Lee's minivan, then kissed her hand. He had never gone on a river trip, but knew Georgie well and respected her immensely. He was particularly moved by the dignity and courage with which she faced her death. Two weeks later, to the day, she was gone.

On May 12, 1992, Georgie passed away peacefully in her sleep. Bishop Bill George officiated at the funeral, and Tom Workman gave a short talk. He said of this later:

> I ended it with the movie and book that just came out. Hook made a quotation when he was about ready to be killed. Peter Pan was going to run him through with the sword, and the quote from Captain Hook was, "Go ahead, finish me through. I've lived an illustrious life, I've done many things, I've traveled around the world, I've sailed magnificent ships. Go ahead, run me through. Death is just another adventure." And that's the way I ended it with Georgie. She's on another adventure. When she gets that trip finished, I'll book a trip with her, maybe when my time is come.[7]

At the request of Bill George, the following verses, which Lee McCurry said were taped on Georgie's desk long before Lee started working for her, were read at the memorial service:

"Miss Me a Little but Let Me Go"

When I come to the end of the road
    And the sun has set for me.
I want no rites in a gloom filled room,
    Why cry for a soul set free?
Miss me a little, but not too long,
    And not with your head bowed low.
Remember the love we once shared,
    Miss me—but let me go.
For this is a journey we all must take,
    And each must go alone.
It's all part of the master's plan,
    A step on the road home.
When you are lonely and sick of heart,
    Go to friends we know,
And bury your sorrows in doing good deeds,
    Miss me but let me go.

Those of Georgie's friends who attended the memorial service vowed that they would keep in touch with each other even though

Georgie was gone, and they have had two or more reunions at the home of Dr. Orville Miller in Sacramento since that time.

Ceremony at Crystal Rapid

Teresa Yates was on the river when Georgie passed away and did not learn of her death until a week after it happened. When she got off the trip, she returned a call from Lee McCurry. Lee told Teresa that the day before Georgie passed on she said she wanted Teresa to carry on the tradition and the spirit of her on the river—Georgie wanted her to wear the leopard print and fly the flag. She was to wear it no matter what anybody thought. Lee said, "Teresa, you've got to wear this leopard print." And she added, "Wear it with pride and carry it on. Carry her spirit on." When her next trip launched on May 27, Teresa began flying a leopard-print flag. She said, "I went to a fabric store and made up a flag and started flying that on my boat and then dedicated it to her."[8]

In addition to flying her flag, Teresa wanted to do more to commemorate Georgie. She talked it over with Tim Whitney, the trip leader of her next run. Then she went out and bought $250 worth of flowers and put them in an ice chest. There were carnations and gladiolus and red and white roses, red being Georgie's favorite color. Tim and Teresa each had a dozen roses for themselves, and there were four or five each for the rest of the crew. The carnations and the gladiolus were to be passed out to the passengers.

During Tim's orientation talk at the beginning of the trip, after getting the people comfortable with what to expect on the river run, he mentioned that "this trip is dedicated to Georgie Clark." He told them a little about her and said that throughout the trip the crew was going to tell them quotes and stories about Georgie. "And, if we go by something on the trip that reminds us of Georgie, we're going to let you know about it." He also told them that, since this trip was dedicated to her, on the third day "we'd like all who want to participate to join in and take part in a special tribute to Georgie."

There were thirty passengers and five crew members on two S-rigs. As they went down the right side of President Harding Rapid they said, "Now Georgie always thought the wimps went down the right side, because she always went down the left!" At almost every point along the river they were reminded of something about Georgie.

They just talked about Georgie until they reached Boucher Rapid. There they tied the two boats together and floated the three miles down to Crystal. In that forty-five-minute period Teresa gave a thumbnail sketch of Georgie's life—told what she knew about Georgie and what she did in her life—about the initiations, and explained some characteristics about her that would give the people an insight as to why they were doing this.

Then they pulled in to scout Crystal. The water was at a lower stage, making a perfect setting for what they would do next. The weather had been rainy until they got to Boucher, and the river was muddy. Then the sun came out. The water was low enough to do a left-side run, which truly fit the occasion, as Georgie nearly always ran left at Crystal.

While Teresa and Tim were scouting the rapid they had their swampers take out the flowers and hand them out to the passengers, reserving the roses for the crew. The crew members wore red t-shirts, in honor of Georgie's favorite color. When Tim and Teresa returned to their boats, they had a sense that this was going to be something really special. When they walked back into their motor wells, the swampers had taken a dozen roses and stuck them in the handle of each motor, so that when they stepped down there were bouquets waiting.

They pulled out into the current and were in a holding pattern facing upstream. At Teresa's suggestion they were organized so that the people started throwing the flowers in from the front of the boat to the back of the boat in a wave, one after another, so the flowers would not all be in one group. The two boats were right together and the flowers spread out at first, then funneled back into the tongue of the rapid. It made a trail of colors as the flowers intertwined. Teresa said:

> And they just floated down in and they went down right where the left run was! They showed us the way! I mean, we were watching them go through and they just went right where we needed to be, to run it left. Then Tim and I threw our roses in last and Tim threw his in in a group and I just started taking mine and was just, one by one, throwing them in. And I threw . . . the last rose I threw was a red rose and I threw it with my left hand, which is awkward enough anyway, but I threw it and it stuck to the back of my boat. It didn't hit the water. So I just left it there and it came off when we ran the rapid. And *that* was pretty neat! But we followed the flowers through: Tim went in first and he had a great run and I

had a fun run and when we came out down below, there were all these flowers just swirling around in the water! You know: just coming in our motor wells and the eddies and it was really beautiful![9]

The passengers were deeply touched. Teresa recalled, "By the time we got to Crystal I think there were about eight or ten people that were crying." She said an older gentleman was sitting next to her in the motor well, and when they were throwing the flowers in he became overcome with emotion. "And we just ended up hugging, right above Crystal!"

Tim said, "It was great! It was meant to happen."

Teresa recalled, "I was pretty happy that day. It was very touching, but I didn't shed a tear. That is one thing I was glad for because Georgie wouldn't have liked that! I was able to hold my composure!"

In their summer newsletter, the Grand Canyon River Guides printed Georgie's picture on the front cover along with this tribute:

Georgie
1910–1992
From her first float trips with
Harry Aleson in the 1940's to
her last trip at the helm of her
triple rig in the fall of '91,
she was unquestionably, incontestably,
The Woman of The River.

She was a renegade from the
get go. Throughout the 50's and
60's she did it herself and she did
it her own way. On through the
70's and 80's. Her folks adored
her. She was never mainstream.
She was Georgie.
Always Georgie.
It was the 1990's
when the river community finally
embraced her for it.
Here's to you, Georgie.[10]

Inside the newsletter was an account by Teresa about the memorial trip.

In reminiscing about Georgie, Jane Foster observed, "She was *not* a woman's libber, and she didn't stand up for woman-kind. She was just an adventurer." Jane said, "She would never have been the bra burning, flag-waving sort of feminist-type person. She was just a *person* and she just did what she wanted to do and gender wasn't a big item!"[11]

Rosalyn Jirge has started a campaign to have a rapid in Grand Canyon named for Georgie. Her first choice is to have Crystal renamed, as it was Georgie's favorite rapid. She is running into resistance in this because Crystal is so famous. But if she accomplishes her goal, it will be a fitting and lasting memorial for a legend.

Appendix
Georgie's Boatmen and Helpers

Signifies Los Angeles Fire Department.

Bob Atherton
Daryl Bates
Carol Bell
Kim and Randy Berg
Kirk "Bing" Bingham*
Bruce "Blacky" Blackwell*
Dave Briggs
Alan Broude
Darlene Brown
Don "Brownie" Brown*
Ron Bruno*
Chester "Chet" Bundy
Ed Burzinski*
Mike Celantano*
Rich Chambers
Jim Coburn*
Jack Cole
Pat Conlan*
Bill Conway
John "Mule" Cooper*
Mike Corcoran*
Jose Couse*
Kathy Couse
Joan DeFato
Paul DeRoss
Glen Dinger*

Paige "Dog" Dougherty
Ray "Pierre" DuBord
Fred Eiseman, Jr.
Margaret "Maggie" Eiseman
Bill Emert
Louise Emert
Dave Fair*
Rick Fair
Jim Falls
Libby Foster
Gerry Foust*
Wink Frandsen*
Mr. & Mrs. Ludwig "Lud" Fromme
Kathy Gambill
Ramon Garcia*
Gene Glidden
Ed Gooch
Ray "Half Breed" Gorospe*
Suzanne Granger
Bob Greenwell
Charles Gripp
Harvey Lee Hall
Vicki Hall
Mr. & Mrs. Ron Hancock
Kjeld Harris
Rick Hay*

Herb Heitmeyer*
Mike Henry*
Richard Hodgson*
Bill Huff*
Kaye Huff
Marty Hunsaker
Dan Hunting
Richard Ingebretsen
Bill Jensen
Roz Jirge
Jim Johnson*
Paula Jones
Chuck Kane*
Red Kastner*
Shaun Kelly
Jack Kelso
Ramsay Kieffer
Reg Kison
Al Korber
Marilyn Moss Korber
Bob Lackey
Jim Lawson
Bob Laxague*
Dave Lingefelt
David Lingefelt
Dana Littlejohn*
Glenn Littlejohn
Harry "Silky" Littlejohn*
Mr. & Mrs. Al Loewe*
Elmer "Peewee" Luckhard
Janet "Kiwi" Macky
Dick McCallum
Robert "Bobby" McCurry
Carolyn McDaniel
Robert McElroy*
Ron McIntyre*
Connie McTaggart
Danny Meeks
Mr. & Mrs. George Melendrez
Penny Meo
Claire Meyer
Orville Miller
Chuck Mills*

Kent Morby
Bob Morse
Karen Morse
Doug Murphy*
Duane Newcomb
Bob Olsen*
Ray Olsen*
Carl Palas*
David Pearson*
Robert Pearson
Tom Prange*
Fred "Rags" Ragland*
Reams Rainey*
Walt Rainey
Mike Reagan*
Jamie Remy*
Frank Rich, Jr.
Dennis Ross
Lee Scott
Don Scutchfield*
Kathleen Scutchfield
Paul Semerjian*
Mr. & Mrs. Bob* Setterberg
Dick Seward
Nancy Sharpe
Tom Shrout*
Tony Silva
Barry Smith
Karen Smith
Richard "Dick" Smith
Ron Smith
Howard Sokol*
Pat Stadt
Clint Stamps*
Jim Stanley
Kim Steiner
Harold Stephens
Harry Stires*
Bob "Smokey" Stover*
Art Suess*
Pete Thompson*
Beth Tierney
Mary Jean Tierney

Pat Tierney*
Eunice Tjaden
Dave Tuckwiller
Tom Vail
John C. Waldron
Bruce Watson*
Jeff Webber
Ken Weeks

John Weisheit
Tanya Wilcox
Phyllis Wilkin
John Wilkins
Bob Witherspoon*
Frank Wommack
Teresa Yates

Notes

Chapter 1

1. Diamond Creek and a nearby pyramid-shaped butte called Diamond Peak were named by Lt. Joseph Christmas Ives and Dr. John S. Newberry during their exploration in 1858. See Nancy Brian, *River to Rim: A Guide to Names along the Colorado River in Grand Canyon from Lake Powell to Lake Mead* (Flagstaff, Ariz.: Earthquest Press, 1992), 125.
2. Georgie White Clark and Duane Newcomb, *Georgie Clark: Thirty Years of River Running* (San Francisco: Chronicle Books, 1977), 31–34.
3. Mile posts on the Colorado River in Grand Canyon are designated as the number of miles downstream from Lee's Ferry, Arizona.
4. Clark and Newcomb, *Georgie Clark*, 32.
5. According to Bureau of Reclamation records, the maximum flow of the river through the Grand Canyon during June 1945 was 50,200 cfs (cubic feet per second).
6. Clark and Newcomb, *Georgie Clark*, 32.
7. Quartermaster Canyon was named for Quartermaster, a Hualapai Indian who lived there between 1900 and 1930. Brian, *River to Rim*, 130.
8. First discovered by Jacob Hamblin, the site was named for Harrison Pierce, who operated a ferry from there across the Colorado River for the Mormon Church from 1876 to 1883. Brian, *River to Rim*, 134.
9. Biographical Notes, Harry L. Aleson Papers, Utah State Historical Society; hereafter cited as Aleson Papers.
10. Ibid.
11. Georgie White Clark, interview by Karen Underhill, Grand Canyon, 6 November 1991, Northern Arizona University Cline Library; also stated in numerous interviews with Georgie by others.
12. Copy of birth certificate in possession of author and in the Georgie Clark Collection at Northern Arizona University Cline Library (hereafter cited as Clark Collection).
13. Clark, interview by Underhill, 1.

14. Colorado Department of Health to Rosalyn J. Jirge, 20 April 1994, in possession of author (regarding verification of birth certificate).
15. The comptometer was the forerunner of the modern calculator.
16. Clark and Newcomb, *Georgie Clark*, 23.
17. Ibid.
18. Ibid, 27.
19. Harry Aleson, quoted in *Boulder City (Colo.) News*, 14 September 1944.
20. Clark and Newcomb, *Georgie Clark*, 28.
21. Ibid.
22. "Aleson Directs Own Boat Rescue while Suffering from Scorpion Sting." *Boulder City (Colo.) News*, 8 September 1944.
23. Clark to Aleson, 1 September 1947, Aleson Papers, box 2, folder 10 (see label included in letter).
24. Aleson Papers, box 1, folder 10.
25. Aleson Papers, box 1, folder 14.

Chapter 2

1. Clark and Newcomb, *Georgie Clark*, 29–30.
2. See J. W. Powell, *The Exploration of the Colorado River and Its Canyons* (New York: Dover Publications, Inc., 1961).
3. David Lavender, *River Runners of the Grand Canyon* (Grand Canyon, Ariz.: Grand Canyon Natural History Association, 1985), 8–9.
4. Aleson Papers, box 2, folder 2.
5. Aleson to Clark, Aleson Papers, box 2, folder 2 (on Johnston Hotel stationery headed only by "Also Sunday AM").
6. Clark to Aleson, 9 May 1946, Aleson Papers, box 1, folder 14.
7. Harry Aleson, Log of June 1946, 1946 Diaries and Journals, Aleson Papers, box 26, folder 2.
8. Ibid.
9. Clark and Newcomb, *Georgie Clark*, 35–36.
10. Aleson, Log of June 1946.
11. Clark to Aleson, Aleson Papers, box 2, folder 6.
12. Clark to Aleson, 7 April 1947, Aleson Papers, box 2, folder 7.
13. Clark to Aleson, 4 August 1947, Aleson Papers, box 2, folder 9.
14. Clark to Aleson, Aleson Papers, box 2, folder 7.
15. Clark and Newcomb, *Georgie Clark*, 40–41.
16. Here and following unless otherwise cited, "Cataract Canyon Boat Trip, 1947," typed copy of original, Clark Collection, box 1, folder 4.
17. Cataract Canyon was named by Major John Wesley Powell in 1869. Powell, *Exploration of the Colorado River*, 216.
18. John Weisheit, "Harry Aleson and Georgie Clark: The Log of the 'Mai Qui,'" *The Confluence: The Journal of Colorado Plateau River Guides* (Moab, Utah), vol. 4, issue 1 (Spring 1997): 22.

Chapter 3

1. Clark to Aleson, 5 February 1948, Aleson Papers, box 3, folder 1.
2. Jeff Wallach, "On River Time," *Sierra: The Magazine of the Sierra Club*, May/June 1994, 66.
3. Harry Aleson to "Lou," 1 June 1948, Marston Collection at the Huntington Library, box 252. Items from this collection are reproduced by permission of the Huntington Library, San Marino, Calif., and are hereafter cited as Marston Collection.
4. Ibid.
5. See David E. Miller, *Hole- in-the-Rock* (Salt Lake City: University of Utah Press, 1975).
6. Discovered and named by Major Powell while on his epic voyage in 1869. Powell, *Exploration of the Colorado River*, 230–31.
7. Clark to Aleson, 1 July 1948, Aleson Papers, box 3, folder 5.
8. Harry Aleson to Otis Marston, 30 November 1948, Aleson Papers, box 3, folder 9.
9. Here and following unless otherwise cited, Bob Rigg and Irish McCalla, interview by author, Scottsdale, Ariz., 15 April 1993. Also see "Six Girls against the Colorado," *Look Magazine*, 8 May 1951.
10. Nancy Nelson, *Any Time, Any Place, Any River: The Nevills of Mexican Hat* (Flagstaff, Ariz.: Red Lake Books, 1991), 64.
11. Bob Rigg, interview by author, Marble Canyon, Ariz., 4 April 1993.
12. Aleson to Marston, 2 January 1951, Aleson Papers, box 5, folder 7.
13. Marie DeRoss to Harry Aleson, 28 August 1951, Aleson Papers, box 6, folder 5.
14. Clark to Aleson, c. 24 September 1951, Aleson Papers, box 6, folder 6.
15. "The 1952 Grand Canyon Trip," copy of Georgie's handwritten account, Clark Collection.
16. Rigg, interview.
17. Legend has it that Mormon explorer Jacob Hamblin shot a badger in the upper reaches of the canyon that comes into the Colorado River just above Mile 8. Later in another canyon he boiled the badger in the alkaline water of the creek. The next morning he discovered that the badger's fat had turned to soap—not a very appetizing breakfast! Thus the names Badger Creek and Soap Creek. Kim Crumbo, *A River Runner's Guide to the History of the Grand Canyon* (Boulder, Colo.: Johnson Books, 1981), 7.
18. This spot was named by Major Powell in 1869 for a botanist friend who had accompanied him on a field trip to Colorado the year before. Powell, *Exploration of the Colorado River*, 238.
19. John Wesley Powell and crew camped at Redwall Cavern in 1869. Brian, *River to Rim*, 30.
20. Rigg, interview.

21. Tad Nichols and Bob Rigg, interview by author, Marble Canyon, Ariz., 2 April 1993.
22. Clark, The 1952 Grand Canyon Trip.

Chapter 4

1. See D. E. Miller, *Hole-in- the-Rock*.
2. Georgie Clark, "Trip from Hole in Rock across to Skelly Oil Field, 10 April 1953," handwritten, Clark Collection. Also see Harry Aleson, "A Pioneer Mormon Road 73 Years Old, 19 April 1953," Clark Collection.
3. See C. Gregory Crampton, *Ghosts of Glen Canyon: History beneath Lake Powell* (St. George, Ut.: Publishers Place, Inc., 1986), 58.
4. Clark, "Trip from Hole in Rock to Skelly."
5. Ibid.
6. Aleson, "A Pioneer Mormon Road."
7. Clark, "Trip from Hole in Rock to Skelly."
8. Here and following unless otherwise cited, Georgie Clark, "Grand Canyon Run—July 10, 1953," Clark Collection.
9. Georgie Clark, "Upset at Cave Springs," handwritten on a torn piece of brown paper, Clark Collection.
10. Powell, *Exploration of the Colorado River*, 238.
11. Brian, *River to Rim*, 38.
12. See Richard E. Westwood, *Rough-Water Man: Elwyn Blake's Colorado River Expeditions* (Reno, Nev.: University of Nevada Press, 1992), 189–90.

Chapter 5

1. Here and following unless otherwise cited, Georgie Clark, "The Mighty Grand Canyon Trip of July 10, 1954," Marston Collection and Aleson Papers.
2. Brian, *River to Rim*, 43.
3. Clark and Newman, *Georgie Clark*, 54.
4. Bill Belknap, letter, Marston Collection, box 289, folder 45.

Chapter 6

1. Georgie White Clark, 1955 Schedule (record kept by Otis Marston), Marston Collection, box 290, folder 19.
2. Here and following unless otherwise cited, Marion Smith to friends after her first trip on the Colorado River, copy in possession of Rosalyn Jirge.
3. Ibid.
4. Clark and Newcomb, *Georgie Clark*, 57–58.
5. Georgie Clark, "Grand Canyon Trip, 1955," Clark Collection.

6. Helen Kendall, "1955 Grand Canyon Trip," Marston Collection, box 110.
7. Ibid.
8. Clark, "Grand Canyon Trip, 1955."
9. Kendall, "1955 Grand Canyon Trip."
10. Here and following unless otherwise cited, Dan Davis, interview by author, Marble Canyon, Ariz., 3 April 1993.
11. Margaret Gorman Eiseman, "River Diary 1955," in possession of author.
12. Joel Sayre, "Georgie's Roaring River," *Sports Illustrated*, 16 June 1958; also in Clark Collection, folder 19.
13. Ibid.
14. Here and following unless otherwise cited, Georgie Clark, "Middle Fork of the Salmon, 1955," Clark Collection.
15. Marybelle Filer, *Idaho County Free Press*, n.d. (September), Clark Collection.

Chapter 7

1. Georgie White Clark, "Biographical Information on Georgie White, 'Woman of the River,'" 1 March 1956, Clark Collection, folder 4, box 1.
2. Otis Marston to Georgie Clark, 6 April 1957, Marston Collection.
3. Lavender, *River Runners of Grand Canyon*.
4. Helen Kendall, "Cataract Canyon Trip of June 4, 1956," Marston Collection, box 110. Also see Allan Boz, letter, 17 January 1957, Marston Collection, regarding 1956 Cataract run.
5. Ibid.
6. Boz, letter.
7. Georgie Clark, "1956 Grand Canyon Trip, July 6–25," Marston Collection, box 252.
8. Dan Davis to Otis Marston, 5 November 1956, Marston Collection.
9. Here and following unless otherwise cited, Orville Miller, interview by Rosalyn Jirge.
10. Ibid.
11. For more on Reverend Shine Smith, see Gladwell Richardson, "Shine Smith's Christmas Party, 1956"; Maurice Kildare, "The Indians Named Him Shine," *Frontier Times*; Toney Richardson, "Shine Smith's Christmas Party for Indians" (all in Clark Collection).

Chapter 8

1. Russell Martin, *A Story that Stands like a Dam: Glen Canyon and the Struggle for the Soul of the West* (New York: Henry Holt and Company, 1989), 215–38. Also see Mark W. T. Harvey, *A Symbol of Wilderness* (Albuquerque: University of New Mexico Press, 1994).

2. Steven W. Carothers and Bryon T. Brown, *The Colorado River through Grand Canyon: Natural History and Human Change* (Tucson, Ariz.: University of Arizona Press, 1991), 4.
3. Here and following unless otherwise cited, Dick McCallum, interview by author, 1 April 1993.
4. Mitch Williams, interview by author, Moab, Ut., 14 July 1992.
5. Randall Henderson, "The Water Was Rough in Cataract Canyon," *Desert Magazine*, February 1958, 5; also in Clark Collection, folder 18.
6. Here and following unless otherwise cited, Margaret Gorman Eiseman, "1957 Grand Canyon Trip," in possession of author.
7. Fred B. Eiseman, Jr., "Back when the Colorado Ran Wild and Free," *River World*, October 1978, 16; also in Marston Collection.
8. Ibid.
9. M. G. Eiseman, "1957 Grand Canyon Trip."
10. Here and following unless otherwise cited, Albert H. Blum to Otis Marston, 10 February 1958, Marston Collection, box 20.
11. Ernst A. Heiniger, *Grand Canyon* (Berne, Switzerland: Kümmerly and Frey, Geographical Publishers, 1971).
12. Here and following unless otherwise cited, Dan Davis, "Incidents etc. Occurring during Georgie White-Heiniger Expedition—1958," Clark Collection.
13. Davis, interview.
14. Heiniger, *Grand Canyon*.

Chapter 9

1. Here and following unless otherwise cited, "Mexico Trip of 1958," compilation of Georgie's detailed narration and the notes of Lillian Lasch, probably typed by Marie DeRoss, Clark Collection.
2. "Journey by Raft Ends Early because of Rain," *Lewiston (Id.) Morning Tribune*, 22 August 1959; also in Marston Collection, box 294.
3. Helen Kendall to Otis Marston, 12 June 1959, Marston Collection.
4. Ken Sleight and Clifford Rayl, interview by author, Marble Canyon, Ariz., 3 April 1993.
5. "Mt. Trumbull News Items," *Washington County (Ut.) News*, 10 September 1959. Also see "Eleven Days of Shooting the Grand Canyon on a Raft," *San Jose Mercury-News*, 9 August 1959, 5; both in Marston Collection, box 294, folder 14.
6. The Grijalva River was named for its discoverer, Juan de Grijalva, who landed at its mouth in 1518. Marshal Bond, Jr., *Pacific Discovery*, November-December 1960, vol. XIII, no. 6:2.
7. Georgie Clark, "The Grijalva River," Clark Collection, folder 21.

Chapter 10

1. "River-Runners Locate Body of Victim," *The Salt Lake Tribune*, 7 June 1960; also in Clark Collection, folder 34.
2. Father John Finbarr Hayes, interview by Rosalyn Jirge, 17 January 1993.
3. Ibid.
4. Barbara Ekker, letter, 9 June 1960, Marston Collection, box 295, folder 16.
5. Here and following unless otherwise cited, Marge Petheram, "The 1960 Petheram Pamphlet, 12th Yuletide Edition," Clark Collection, folder 37.
6. Clark and Newcomb, *Georgie Clark*, 177.
7. Georgie Clark, "River Rats Exploratory Trek on Chetina and Copper Rivers of Alaska Proves Very Successful," Clark Collection.
8. Ibid.
9. Clark and Newcomb, *Georgie Clark*, 123.
10. McCallum, interview.
11. Joyce Hamilton, *White Water: The Colorado Jet Boat Expedition* (Christchurch, New Zealand: The Caxton Press, 1963), 64–65.
12. Ibid, 217–18.
13. Information for this section from Orville H. Miller, "Medical Folklore of North America," *Let's Live*, February 1961; Ellis L. Spackman, "Down the Rio Balsas—A Journey of Daring, Nerve," *Sun-Telegram*, 10 July 1964; and Rose Marie DeRoss, "The Balsas River Experience," *Let's Live*, February 1961 (all in Clark Collection, folder 32).
14. Mrs. James Bundy, *Washington County (Ut.) News*, 3 August 1961; also in Marston Collection, box 17.
15. Sylvia Tone, interview by Rosalyn Jirge, 14 November 1992.

Chapter 11

1. Sylvia Tone, "Glen Canyon Trip, 1–8 May 1962," copy in possession of author.
2. Art Gallenson to Otis Marston, 22 September 1962, Marston Collection, box 298, folder 9.
3. Sylvia Tone, "Grand Canyon Trip, May 1962," in possession of author.
4. Marjorie Steurt, "Christmas 1962," Marston Collection, box 298, folder 9.
5. *(Los Angeles) Southwestern Sun*, 6 September 1962.

Chapter 12

1. Here and following unless otherwise cited, Delphine Mohrline, "Colorado River Trip with Georgie White, Moab to Hite, Utah, through Cataract Canyon, June 3–7, 1963," in possession of author.

2. Information for this section from Marjorie Steurt, Journals, Marston Collection, box 252; and Sylvia Tone, Journal, in possession of author.
3. Bob Atherton, telephone interview by author, June 1993.
4. *The Province*, 25 July 1963 (probably a Canadian publication), clipping in Clark Collection.
5. Here and following unless otherwise cited, *Canada Weekly, The Star Weekly Magazine*, 2 November 1963.
6. Steurt, Journals.
7. Ibid.

Chapter 13

1. Spackman, "Down the Rio Balsas."
2. Here and following unless otherwise cited, Delphine Mohrline, "Balsas River Trip-Mexico with Georgie White, August 1963," Clark Collection, folder 32.
3. Spackman, "Down the Rio Balsas."
4. Ibid.
5. Mohrline, "Balsas River Trip-Mexico."
6. Georgie Clark to Sylvia Tone, 3 November 1963, in possession of author.
7. Joyce Rockwood Muench, "Georgie White, Queen of the Rivers" and "River Trip through the Marble and Grand Canyons, by Josef Muench as Told to Joyce Rockwood Muench," *Arizona Highways*, April 1965, 3; hereafter cited as J. R. Muench, *Arizona Highways*.
8. Clark to Tone, n.d., in possession of author.
9. Martin, *A Story that Stands like a Dam*, chap. 1.
10. Josef Muench, interview by author, Sacramento, Calif., 4 October 1992.
11. J. R. Muench, *Arizona Highways*.

Chapter 14

1. "Share the Expense Plan River Trips, 1965," Schedule of Trips, Marston Collection, box 301, folder 8.
2. John G. Schmitz to Georgie Clark, 4 March 1965, Clark Collection.
3. McCallum, interview.
4. Carol Hintze, interview by author, 1993, pt. 2.
5. Tone, Journal, 3 May 1965.
6. Here and following unless otherwise cited, Delphine Mohrline, "Marble Canyon, 17–31 May 1965," Clark Collection, folder 37.
7. Marion Smith, "A 1965 Trip through Grand Canyon," Clark Collection.
8. Ibid.
9. Here and following unless otherwise cited, Orville Miller, interview by author, 4 October 1992.

Chapter 15

1. Congressional House Report (H.R.) 4671.
2. Hugh Nash, *Sierra Club Bulletin*, May 1966, vol. 51, no. 5:4; also see Douglas W. Steeples, letter in "The Forum," *The (Richmond, Ind.) Palladim-Item and Sun-Telegram*, 1 May 1966 (both also in Clark Collection, folder 35).
3. Kenneth Catlin to Stewart Udall, 15 July 1966, Clark Collection.
4. M. E. Cooley, B. N. Aldridge, and R. C. Euler, "Effects of the Catastrophic Flood of December 1966, North Rim Area, Eastern Grand Canyon, Arizona," Geological Survey Professional Paper 980.
5. Don Dedera, "Flood Deals Destruction," clipping, Clark Collection, folder 36 (probably appeared in the *Arizona Republic*).
6. Georgie Clark, "Santiago River Trip, 1967," Clark Collection.
7. Here and following unless otherwise cited, Orville's story from O. Miller, interview by Jirge.
8. Clark, "Santiago River Trip."
9. Here and following unless otherwise cited, Bob or Jean's story from Jean and Robert Baer, interview by Rosalyn Jirge, San Jose, Calif., 25 September 1993.
10. Clark, "Santiago River Trip."

Chapter 16

1. Orville Miller and Joan DeFato, interview by author.
2. Ibid.
3. Brian Dierker, interview by author, 30 October 1992.
4. Al Loewe, interview by author, Sacramento, Calif., 11 September 1993.
5. Ken Sleight and Clifford Rayl, interview by author, Marble Canyon, Ariz., 3 April 1993.
6. Igor de Lissovoy, "The Royal River Rats of the Mighty Colorado," *The Donnelley Printer*, Summer 1970; also in Clark Collection, folder 37.
7. Here and following unless otherwise cited, Bill Jensen and Jim Falls, interview by author, Phoenix, Ariz., 26 January 1993.
8. Jane Foster, interview by author, 5 April 1993.
9. Patty Ellwanger, interview by author, Marble Canyon, Ariz., 5 April 1993.
10. Sylvia Tone, Letters, copies in possession of author.
11. O. Miller, interview by author.
12. Tone, Letters.
13. Foster, interview.
14. Tone, Letters.
15. Paul DeRoss, Jr., interview by Rosalyn Jirge, Norwalk, Calif., 29 November 1992.
16. Tone, Letters.
17. John Kelly to River Rats, copy in Clark Collection.

Chapter 17

1. Barbara G. Phillips, Robert A. Johnson, Robert M. Phillips, III, and Nancy J. Brian, *Monitoring the Effects of Recreational Use on the Colorado River Beaches in Grand Canyon National Park* (Flagstaff, Ariz.: Museum of Northern Arizona Press, 1986), bulletin series 55:3.
2. Pete Czura, "River Running: Conflict on the Colorado," *True Magazine*, 1974; clipping in Clark Collection, folder 3.
3. Ibid.
4. Sylvia Tone, interview by Deborah Whiteford.
5. Bob Pearson, interview by author, Sacramento, Calif., 4 October 1992.
6. Harvey Lee Hall, interview by Rosalyn Jirge, 21 April 1994.
7. Here and following unless otherwise cited, Dan Dierker, interview by author, 30 October 1992.
8. Penny Meo, interview by author, Sacramento, Calif., 4 October 1992.
9. Jeff Webber, interview by author, Sacramento, Calif., 4 October 1992.
10. Ludwig H. Fromme to author, 1 May 1993.
11. Here and following unless otherwise cited, Michael Denoyer, interview by author, Kanab, Ut., 25 May 1994.
12. Foxy (Libby) Weimer, "Colorado, Here I Am! (A Journal of Rafting the Grand Canyon), 14–23 July 1975," Clark Collection, folder 39.

Chapter 18

1. Here and following unless otherwise cited, Tom Workman, interview by author, 1 November 1992.
2. Here and following unless otherwise cited, Tom Prange, interview by Rosalyn Jirge, 26 November 1993.
3. Tom Bradshaw and friends, interview by Rosalyn Jirge, 4 December 1993.
4. Michele Strutin, *New West (San Francisco)*, 27 August 1979.
5. Ibid.
6. Ibid.
7. Here and following unless otherwise cited, Hayley Weisner, "Hayley's River Trip, 9–18 July 1978."
8. Asha Jirge, "My Grand Canyon Trip down the Colorado River, 9–18 July 1978."

Chapter 19

1. Tom Vail, interview by author, 9 November 1992.
2. Brian Rasmussen, interview by author, 30 October 1992.
3. Rosalyn Jirge, "Trip Journals—1981 Working Trip," in possession of author.

4. Rosalyn Jirge, "Thoughts and Memories," in possession of author.
5. Ibid.
6. Rosalyn Jirge, "Trip—Year 5, 'Holiday Trip,'" in possession of author.
7. Ibid.
8. Jirge, "Trip Journals."

Chapter 20

1. "Dam Facts & Figures," pamphlet, Carl Hayden Visitor Center, Glen Canyon Dam.
2. "Officials Confident Canyon Flow Will Ease," *(Flagstaff) Arizona Daily Sun*, 29 June 1983.
3. Ibid.
4. *(Grand Canyon) Visitor Information*, vol. 94, 30 June 1983.
5. Here and following unless otherwise cited, Daryl Bates, telephone interview by author, 11 January 1995.
6. Roy Webb, "A Grand Party for a Grand Lady: Georgie White's 80th Birthday" (unpublished article written after his return from the party).
7. Chuck Mills, telephone interview by author, 15 January 1995.
8. Here and following unless otherwise cited, Raymond Gorospe, telephone interview by author, 16 January 1995.
9. Mills, interview.
10. Here and following unless otherwise cited, Mark L. Austin, interview by author.
11. Gill Ediger, "Fear & Loathing on the Grand during the High Water of June 1983," in possession of author.

Chapter 21

1. Ray Abrams, telephone interview by Brien Culhane, 26 August 1984, U.S. Department of the Interior, National Park Service, supplementary case/incident record no. 2832, Grand Canyon Library.
2. Here and following unless otherwise cited, Fromme to author.
3. Don Scott, testimony, 11 September 1984.
4. Abrams, interview.
5. Hall, interview.
6. Here and following unless otherwise cited, Paul Miller, interview by author, Sacramento, Calif., 4 October 1992.
7. Here and following unless otherwise cited, Lee McCurry, interview by author, Las Vegas, Nev., 25 September 1992.
8. O. Miller, interview by author.
9. Ibid.
10. Rosalyn Jirge, interview by author, 2 October 1992.

11. Ibid.
12. Teresa Yates (Georgie's heir to the title of "Woman of the River"), interview by Rosalyn Jirge.
13. Teresa Yates, interview by author, 17 April 1994.

Chapter 22

1. Karen Smith, interview by author, Sacramento, Calif., 4 October 1992.
2. Kjeld Harris, telephone interview by author, 4 October 1994.
3. Tanya Wilcox, telephone interview by author, 1 March 1995.
4. Here and following unless otherwise cited, Tanya Wilcox Falls to author, 6 March 1995.
5. Wilcox, interview.
6. Chuck Kane, interview by author.
7. McCurry, interview.
8. Harris, interview.
9. Curtis "Whale" Hansen, interview by author, 31 August 1993.
10. Steve Hatch, interview by author.
11. Ibid.
12. Ibid.
13. Mark E. Law, narrative report, U.S. Department of the Interior, National Park Service, case/incident record no. 892092, Grand Canyon Library.
14. Hansen, interview.
15. Wilcox, interview.

Chapter 23

1. Carol Fritzsinger, interview by author, 30 October 1992.
2. D. Dierker, interview.
3. Foster, interview.
4. Ibid.
5. Yates, interview by Jirge.
6. Garrett Schniewind, interview by author, 30 October 1992.
7. Pat Stadt, interview by author, 4 October 1992.
8. Hatch, interview.
9. D. Dierker, interview.
10. B. Dierker, interview.
11. Here and following unless otherwise cited, Lew Steiger, "We Could Have Danced All Night," *Grand Canyon River Guides, The News*, vol. 4, no. 1 (February 1991).
12. Here and following unless otherwise cited, Don Briggs, interview.
13. Roy Webb, "A Grand Party for a Grand Lady."
14. Steiger, "We Could Have Danced."

Chapter 24

1. David Brown (of "America Outdoors," an alliance of Western River Guides Association and Eastern Professional River Outfitters), telephone interview by author.
2. Susan Cherry (Grand Canyon National Park ranger in charge of permits), interview by author.
3. Ken Sleight, qtd. in Donovan Webster, "Utah: Land of Promise, Kingdom of Stone," *National Geographic*, vol. 189, no. 1 (January 1996): 62.
4. Mark Law, interview by author.
5. Here and following unless otherwise cited, Dan Cassidy, interview by author, 1 December 1992.
6. Jirge, "Thoughts and Memories."
7. Here and following unless otherwise cited, Yates, interview by author.
8. Tom Bradshaw and friends, interview by Rosalyn Jirge.
9. Karen Smith, interview by author, 4 October 1992.
10. Here and following unless otherwise cited, Natalie A. Jensen and Marnie Bellows, interview by author, 4 April 1993.
11. McCurry, interview.

Chapter 25

1. McCurry, interview.
2. Bob Pearson, interview by author, 4 October 1992.
3. Prange, interview.
4. Ibid.
5. Patty Ellwanger, interview.
6. Yates, interview by Jirge.
7. Workman, interview.
8. Yates, interview by author.
9. Ibid.
10. *Grand Canyon River Guides, The News*, vol. 5, no. 3 (Summer 1992).
11. Foster, interview.

Related Works

Beer, Bill. *We Swam the Grand Canyon: The True Story of a Cheap Vacation that Got a Little Out of Hand*. Seattle: The Mountaineers, 1988.

Beus, Stanley S., and Michael Morales. *Grand Canyon Geology*. New York: New York Oxford Press/University of Northern Arizona Press, 1990.

Brian, Nancy. *River to Rim: A Guide to Names along the Colorado River in Grand Canyon from Lake Powell to Lake Mead*. Flagstaff, Ariz.: Earthquest Press, 1992.

Carothers, Steven W., and Bryon T. Brown. *The Colorado River through Grand Canyon: Natural History and Human Change*. Tucson: University of Arizona Press, 1991.

Clark, Georgie White, and Duane Newcomb. *Georgie Clark: Thirty Years of River Running*. San Francisco: Chronicle Books, 1977.

Cook, William. *The Wen, the Botany, and the Mexican Hat: The Adventures of the First Women through Grand Canyon, on the Nevills Expedition*. Orangeville, Calif.: Callisto Books, 1987.

Crampton, C. Gregory. *Ghosts of Glen Canyon: History beneath Lake Powell*. St. George, Utah: Publishers Place, 1986.

Crumbo, Kim. *A River Runner's Guide to the History of the Grand Canyon*. Boulder, Colo.: Johnson Books, 1981.

DeRoss, Rose Marie. *Woman of the Rivers*. Palm Desert, Calif.: Desert Magazine Press, 1958.

Hamilton, Joyce. *White Water: The Colorado Jet Boat Expedition*. Christchurch, New Zealand: The Caxton Press, 1963.

Harvey, Mark W. T., *A Symbol of Wilderness*. Albuquerque: University of New Mexico Press, 1994.

Heiniger, Ernst A. *Grand Canyon*. Berne, Switzerland: Kümmerly and Frey, Geographical Publishers, 1971.

Kolb, Ellsworth L. *Through the Grand Canyon from Wyoming to Mexico*. New York: Macmillan, 1914, 1942.

Lavender, David. *River Runners of the Grand Canyon*. Grand Canyon, Ariz.: Grand Canyon Natural History Association, 1985.

Martin, Russell. *A Story that Stands like a Dam: Glen Canyon and the Struggle for the Soul of the West*. New York: Henry Holt and Company, 1989.

Miller, David E. *Hole-in-the-Rock*. Salt Lake City: University of Utah Press, 1975.

Nelson, Nancy. *Any Time, Any Place, Any River: The Nevills of Mexican Hat*. Flagstaff, Ariz.: Red Lake Books, 1991.

Phillips, Barbara G.; Robert A. Johnson; Robert M. Phillips, III; and Nancy J. Brian. *Monitoring the Effects of Recreational Use on the Colorado River Beaches in Grand Canyon National Park*. Flagstaff, Ariz.: Museum of Northern Arizona Press, 1986.

Powell, J. W. *The Exploration of the Colorado River and Its Canyons*. New York: Dover Publications, 1961.

Ringholz, Raye. *Uranium Frenzy: Boom and Bust on the Colorado Plateau*. New York: W. W. Martin and Company, 1989.

Rusho, W. R., and C. Gregory Crampton, *Lee's Ferry: Desert River Crossing*. Salt Lake City: Cricket Productions, 1992.

Stanton, Robert Brewster. *Colorado River Controversies*. Boulder, Colo.: Westwater Books, 1982.

Teal, Louise. *Breaking into the Current*. Tucson: University of Arizona Press, 1994.

Topping, Gary. "Harry Aleson and the Place No One Knew." *Utah Historical Quarterly*, vol. 52 (Spring 1984).

Webb, Roy. *Call of the Colorado*. Moscow, Id.: University of Idaho Press, 1994.

Webb, Roy D. *If We Had a Boat: Green River Explorers, Adventurers, and Runners*. Salt Lake City: University of Utah Press, 1986.

Westwood, Richard E. *Rough-Water Man: Elwyn Blake's Colorado River Expeditions*. Reno: University of Nevada Press, 1992.

Index